D0119131

MARCOS AGAINST THE CHURCH

MARCOS AGAINST THE CHURCH

Economic Development and Political Repression in the Philippines

ROBERT L. YOUNGBLOOD

Cornell University Press

Ithaca and London

First published 1990 by Cornell University Press.

International Standard Book Number 0-8014-2305-8
Library of Congress Catalog Card Number 90-55135

Printed in the United States of America

Librarians: Library of Congress cataloging information appears on the last page of the book.

∞ The paper in this book meets the minimum requirements of the American National Standard for Information Sciences—Permanence of Paper for Printed Library Materials, ANSI Z39.48-1984.

FOR GAIL

Contents

Tables

Preface

The February 1986 call of Jaime Cardinal Sin, the archbishop of Manila, for Filipinos to surround Camp Crame and Camp Aguinaldo in support of a military revolt against President Ferdinand Marcos, was the culmination of a growing dissatisfaction within the Philippine Roman Catholic and Protestant churches with the Marcos regime. Thousands responded to Sin's call, and within days President Marcos was forced into political exile in the United States.

The role of the Philippine churches, especially the Roman Catholic church, in the events that led to the termination of Marcos' twenty-year rule, dramatically underscored the depth to which church-state relations had fallen since Marcos' first term as president (1966–69). This book examines church-state conflict during the Marcos years in the context of Philippine development policy and in the context of the churches' commitment, since the Second Vatican Council (1962–65), to work for social justice among the poor. Marcos' dealings with the churches remained cordial until the late 1960s, but following the imposition of martial rule in September 1972, church-state relations began to deteriorate with the loss of civil liberties, increased abuses of human rights by the military, and the rise of graft, corruption, and economic mismanagement. Inevitably government policies serving the interests of the president, his relatives, close associates, and other political allies clashed with church programs aimed at assisting the poor.

Although much of Marcos' rhetoric concerning the economy focused on improving the living standards of the poor, economic conditions for all but a privileged few deteriorated during the Marcos presidency. While Marcos and his cronies were looting the country, the percentage of families below the poverty line increased, and the income of the bottom 60 percent of households decreased. At the same time, the international debt of the Philippines soared to $26 billion, precipitating an economic crisis and stalling economic growth. Critics of the regime, including members of the clergy, were routinely branded as communists or communist sympathizers and often jailed as threats to the country's national security. When church officials denied engaging in antigovernment activities and clarified the objectives of church programs among the poor, government-controlled media largely ignored them. Indeed, the regime increased its attacks on the clergy in the late 1970s and early 1980s.

In the absence of genuine reform, and particularly after the assassination of Benigno Aquino, Jr., in August 1983 while in the custody of the military, Marcos' relations with the churches became increasingly acrimonious. Despite intermittent attempts at reconciliation, a breach with the Catholic bishops remained unrepaired at the time of Marcos' departure from the Philippines. The regime's intransigence convinced some conservative and moderate bishops who had previously supported Marcos to join progressive bishops in an intensified critique of the government, including a renewed call for free and honest elections.[1] The new coalition strengthened the voice of the Catholic Bishops' Conference of the Philippines (CBCP), as the 1986 presidential election made clear. Before the election the CBCP issued a pastoral letter urging Filipinos to vote and warning against fraud; immediately after the election, when it became obvious that Marcos planned to remain in office regardless of the vote, the bishops took the unparalleled step of issuing another pastoral letter, accusing the regime of using fear and intimidation in a "criminal" attempt to steal the election. The bishops went on to say that a government which attempts to gain or retain power though fraudulence was immoral, and they recommended that Filipinos seek justice through nonviolent struggle. The letter stripped Marcos of any remaining threads of political legitimacy; even if he had not been forced into exile, he would not have been able to govern.

The way church leaders, especially Cardinal Sin, participated in ousting Marcos and returning the Philippines to democracy was uniquely Filipino.

[1]Consult Chapter 4, pp. 72–73, for a discussion of how the terms *conservative*, *moderate*, and *progressive* are used. I should emphasize that my use of the term *progressive* in connection with the Philippine Roman Catholic and Protestant churches is not an indication of support for the NDF.

Yet many aspects of church-state relations in the Philippines leading up to the "EDSA Revolution" (EDSA refers to Epifanio de los Santos Avenue, which runs between Camp Aguinaldo and Camp Crame) have broader application. The renewed commitment of the Philippine churches to the poor and to social justice, that is, to a more equitable distribution of goods and services, is being duplicated simultaneously by churches in other developing countries, particularly in Latin America, and is resulting in similar conflicts with secular authority. Church-state relations during the Marcos years are thus an important case study for understanding the nature of socioeconomic and political change in the Third World.

I take pleasure in thanking a few of those institutions and people who have helped me with this book. A Fulbright-Hays Research Fellowship sustained me in the Philippines for nearly six months in 1979 while I conducted interviews and gathered documentary information. Research grants from the Faculty Grant-in-Aid Program and from the College of Liberal Arts at Arizona State University allowed me to devote the summers of 1980 and 1981 to writing. The College of Liberal Arts also provided me with additional research assistance during 1981 and 1982, while the university's Small Grants Program made funds available for photocopying documents during 1984 and 1985. I also benefited from a generous fellowship from the Earhart Foundation during the summer of 1984. I am grateful to Russell Fifield, Sheldon Simon, Kent Jennings, David Berman, and Patrick McGowan for helping me obtain financial assistance for my research.

During my stay in the Philippines in 1979, I received assistance from many individuals and institutions. I especially thank Raul de Guzman for giving me an academic home as a visiting research associate at the College of Public Administration of the University of the Philippines and Belinda Aquino for helping me obtain the affiliation. Colleagues at the college to whom I owe a special debt of gratitude for their kindness, encouragement, and assistance are Ledivina Cariño, Maria Concepcion Alfiler, and Adelwisa Agus Weller, now of Ann Arbor, Michigan. My appreciation also goes to the administrative staff of the college for their assistance in facilitating my research.

I also acknowledge Juan Francisco, Artemio Dolor, and the staff of the Philippine-American Educational Foundation for handling the administrative details of my Fulbright Fellowship, helping me get settled in Manila, and assisting my research travel.

I am deeply grateful to John Carroll, S.J., John Doherty, S.J., the Reverend Cirilo Rigos, James Ferry, M.M., Ralph Kroes, M.M., Thomas

Marti, M.M., and the Reverend Henry Aguilan for their generosity in aiding my research. Each went out of his way to help me obtain documents and interviews crucial to my research. Frs. Carroll, Doherty, Kroes, and Marti sharpened my analysis by reading either parts or all of the manuscript. I also thank the Philippine Province of the Society of Jesus for allowing me to use the library of La Ignaciana Apostolic Center, where I was graciously assisted by Virginia Abadia and Angel de la Cruz.

I owe a special debt to Senator Jovito Salonga for his interest and support of my work; to a large number of priests, nuns, pastors, and layworkers who anonymously assisted my research; to Lela Noble and Stephen Walker, who took time away from their busy schedules to read and comment on the entire manuscript; and to Kenneth and Gloria Fry for their encouragement and help.

Numerous individuals, some of whom I have never met, have provided me with information on the Philippines. I am grateful to Walden Bello, Sophie Bodegon, F. Dale Bruner, Mimi Camins, Bishop Fernando Capalla, Daphne Chapin, Bishop Francisco Claver, S.J., Arsenio Dominguez, Ronald Edgerton, Lynn Fagot, Carlos Fernandez, Doreen Fernandez, Edwin Fisher, Karl Gaspar, Marion Kline, Edwin Luidens, Rosemary McKenna, the late Perla Makil, Patricia Mullen, James Palm, Mary Racelis, Dennis Shoesmith, G. Sidney Silliman, Dante Simbulan, Anthony Sistrom, the late Joseph Stoffel, S.J., Enrique Syquia, Benjamin Tayabas, Deborah Wall, and William Yap, Jr. I also thank Terry Rusch for helping me mail my data from Manila.

The Department of Political Science and the Center for Asian Studies at Arizona State University have contributed significantly. Department chair Patrick McGowan allowed me to devote my full time to writing during the spring semester of 1985. The department also provided me with excellent research assistance. I owe a special debt to Melba Solidum Lim, who organized much of the data in the early phase of the research, and I thank David Crowe, Matthew Guenning, and Roxanne Doty for assisting in other phases of the research. I also acknowledge the help of the Center for Asian Studies in providing travel funds and other support for the research.

I thank the many institutions and publishers who graciously granted me permission to reprint portions of articles for this book. Parts of Chapters 3, 4, and 5 were originally published in "Church Opposition to Martial Law in the Philippines," *Asian Survey* 18 (May 1978): 505–520; "The Protestant Church in the Philippines' New Society," *Bulletin of Concerned Asian Scholars* 12 (July–September 1980): 19–29; "Government-Media Relations in the Philippines," *Asian Survey* 21 (July 1981): 710–728; "Church-

Military Relations in the Philippines," *Australian Outlook* 35 (December 1981): 250–261; "Structural Imperialism: An Analysis of the Catholic Bishops' Conference of the Philippines," *Comparative Political Studies* 15 (April 1982): 29–56; "Ideology and Christian Liberation in the New Society," *Kabar Seberang* nos. 10–11 (December 1982): 102–110; "Church and State in the New Republic of the Philippines," *Contemporary Southeast Asia* 6 (December 1984): 205–220.

My stay in the Philippines in 1979 without my family was made more enjoyable by the good friendship of Ulrich and Madeleine Rausch, and James and Pia Eder, while my research and writing here in Tempe, Arizona, have been delightfully interrupted and put into proper perspective by my children, Erik and Ingrid.

Finally, I thank my wife, Gail, for her steadfast support during my long absences while researching and writing, for enduring my expatiations about my work, and for tirelessly reading the manuscript for its inevitable lapses. I can never adequately express my appreciation and love for her help.

ROBERT L. YOUNGBLOOD

Tempe, Arizona

Abbreviations

AFP	Armed Forces of the Philippines
AI	Amnesty International
AMRSP	Association of Major Religious Superiors of the Philippines
ASSO	Arrest, Search, and Seizure Order
BCC	Basic Christian Community
BISA	Bishops' Institutes for Social Action
BLISS	*Bagong Lipunan* Sites and Services
BOI	Board of Investment
BUSCO	Bukidnon Sugar Corporation
CAE	Commercial Arms Export
CANU	Constabulary Anti-Narcotics Unit
CBCP	Catholic Bishops' Conference of the Philippines
CCA	Christian Conference of Asia
CCHR	Concerned Citizens for Human Rights
CCJP	Citizens Council for Justice and Peace
CCJP-Aust.	Catholic Commission for Justice and Peace in Australia
CDSC	Commission on Development and Social Concerns
CELAM	Latin American Episcopal Conference
CFIC	Franciscan Sisters of the Immaculate Conception of the Mother of God
CHDF	Civilian Home Defense Force (see also ICHDF)
CIA	Central Intelligence Agency
CICM	Congregation of the Immaculate Heart of Mary
CISA	Central Intelligence Service Agency

CLUP	Civil Liberties Union of the Philippines
CMLC	Church-Military Liaison Committee
CNL	Christians for National Liberation
COACCA	Cagayan de Oro Archdiocesan Center for Community Action
COMCAD	Command for the Administration of Detainees
COMELEC	Commission on Elections
CPBC	Convention of Philippine Baptist Churches
CPP	Communist Party of the Philippines
CRBDP	Chico River Basin Development Project
CSU	Constabulary Security Unit
CTFCO	Confederation of Tondo-Foreshore and Community Organizations
CWA	Church Workers Assembly
CWL	Catholic Women's League
CWO	Catholic Welfare Organization
DAP	Development Academy of the Philippines
DAPECOL	Davao Penal Colony
FABC	Federation of Asian Bishops' Conferences
FFF	Federation of Free Farmers
FFW	Federation of Free Workers
FLAG	Free Legal Assistance Group
FMS	Foreign Military Sales
IBP	Interim *Batasang Pambansa*
ICHDF	Integrated Civilian Home Defense Force
ICJ	International Commission of Jurists
ICM	Missionary Sisters of the Immaculate Heart of Mary
ICRC	International Committee of the Red Cross
IMF	International Monetary Fund
INP	Integrated National Police
ISAFP	Intelligence Service of the Armed Forces of the Philippines
ISO	Institute of Social Order
JAGO	Judge Advocate General Office
KAPATID	*Kapisanan Para sa Pagpapalaya at Amnestiya ng mga Detenido sa Pilipinas*
KASAPI	*Kapulungan ng mga Sandigan ng Pilipinas*
KBL	*Kilusang Bagong Lipunan*
KBS	Kanlaon Broadcasting System
KDSP	*Katipunan ng Demokratikong Sosyalista ng Pilipinas*
KKK	*Kilusan Para sa Katarungan at Kapayapaan*
KKKP	*Kilusang Kristiyano ng Kabataang Pilipino*
KKRP	*Kilusang Khi Rho ng Pilipinas*

KM	*Kabataang Makabayan*
LABAN	*Lakas ng Bayan*
LAPVIIR	Laymen's Association for Post–Vatican II Reforms
LISA	Lay Institute of Social Action
LOI	Letter of Instruction
LP	Liberal Party
LUSSA	Luzon Secretariat of Social Action
MAG	Medical Action Group
METROCOM	Metropolitan Command
MISG	Metrocom Intelligence and Security Group
MISSACPA	Mindanao-Sulu Social Action Personnel Assembly
MISSSA	Mindanao-Sulu Secretariat of Social Action
MM	Maryknoll Fathers
MNLF	Moro National Liberation Front
MSPC	Mindanao-Sulu Pastoral Conference
MSPCS	Mindanao-Sulu Pastoral Conference Secretariat
NAMFREL	National Citizens' Movement for Free Elections
NASSA	National Secretariat for Social Action, Justice and Peace
NASUTRA	National Sugar Trading Corporation
Nat-Dem	National Democrats
NCCP	National Council of Churches in the Philippines
NDC	National Development Corporation
NDF	National Democratic Front
NEDA	National Economic and Development Authority
NFSW	National Federation of Sugar Workers
NISA	National Intelligence and Security Authority
NP	Nacionalista Party
NPA	New People's Army
NPDSP	*Nagkakaisang Partido Demokratikong Sosyalista ng Pilipinas*
NUL	National Union for Liberation
NUSP	National Union of Students of the Philippines
OLH	Operation Leasehold
OLT	Operation Land Transfer
PANAMIN	Presidential Assistant on National Minorities
PC	Philippine Constabulary
PCA	Philippine Coconut Authority
PCHR	Philippine Coalition for Human Rights
PCO	Presidential Commitment Order
PCPM	Philippine Council for Print Media
PD	Presidential Decree

PDA	Preventative Detention Action
PDP	Philippine Democratic Party
PEACE	Philippine Ecumenical Action for Community Development
PECCO	Philippine Ecumenical Council for Community Organizations
PEFTOK-IDC	Philippine Expeditionary Force to Korea Investment and Development Corporation
PES	Presidential Economic Staff
PHILCAG	Philippine Civic Action Group
PHILPACK	Philippine Packing Corporation
PHILSUCOM	Philippine Sugar Commission
PISA	Priests' Institute for Social Action
PLDT	Philippine Long Distance Telephone Company
PLISA	Priests' and Laymens' Institute of Social Action
PLMP	Philippine Lay Missionaries Program
POV	Public Order Violator
PPI	Philippine Priests Incorporated
PROD	President's Regional Officers for Development
PSC	Presidential Security Command
PVIDC	Philippine Veterans Investment Development Company
RETELCO	Republic Telephone Company
RPN	Radio Philippines Network
RUC	Regional Unified Command
SCAPS	Share and Care Apostolate for Poor Squatters
SDP	Social Democratic Party
SEAMS	Southeast Asian Major Superiors' Conference
SELDA	*Samahan ng mga Ex-detainee Laban sa Detensyon at Para sa Amnestiya*
SIFI	Sugar Industry Foundation, Incorporated
SJ	Society of Jesus
SKK	*Samahan ng Kristiyanong Komunidad*
SMRPC	Southern Mindanao Regional Party Committee
Soc-Dem	Social Democrats
SSC	Society of St. Columban
SUAFP	Special Unit of the Armed Forces of the Philippines
TADECO	Tagum Agricultural Development Corporation
TFD	Task Force Detainees
TFRC	Task Force Rural Conscientization
TFUC	Task Force Urban Conscientization
TNC/TNB	Transnational Corporations and Banks
UCCP	United Church of Christ in the Philippines

UCPB	United Coconut Planters' Bank
UIM	Urban Industrial Mission
UNICOM	United Coconut Mills, Incorporated
UNIDO	United Democratic Opposition
USTE	*Ugnayan ng mga Samahan sa Tatalon Estate*
VISSA	Visaya Secretariat of Social Action
WCC	World Council of Churches
YCSP	Young Christian Socialists of the Philippines
YCW	Young Christian Workers
ZOTO	Zone One Tondo Organization

MARCOS AGAINST THE CHURCH

1

Introduction

Among the major historical roles of the Roman Catholic and Protestant churches in the Philippines was the legitimation of the political control of the colonizing powers—Spain (1565–1898) and the United States (1898–1946)—and, since independence, of the dominant Filipino political elites. The Roman Catholic church played an especially strong part, for the propagation of the Christian faith was one of the primary reasons for the Spanish conquest of the Philippines. Augustinian missionaries accompanied Legaspi's colonizing mission in 1565, and over the next forty years the Discalced Franciscans (1578), the Jesuits (1581), the Dominicans (1587), and the Augustinian Recollccts (1606) all established mission outposts in the archipelago. Under the terms of the *patronato real de las Indias*, which committed the Spanish monarch to support and to protect the Roman Catholic religion, missionaries traveled to the Philippines at the crown's expense and received a stipend either from the colonial government directly or from the *encomendero* of the jurisdiction (*encomienda*) to which they were assigned.[1] In return, the Spanish crown received the right to nominate candidates to the Holy See for appointment as colonial bishops, and in the Philippines the captain-general, as the king's representative and "vice-patron," approved the bishop's appointment of parish priests.

[1]An *encomienda* was a royal grant of jurisdiction over the inhabitants of a certain area that allowed the *encomendero* to collect tribute, but also imposed on him a series of obligations, such as propagating the Catholic faith and providing law and order and justice, to the people in his trust.

Directives from Rome to the colonial churches were also not considered binding unless they were officially endorsed by the king through the Royal Council of the Indies; in 1594 Philip II himself partitioned the country into missionary areas and assigned each religious order a separate region to evangelize.

The symbiotic relationship between the church and the Spanish government was further underscored by the fact that in the early years of the colony, especially, the religious were often consulted on governmental administrative matters, such as the strict observance of laws involving *encomiendas*, the collection of taxes, and whether to engage in punitive military expeditions. They likewise served the colonial government in diplomatic missions abroad. At the local level, the parish priest, as a salaried representative of the crown and often the only Spanish resident in most Philippine villages, was also entrusted with a variety of purely civil duties. Among these duties were the organization of the tribute list; the direction of the local elementary school; the supervision of the election of local officials; the management of town council meetings and the approval of local ordinances; and the administration of public works projects, including the maintenance of roads and bridges.[2]

To be sure, as de la Costa points out, the Spanish Patronato regime required "the closest possible collaboration between the bishops, the religious orders, and the civil officials." At the same time, however, "a series of more or less serious jurisdictional conflicts between . . . the religious orders and the civil government" and "between the civil government and the bishops" emerged as a minor theme in church-state relations.[3] The conflict between the church and the state often revolved around questions of social justice, with the friars denouncing the Spanish colonial government for atrocities against the native population and periodically refusing the sacraments to those guilty of abuses.[4]

The rapid Christianization of most of the lowland Philippines by a small number of missionaries was attributable, according to Schumacher, to the fact that the religious as early as the 1570s stood up for the rights of the

[2]Horacio de la Costa, "The Filipino Priest . . . Yesterday and Today," *Philippine Priests' Forum* 2 (June 1970): 10–11; and Horacio de la Costa, "Episcopal Jurisdiction in the Philippines during the Spanish Regime," in *Studies in Philippine Church History*, ed. Gerald H. Anderson (Ithaca: Cornell University Press, 1969), pp. 44–46.

[3]De la Costa, "The Filipino Priest," pp. 11–12.

[4]See John N. Schumacher, *Readings in Philippine Church History* (Quezon City: Loyola School of Theology, Ateneo de Manila University, 1979), chap. 3, "The Struggle for Justice," pp. 22–38.

native population.[5] Although church involvement in the galleon trade and in the management of the friar lands subsequently tainted the Roman Catholic clergy with commercialism and exploitation, resulting in considerable anticlericalism by the nineteenth century, the administration of schools, hospitals, orphanages, and other charitable organizations "were almost exclusively the concern of the church during the entire period of Spanish rule."[6] Significantly, the population remained staunchly Catholic and, in general, continued to believe and to expect that the church would defend their rights and protect them.

Notwithstanding a continuing commitment to schools, hospitals, and charitable institutions, the social action profile of the Philippine Roman Catholic church remained low throughout the first half of the twentieth century. New initiatives, such as Catholic Action in the 1920s and the Bellarmine Evidence Guild in the early 1930s,[7] were organized to address social issues, but the church's involvement in the problems of the poor fell far short of its earlier historical role. This lack of involvement on issues of social justice was due in part to a shortage of financial resources and church personnel; to continued anticlericalism by Filipino economic and political elites; and to a demoralization resulting from the Aglipayan schism that led to the creation of the Philippine Independent church and to the appearance, during the early part of the American colonial period, of several Protestant denominations, which tended to combine religious faith and social action more easily.[8]

Following World War II, however, the immediate need for reconstruction and the threat of a communist takeover in the 1950s, coupled with a heightened concern about the conditions of labor as a result of the social encyclicals of Pope Leo XIII (*Rerum Novarum* [1891]) and Pope Pius XI (*Quadragesimo Anno* [1931]), galvanized the Philippine Roman Catholic church to greater efforts in the social sphere. Even before the end of the war, in February 1945, the church established the Catholic Welfare Organization (CWO) to assist in relief work, while in 1947, the Institute of Social Order (ISO) and the Young Christian Workers movement (YCW) were organized to disseminate Catholic social doctrine and to apply it to commu-

[5]John N. Schumacher, "Justice," *Life Forum* 15 (June 1983): 26–29.

[6]*New Catholic Encyclopedia*, 1967 ed., s.v. "Philippines," by Horacio de la Costa.

[7]Arthur A. Weiss, "Jesuit Social Apostolate: 1859–1956," *Philippine Studies* 4 (Ignatian Number, 1956): 278–284.

[8]James H. Kroeger, "Human Promotion as an Integral Dimension of the Church's Mission of Evangelization: A Philippine Experience and Perspective since Vatican II—1965–1984" (Ph.D. diss., Pontificia Universitas Gregoriana, 1985), pp. 109–115.

nity problems. In June 1950, Father Walter Hogan, the founder of the ISO, and a group of young Filipinos led by Juan "Johnny" Tan started the Federation of Free Workers (FFW), a democratic, anticommunist labor union.[9] In October 1953, Jeremias Montemayor and Fernando Esguerra, two laymen with close connections to the Catholic church, established the Federation of Free Farmers (FFF) to assist small farmers fight for their rights, especially in land disputes.[10] The philosophies of both the FFW and the FFF reflected Catholic social doctrine; the FFF, like the FFW, was staunchly anticommunist, having been organized to offer peasant farmers an alternative to the Huk movement.[11]

The commitment to social action within the Catholic church was also given a boost in the late 1940s by the Philippine hierarchy and by the apostolic delegate, Archbishop Egidio Vagnozzi. The bishops, echoing the papal teachings in *Rerum Novarum* and *Quadragesimo Anno*, issued three important pastoral letters, one in 1948 and two in 1949, that addressed the rights and obligations of employers and employees and that expressed concern for the welfare of the poor.[12] In addition, the hierarchy, along with Archbishop Vagnozzi, criticized the injustices of capitalism which were creating an atmosphere for the spread of communism. The bishops maintained the defenders of private property must take care that it is a system which brings private property to all, and not a system of ever increasing concentration of that property within the hands of a few, leaving millions of people with no private property at all.

The bishops went on to warn that only a "vigorous, sustained execution of reforms" would "stop the advances of Communism."[13] Vagnozzi expressed similar anxieties about social injustices in Philippine society and the obligation of the church to address them.[14]

[9]Ibid., pp. 116–118; and Pasquale T. Giordano, "A Theological Analysis of the Changing Understanding of the Social Mission in the Philippine Church after Vatican II: 1965–81" (Ph.D. diss., Catholic University of America, 1983), p. 33.

[10]Leo A. Cullum, "Federation of Free Farmers," *Philippine Studies* 2 (June 1954): 171–174; Jeremias U. Montemayor, "The Free Farmers Re-examined," *Philippine Studies* 8 (April 1960): 418–426; and Giordano, "A Theological Analysis," p. 34.

[11]The origin of the term *Huk* is explained in Chapter 2, note 7.

[12]"Statement of the Ecclesiastical Hierarchy of the Philippines on the Social Principles," *Boletin Eclesiastico de Filipinas* 20 (March 1948): 155–156; "Joint Pastoral Letter of the Hierarchy of the Philippines on the Virtue of Justice," *Boletin Eclesiastico de Filipinas* 23 (March 1949): 165–176; and "Pastoral Letter of the Philippine Catholic Hierarchy on 'Social Justice,' " in Jeremias U. Montemayor, *Ours to Share* (Manila: Rex Book Store, 1966), Appendix 5, pp. 511–520.

[13]"Pastoral Letter on 'Social Justice,' " in Montemayor, *Ours to Share*, p. 518.

[14]Egidio Vagnozzi, "Sermon of Apostolic Delegate to the Philippine Nation on the Hour of Pax Roma," *Boletin Eclesiastico de Filipinas* 23 (September 1949): 582–585; and

Other efforts throughout the 1950s and 1960s also indicated an increase in the Catholic church's commitments to social action. Among them were the organization of the first Priests' Institute of Social Action (PISA) in April 1950, the holding of the initial Lay Institute of Social Action (LISA) in January 1952, the meeting of the Priests' and Laymen's Institute of Social Action (PLISA) in April 1953, and the hosting of the First Asian Meeting for Lay Apostolates in December 1955. The Asian Social Institute was established in 1962, followed by the creation of the Sister Formation Institute in 1963.[15] Nevertheless, prior to 1965 the bishops' efforts within the social sphere were uncoordinated, sometimes contradictory, and focused primarily on charitable works, reflecting a continuing paternalism within the church. For instance, in 1953 Rufino Santos announced the creation of a charitable fund to assist the poor in celebration of his installation as the archbishop of Manila. In 1956, despite earlier pastoral letters by the CWO and speeches by Archbishop Vagnozzi on the need to support labor, the hierarchy declared a strike by the University of Santo Tomas Employees Association, which was affiliated with the FFW, to be immoral. Subsequently, Archbishop Santos banned Fr. Hogan, who was involved in the strike, from making public addresses and issuing press releases on social justice questions in the Archdiocese of Manila; asked for the exclusion of several laymen, including FFW organizer "Johnny" Tan, from the labor management school of the ISO; and, according to James Kroeger, took steps to destroy the ISO itself.[16]

Policy changes within the Holy See as well as within the World Council of Churches during the 1960s, combined with a surge in Philippine nationalism, presaged a qualitative shift in the social action orientations of the Philippine Catholic and Protestant churches.[17] Since 1960 the emphasis on social justice as an integral part of evangelization has received additional attention in the Roman Catholic church, especially, as well as in various

---

"Address to the Knights of Columbus," *Boletin Eclesiastico de Filipinas* 24 (February 1950): 84–101.

[15]Kroeger, "Human Promotion," pp. 121–130.

[16]Mario Bolasco, "Marxism and Christianity in the Philippines: 1930–1983," in *Marxism in the Philippines: Marx Centennial Lectures*, ed. Third World Studies (Quezon City: Third World Studies Center, University of the Philippines, 1984), pp. 111–112; Giordano, "A Theological Analysis," p. 33; and Kroeger, "Human Promotion," pp. 125–126.

[17]World Council of Churches (WCC), "World Conference on Church and Society: Message to the Conference," *Ecumenical Chronicle* 19 (January 1967): 59–61, is the major statement of the WCC's Church and Society meeting in July 1966. See also Philippine Ecumenical Writing Group, *Moving Heaven and Earth: An Account of Filipinos Struggling to Change Their Lives and Society* (Manila: Commission on the Churches' Participation in Development, World Council of Churches, 1982), pp. 26–31.

Protestant denominations. Encyclicals issued during the papacies of John XXIII, Paul VI, and John Paul II, coupled with documents produced during the Second Vatican Council (1962–65) and several international synods and convocations of bishops, have all underscored the Roman Catholic church's renewed commitment to human rights, freedom, and social justice. Perhaps nowhere has the connection between the Catholic faith and social justice been made more explicit than in the declaration of the 1971 synod of bishops in Rome that "action on behalf of justice and participation in the transformation of the world" represents a "constitutive dimension of the preaching of the Gospel."[18]

The deliberations of Vatican II and other international Catholic and Protestant convocations have had a profound effect on the Philippine churches, but at the same time, ironically, they contributed to increasing church-state conflict during the Marcos presidency (1965–86). The churches' emphasis on social justice collided with the development programs and the national security concerns of the Marcos regime. An analysis of this conflict against the background of Philippine development policy is important for several reasons. First, given that both the Philippine churches and successive administrations since 1946 have stressed the need to improve the socioeconomic and political conditions of the poor in the process of creating a more just society, an examination of church-state conflict provides not only insights into why the development policies of the Marcos regime failed, but also reveals the human costs of those policies. These insights are additionally significant because President Marcos adopted, at least rhetorically, the liberal Western model for economic development that emphasized the importance of foreign investment and export promotion. Second, an analysis of the root causes of church-state conflict during the Marcos presidency provides a framework for better understanding of the evolving role of the churches (especially the Philippine Roman Catholic church) in contemporary Philippine society, and within the broader context of the Catholic and Protestant churches' commitment to fostering integral human development, clarifies the involvement of the clergy, particularly that of the Catholic bishops, in the overthrow of the Marcos regime. Third, an investigation of church-state conflict focuses perforce on the prophetic role played by a vocal and committed minority within the Catholic and Protestant churches in sustaining the ideals of democracy while defending human rights, social justice, and freedom in the name of the gospel.

[18]Joseph Gremillion, *The Gospel of Peace and Justice: Catholic Social Teaching since Pope John* (Maryknoll, N.Y.: Orbis Books, 1976), p. 514.

Finally, an analysis of church-state relations in the Philippines serves as a context for comparing the activities of the Catholic and Protestant churches in the Third World since Vatican II, for just as the impetus for change within the Philippine churches was externally generated, church involvement in social transformation in the Philippines has influenced other Christian churches in Asia.

Procedures and Data

The research for this book was initially stimulated by the appearance in the mid-1970s of numerous accounts of church-state conflict in the Philippines stemming from opposition to martial law from elements within both the Roman Catholic and the Protestant churches. After reviewing documentary data in the United States and corresponding with church officials and others knowledgeable about Philippine church-state relations, I conducted research in the Philippines for nearly six months in 1979. While in the field, I interviewed scores of Filipino priests, nuns, pastors, foreign missionaries, and lay workers familiar with the activities of the Catholic and Protestant churches under martial law; I also gathered a large amount of fugitive documentation on church-state relations. Many of those with whom I talked were engaged in social justice activities deemed "subversive" by the Marcos regime; a number had either previously been detained or subsequently jailed and/or deported; several had endured physical and psychological abuse—in two cases, torture—while in custody. Since 1979, I have continued to correspond with priests, pastors, and scholars interested in and knowledgeable about the churches in the Philippines and to gather additional documentation on Philippine church–state relations.

The interviews, documents, and letters have all been used in analyzing church-state relations during the Marcos years. In the chapters that follow, I focus on church-state interactions within the context of Philippine development policy; with seemingly identical goals of uplifting the poor, the relations between the Catholic and Protestant churches and the Marcos regime nonetheless steadily deteriorated, especially after 1975. While embracing a rhetoric of social justice, the Marcos government became increasingly abusive and corrupt and, ultimately, isolated and incapable of dealing with the problems facing the country. It is significant that the Philippine churches, particularly the Roman Catholic church, were at the forefront of those calling for reform and subsequently for the replacement of Marcos as president; such calls demonstrated the power and influence of the churches as institutions in Philippine society. They also underscored the degree to which important elements within the Philippine Catholic and Protestant hierarchies were morally committed to the gospel ideals of social justice and human liberation.

Chapter 2 places the economic development program of the Marcos government within the context of political development theory and Philippine economic policy since the early 1960s. I examine Philippine economic policy in terms of the shift in development (modernization) theory from an emphasis on the growth of liberal democracy as a concomitant of economic development to an emphasis on political order and bureaucratic authoritarianism, along with depoliticization, as a condition (if only a temporary onc) for economic development. I use the evolution both of general development theory and Philippine economic policy since 1965 as a basis for understanding the successes and failures of Marcos' choice of an authoritarian model for achieving economic and political development for the Philippines. Special emphasis is given to policies resulting in the growth of foreign debt after 1965, to the influence of Western trained technocrats, and to the expansion of the role of the Philippine military.

Chapter 3 focuses on the "ideology" of the New Society, which Marcos dubbed the "Revolution from the Center." Central to Marcos' "revolution" was an avowed commitment to social justice and economic prosperity for the poor through the employment of authoritarian methods. After presenting the major tenets of Marcos' New Society "ideology," I examine the expansion of the military, the control of the mass media, the creation of a new system of local government, and the manipulation of referenda and elections; Marcos viewed control of these institutions as a necessary condition for instilling the discipline needed to achieve the goals of the "Revolution from the Center."

Chapter 4 discusses the major divisions—conservative, moderate, and progressive—within the Philippine Catholic and Protestant churches and traces the evolution since Vatican II of Catholic and Protestant social action, which shifted from an emphasis on small self-help projects in the late 1960s to an emphasis on liberation and the creation of Basic Christian Communities (BCCs) by the mid-1970s. I also note the influence of Latin American liberation theology on the Philippine churches, and in a final section of the chapter, I address the conflict that resulted from the Marcos regime's attempt to control and repress those involved in the social justice and BCC programs of the churches.

Chapter 5 deals with the conflict that arose from Marcos' use of the military to foster the development programs of the government. Here I give special attention to church-military clashes over the military's involvement in agribusiness development in Mindanao and natural resource exploitation in northern Luzon, which resulted in repression against small farmers and minority tribesmen. In addition, I detail a series of major military raids on Protestant and Catholic church institutions after 1972, and discuss the reaction of the churches to the assaults.

Chapter 6 examines the problems surrounding the detention of thousands of Filipinos between 1972 and February 1986 and discusses the detention of political prisoners, their treatment in prison, the role of the churches in monitoring the problem, and the position of the government on the jailing of political prisoners. The chapter also includes an analysis of the upsurge of "disappearances" and extrajudicial killings in the Philippines since the late 1970s.

Chapter 7 presents the varied reactions within the Catholic and Protestant churches to the declaration of martial law and to the government's socioeconomic and political development policies. I also discuss the conflict within the Philippine Roman Catholic church over the negative stance of powerful members of the Roman curia to opposition among some church leaders to the Marcos government's policies. I use President Marcos' proclamation terminating martial rule (Proclamation 2045) as a vehicle for cataloging the successes and failures of the regime's socioeconomic and political development programs and as a standard by which to analyze the evolution of the churches' stance toward the policies of the New Society. Although church leaders initially disagreed over the efficacy and morality of martial law as well as over the proper role of the churches in the New Society, the cumulative abuses of the regime, detailed in Chapters 3 through 6, had the effect of uniting many church leaders of different ecclesiological orientations against the regime and of reinforcing the commitment of the churches to the ideals of social justice and total human liberation.

2

Development and Political Order in the Philippines

A major assumption of the U.S. government immediately after World War II was that economic development (measured in terms of per capita GNP) in the Third World would result in greater political participation and in the growth of democratic representative institutions. Economic development was to be brought about by a global application of the principles of the free market; while income inequality would increase in the short run, economic benefits would eventually "trickle down" to the general public. The United States stood ready with foreign aid and technical assistance to accelerate the processes of development, and as a consequence of greater affluence, the newly independent nations of Asia and Africa were expected to establish pro-Western (especially pro-American) foreign policies. Without economic development and political stability, provided in part by an American willingness to exercise its military power in the defense of the capitalist system, these nations were likely to fall under Communist domination. The American success in rebuilding Western Europe and Japan with capitalist economies and democratic political structures encouraged U.S. government officials and academics in their belief that economic development could be achieved rapidly in the Third World, serving as it had in Western Europe and Japan as a bulwark against the spread of Communism. Moreover, the establishment of democratic, capitalist regimes in developing areas of the globe increased the likelihood of the creation of a world community in the American image that would more effectively serve U.S. economic and political interests abroad.

A related assumption was that the existence of liberal democratic political institutions was largely responsible for the high standards of living and the political stability of the Western industrial nations, particularly the United States. Such achievements were contrasted with the economic and political failures of Fascism and Nazism and the obvious excesses of Stalinism and Maoism. Thus liberal democracy was equated with economic development and political modernization (or development) and was offered as a model for the newly independent nations just emerging from colonialism. The equating of the growth of liberal democracy in the Third World with the attainment of political modernization is clearly reflected in much of the political development literature of the 1950s and early 1960s. Political modernization, like economic development, was understood as a series of stages through which traditional polities made a "transition" to modern polities approximating the political systems of the United States and Great Britain. Progress toward democracy was increasingly quantified in measures that embraced a variety of socioeconomic, political, and cultural variables, including levels of communication, education, literacy, urbanization, cultural and attitudinal change, and political participation.

Embedded within the "liberal" approach to the Third World in the 1950s and early 1960s was a belief by many American government officials and social scientists that economic development and political modernization were easily attainable and that the process was amenable to acceleration through the judicious application of foreign economic aid and technical advice, *if*, at the same time, indigenous leaders were willing to make tough socioeconomic and political decisions. All that developing nations had to do was duplicate the successes of the Western industrial nations. Often the solutions were presented in formula-like fashion, giving the impression that economic "take-off" was (if not a relatively simple process) almost inevitable, providing certain preconditions were met.

American confidence in the tractability of the problems of economic development and political modernization stemmed in part from a belief that the stresses of industrial society, such as poverty, unemployment, and inequality, were not only decreasing in absolute terms, but were essentially technical questions that were open to technological solutions. Such solutions could also be applied (perhaps with modifications) to similar problems in the Third World, and stemmed in part from a growing confidence in the efficacy of social engineering for economic and political development that was associated with the rise of "scientific" social science after the war. The Truman Doctrine and the Marshall Plan of the late 1940s and 1950s as well as the Alliance for Progress and the Peace Corps of the early 1960s were clear testimony to the boundless, if naive, optimism about the simplicity with which economic and political development could be achieved abroad with U.S. assistance and advice.[1]

By the mid-1960s considerable evidence existed that contradicted the earlier assumptions about the inevitability of economic development and political modernization in the Third World. By the early 1970s, research demonstrated unequivocally that increased levels of political participation (i.e. democracy) were, as Irma Adelman and Cynthia Morris put it, "by no means automatic consequences of socioeconomic development in underdeveloped countries."[2] Paradoxically, increases in literacy, urbanization, communications, and political mobilization appeared to contribute to economic stagnation and political disorder rather than to economic growth and political stability.[3] Many newly independent nations, such as Pakistan, Burma, Indonesia, and Nigeria, which originally established liberal democratic political regimes similar to the American and British models, later discarded them in favor of military or authoritarian political structures. The case was often made that liberal democracy was unsuitable to the cultural traditions and levels of development of much of the Third World. Instead, what was needed was less mass participation and political competition and more discipline and direction from above; unsatisfied demands for material progress were frequently generating, in the words of Daniel Lerner, "a 'revolution of rising frustrations' " that threatened the stability of newly independent nations.[4]

Political Development Theory and Political Order

The failure of steady, linear progress in economic development and political modernization in the underdeveloped nations during the 1950s and

[1]Richard A. Higgott, *Political Development Theory: The Contemporary Debate* (London: Croom Helm, 1983), pp. 15–16. For other excellent reviews of the political development literature, see Ronald H. Chilcote, *Theories of Comparative Politics: The Search for a Paradigm* (Boulder, Colo.: Westview Press, 1981); Robert A. Packenham, *Liberal America and the Third World: Political Development Ideas in Foreign Aid and Social Science* (Princeton: Princeton University Press, 1973); and Donal C. O'Brien, "Modernization, Order, and the Erosion of a Democratic Ideal: American Political Science, 1960–70," *Journal of Development Studies* 8 (July 1972): 351–378. My discussion uses *political modernization* and *political development* interchangeably.

[2]Irma Adelman and Cynthia T. Morris, *Economic Growth and Social Equity in Developing Countries* (Stanford: Stanford University Press, 1973), p. 139.

[3]Mark Kesselman, "Order or Movement? The Literature of Political Development as Ideology," *World Politics* 26 (October 1973): 140.

[4]Daniel Lerner, *The Passing of Traditional Society: Modernizing the Middle East* (New York: Free Press, 1964), p. vii.

early 1960s presaged attitude changes among U.S. policymakers and social scientists. No longer were representative institutions and mass political participation in the Third World viewed with confidence. Indeed, participation of the masses was increasingly viewed as contributing to political instability and chaos. As Ithiel de Sola Pool pointed out:

> It is clear that order depends on somehow compelling newly mobilized strata to return to a measure of passivity and defeatism from which they have recently been aroused by the process of modernization. At least temporarily, the maintenance of order requires a lowering of newly acquired aspirations and levels of political activity. The so-called "revolution of rising expectations" creates turmoil as new citizens demand things which the society is unable to supply. Movements which express demands that cannot be satisfied do threaten the cohesion of those commonwealths.[5]

Thus the previous advocacy of pluralism, the distribution of political power, and the importance of political mobilization (that is, the establishment of liberal democracies) was superseded in the late 1960s and the 1970s by an emphasis on the maintenance of political order and the enhancement of governmental capacities. The shift in American thinking, according to O'Brien, was observable in a growing preoccupation with anti-insurgency programs abroad, and in an emphasis on bureaucratic authoritarianism in the political development literature.[6]

Although counterinsurgency received a boost from U.S. involvement in Vietnam, the correspondence between the advent of political order research and the ascendancy of counterinsurgency was deeply rooted in a fear of the destabilizing affects of Communist-inspired wars of "national liberation." The success in the early 1950s of American assistance in the suppression of the Huks in the Philippines and of the British against the Communists in Malaya convinced influential American policymakers and social scientists of the applicability of counterinsurgency for the maintenance of political stability in underdeveloped nations.[7] By the mid-1960s the U.S. government was funding security training programs in a number of countries, including the Philippines, Vietnam, and Thailand. In 1966 Lucian Pye

[5]Ithiel de Sola Pool, "The Public and the Polity," in *Contemporary Political Science: Towards Empirical Theory*, ed. Ithiel de Sola Pool (New York: McGraw-Hill, 1967), p. 26.

[6]O'Brien, "Modernization," pp. 363–369.

[7]The term *Huk* has been used to refer to both the *Hukbo ng Bayan Laban sa Hapon* ([Hukbalahap] Peoples's Army to Fight the Japanese) and the *Hukbong Mapagpalaya ng Bayan* ([HMB] People's Liberation Army). The Hukbalahap was an anti-Japanese guerrilla movement, organized under the leadership of the *Partido Komunista ng Pilipinas* (PKP—Communist Party of the Philippines), that evolved after 1945 into the HMB, a peasant rebellion in Central Luzon which threatened the stability of the Philippine government.

wrote of the necessity to protect developing countries politically and militarily "from the calculated attempts of well organized enemies of freedom to use violence to gain totalitarian control."[8] Pye was not alone, however; other American academics advocated the use of anti-insurgency techniques to provide political stability, regardless of regime type, to pro-Western Third World countries, creating in the process a climate in the United States for accepting authoritarian governments abroad so long as American economic and political interests were served.

Perhaps the two most influential works on the primacy of political order for economic development and political modernization were Samuel Huntington's *Political Order in Changing Societies* and Leonard Binder et al.'s *Crises and Sequences in Political Development.*[9] Both Huntington and Binder were concerned with the decline of political order in Asia, Africa, and Latin America brought about by accelerated socioeconomic changes and the rapid inclusion (social mobilization) of new groups into the political process without an equally rapid development of political institutions capable of processing the multiplication of demands. The result, instead of economic and political development, was political decay. Huntington saw political modernization as a process of buttressing political institutions in order to deal with the stresses of social mobilization and political participation, while Binder et al. emphasized the importance of increasing governmental capacities to deal with five major crises—legitimacy, identity, participation, penetration, and distribution—faced by developing nations. Both Huntington's institutionalization and Binder's capacities enhancement were aimed at strengthening the abilities of governing elites to rule more effectively, and as such served as a rationalization for accepting the establishment of bureaucratic authoritarianism in the Third World.

The appearance in increasing frequency of authoritarian regimes in underdeveloped nations facing instability and development problems has been explained as predictable from an analysis of aggregate socioeconomic and political indicators, as consistent with the lower-class composition of poor nations, and as rational from the perspective of managing what David Korten terms system "stress," resulting from a high need for goal attainment.[10] Yet not all social scientists have viewed the failure of economic and

[8]Lucian W. Pye, *Aspects of Political Development* (Boston: Little, Brown, 1966), p. 128.

[9]Samuel P. Huntington, *Political Order in Changing Societies* (New Haven: Yale University Press, 1968); and Leonard Binder et al., *Crises and Sequences in Political Development* (Princeton: Princeton University Press, 1971).

[10]Phillips Cutright, "National Political Development: Measurement and Analysis," *American Sociological Review* 28 (April 1963): 253–264; Seymour Martin Lipset, *Political Man:*

political development, coupled with the turn toward authoritarianism in the Third World, as either natural or appropriate. Some social scientists have viewed the emergence of authoritarian regimes, at least in part, as a consequence of a symbiotic relationship between overdevelopment and underdevelopment, in which the asymmetries of the capitalist global economy work to the advantage of the industrial nations of North America and Europe and to the disadvantage of underdeveloped nations on the periphery. From this perspective, political order is needed to uphold the interests of international capital in developing nations. Although domestic forces may play a significant part in the appearance of authoritarian regimes, external forces such as imperialism, neocolonialism, and transnational corporations and banks (TNCs and TNBs) are considered equally, if not more, important.[11]

Modernization and Political Order during the Marcos Era

The Philippines was an American colony from after the Spanish American War until after the defeat of Japan in World War II; perhaps no other Third World country's economic and political development strategies have been so profoundly influenced by the United States. At the time of independence in 1946, the Philippines established an American-style presidential system of government, and although controlled by a landed elite and plagued by myriad economic and political problems, including deeply entrenched graft and corruption, the political system was nevertheless viewed in Washington as an American "showcase" of democracy in Asia and the Third World. Politics in the Philippines tended to reinforce the belief that liberal democracy, with all of its shortcomings, could take root in underdeveloped countries and serve as an effective instrument for economic development and political modernization.

The Social Bases of Politics (Garden City, N.Y.: Doubleday, 1960), chap. 4; and David C. Korten, "Situational Determinants of Leadership Structure," *Journal of Conflict Resolution* 4 (September 1962): 222–235.

[11]See, inter alia, Robert B. Stauffer, "The Political Economy of a Coup: Transnational Linkages and Philippine Political Response," *Journal of Peace Research* 10 (1974): 161–177; "Philippine Authoritarianism: Framework for Peripheral 'Development,'" *Pacific Affairs* 50 (Fall 1977): 365–386; and "The Political Economy of Refeudalization," in *Marcos and Martial Law in the Philippines*, ed. David A. Rosenberg (Ithaca: Cornell University Press, 1979), pp. 180–218.

In 1965, when Ferdinand Marcos was first elected president, the Philippines was still considered a showcase of democracy in Asia, with regular and relatively honest elections, a functioning Congress, and an independent judiciary. Over the next twenty years, Marcos dismantled Philippine democracy and established a dictatorship that lasted until he was ousted from power in February 1986. Economic and political factors, both domestic and foreign, were part and parcel of Marcos' shift to an authoritarian form of government. Among the most important were (1) economic liberalization and the marked growth of the Philippine foreign debt after 1965; (2) the rise in influence of Western-trained technocrats in the formulation of government economic and development policies; and (3) an enlargement of the Philippine military and an expansion of its role in governmental affairs. Significantly, all three factors were influenced by U.S. policies toward the Philippines that emphasized export-led economic development, an enhancement of bureaucratic capabilities, and a strengthening of the military's anti-insurgency skills.

The Growth of External Debt

Upon becoming president, Marcos continued the economic liberalization policies of his predecessor Diosdado Macapagal and reaffirmed (at least partially) the "special relationship" with the United States in matters of military and economic policy. In doing so, Marcos, like Macapagal, sided with a segment of the Filipino business elite and the American business community in the Philippines that favored increasing exports and opposed continuing import and exchange controls. Economic liberalization signified a major shift in Philippine economic policy toward an emphasis on export-oriented industrialization and a concomitant reliance on foreign borrowing to pay for development and finance deficits. The logic of these policy shifts resulted in the Marcos administration's acceptance of an international division of labor based on principles of comparative advantage, which in the Philippine case meant the utilization of cheap labor for the assembly of products for export (and reexport) to the developed nations of the West and Japan and a continued emphasis on the export of tropical agricultural commodities.

One of the major consequences was an increase in the total external debt of the Philippines, which tripled in the eight years between Macapagal's election in 1961 and the end of Marcos' first term in 1969, rising from $277.7 million to $840.2 million. During the same period Manila's external obligations to the International Monetary Fund (IMF) and the World Bank soared from $58 million to $286 million.[12] Mounting trade and payment deficits, aggravated by government overspending in Marcos' successful reelection bid in 1969, culminated in an acute foreign exchange crisis in late 1969, forcing the Philippines to devalue the peso in 1970 in order to secure a stabilization loan from the IMF. Although Marcos at first resisted devaluation because of its adverse economic consequences for "low income groups," he had little choice but to accept the financial package of the IMF and the establishment of a Philippine Consultive Group, under the leadership of the World Bank, to monitor the Philippine economy.[13]

The price for the accumulating external debt was more comprehensive monitoring of the economy by the IMF and the World Bank. The first two major stabilization loans, in 1962 (during the Macapagal administration) and 1970, required, in addition to the elimination of import and exchange controls and the devaluation of the peso, the liberalization of regulations for foreign investors and a constriction of domestic credit.[14] Ironically, although Marcos' overspending in the 1969 presidential election damaged the economy, resulting in considerable anti-Marcos sentiment in early 1970, increased supervision of the Philippine economy by the IMF and World Bank gave Marcos and government technocrats more leverage against nationalist economists and businessmen and, ultimately, more control over the economy, which Marcos increasingly used to enrich himself, his relatives, and close associates.[15]

The Technocrats

The decision to increase foreign borrowing was due in large measure to the advice of a group of American-trained technocrats, who, although they had diverse backgrounds in economics, law, political science, and business administration, shared a similar commitment to economic development and political modernization within the context of the free enterprise system

[12]Computed from Philippines (Republic), Central Bank of the Philippines, Department of Economic Research, *Twenty Five Years of Economic and Financial Statistics in the Philippines, Public Finance & Prices*, vol. 4 (Manila: Central Bank of the Philippines, 1974), Table 89, pp. 976–978, and Table 92, pp. 1006–1008. World Bank refers to the International Bank for Reconstruction (IBRD), organized in 1945, and its affiliate the International Development Authority (IDA), organized in 1960.

[13]*Japan Times*, 22 December 1969, p. 9.

[14]Robin Broad, *Unequal Alliance: The World Bank, the International Monetary Fund, and the Philippines* (Berkeley: University of California Press, 1988), pp. 33–35.

[15]On Marcos' use of the presidency for self-enrichment, see Belinda A. Aquino, *The Politics of Plunder: The Philippines under Marcos* (Manila: College of Public Administration, University of the Philippines, 1987).

and a capitalist international division of labor based on comparative advantage. Generally, they eschewed partisan politics, favored government planning, and saw deficit financing, both from domestic and foreign sources, as an opportunity to accelerate economic development. Many circulated easily from positions in prestigious academic institutions, such as the University of the Philippines, Ateneo de Manila University, De la Salle University, and private enterprise to important decision-making positions in the government.[16] While some technocrats had served in previous administrations, especially Macapagal's, they became especially prominent during Marcos' first term as members of the Presidential Economic Staff (PES) and the Board of Investment (BOI).

The rise in influence of the technocrats, as Stauffer points out, was not due initially to direct American involvement; nonetheless, U.S. policies throughout the postwar period concentrated on strengthening the bureaucracy's ability to deliver more programs and to expand its control geographically. The aid encompassed a variety of projects, including irrigation improvement, agricultural extension, nutrition and child care centers, community development, population planning, and in the 1960s, programs to familiarize Filipino public administrators with the latest methodologies of administrative science. The 1960s was also a period when U.S. technical specialists, along with experts from international organizations such as the United Nations, the IMF and World Bank, and the Asian Development Bank, began to assist in modernizing the bureaucracy to handle the increasingly complex problems of economic and political development. The relationships forged between Filipino technocrats and foreign advisers not only tended to strengthen administrative and planning capabilities but also reinforced an ideology of modernization that worked to bind the Philippines more tightly to the capitalist world system.[17]

The Military

Unlike the indirect American contribution to the prominence of the civilian technocrats, the U.S. role in fostering the growing influence and power of the Armed Forces of the Philippines (AFP) in the 1960s was straightforward. The anti-Huk campaigns of the 1950s established a framework for continued U.S.–Philippine cooperation during Marcos' first term.

[16]Romeo B. Ocampo, "Technocrats and Planning: Sketch and Exploration," *Philippine Journal of Public Administration* 15 (January 1971): 31–64.

[17]Robert B. Stauffer, *The Philippine Congress: Causes of Structural Change* (Beverly Hills, Calif.: Sage, 1975), p. 49.

With the ascendancy of the doctrine of counterinsurgency in the Kennedy administration, considerable emphasis in Philippine-American military relations in the 1960s was on "civic action," that is, winning the hearts and minds of the population in the countryside by utilizing excess military capacity for the construction of civilian projects and the suppression of dissidence. The kinds and amount of American aid from the mid-1960s to the early 1970s underscored Washington's support for the civic action/counterinsurgency thrust in Marcos' military strategy, as much of the assistance went for heavy equipment needed in road and bridge construction and for military and public safety training programs. Marcos used the U.S.-funded civic action and security training programs very effectively to expand the administrative role of the AFP and to enhance his political authority, especially at the grass roots. There is little doubt, for example, that all of the roads, bridges, child care centers, and schools built during Marcos' first term contributed to his reelection in 1969 or that the American-trained and equipped police were a significant factor in controlling urban demonstrations and riots in the late 1960s and early 1970s.[18]

By 1973 millions of dollars had been invested in civic action and thousands of Filipino officers and policemen had received security training both in the Philippines and the United States.[19] Yet American involvement went beyond mere funding and training activities, as indicated by the fact that in the late 1960s and early 1970s U.S. personnel often participated directly in rural development projects and also occasionally served in advisory capacities during counterinsurgency campaigns conducted by the Philippine military.[20] Such cooperation was facilitated by the AFP's growing dependence on sophisticated U.S. weapons and on American coun-

[18]Stauffer, "Philippine Authoritarianism," pp. 368–371, and "The Political Economy of Refeudalization," pp. 191–192; Stephen R. Shalom, *The United States and the Philippines: A Study of Neocolonialism* (Philadelphia: Institute for the Study of Human Issues, 1981), pp. 104–114; and Carolina G. Hernandez, "The Extent of Civilian Control of the Military in the Philippines: 1946–1976" (Ph.D. diss., State University of New York at Buffalo, 1979), pp. 207–208.

[19]U.S. Congress, Senate, Committee on Foreign Relations, *Korea and the Philippines: November 1972*, 93d Cong., 1st sess., staff report, 18 February 1973, pp. 38–39 (hereafter cited as Senate Staff Report, 1972); Michael Klar, "The Police Apparatus Courtesy of USAID," *Philippines Information Bulletin* 1 (January 1973): 18–20; and Shalom, *United States and the Philippines*, p. 114.

[20]Tad Szulc, "The Movable War," *New Republic*, 12 May 1973, pp. 21–23; prepared statements of Benedict J. Kerkvliet and Russell Johnson, U.S. Congress, Senate, Committee on Appropriations, *Foreign Assistance and Related Programs, Appropriations for Fiscal Year 1975, Hearings before a Subcommittee of the Committee on Appropriations*, 93d Cong., 2d sess., 1974, pp. 458–461, 477–478; and Shalom, *United States and the Philippines*, pp. 180–181.

terinsurgency techniques as well as boosted by Marcos' decision, in violation of a 1965 campaign promise, to dispatch a military contingent, the Philippine Civic Action Group (PHILCAG), to Vietnam in 1966.[21] Marcos received substantial material and psychological rewards from a U.S. government eager to "internationalize" the war. Not only did the Johnson administration shoulder the expenses of the unit in Vietnam and give Marcos a lavish welcome during an official visit to the United States in 1966, which included an address to a joint session of Congress, but American military assistance to the Philippines also increased by 20 percent during Marcos' first term over what it had been during the Macapagal presidency.[22]

Additional U.S. military assistance to the Philippines during Marcos' first term, while undoubtedly linked in the first instance to the willingness of Manila to send a civic action unit to Vietnam, reflected a broader concern both in Washington and Manila (particularly within the American business community in the Philippines) with the political stability of the republic and the prospects for accelerated economic development. The revival of nationalism in the 1960s, which resulted in a number of unprecedented anti-American demonstrations in 1964 and 1965 and in the establishment of a variety of nationalist organizations, especially within the student, labor, and leftist movements, contributed to an atmosphere of political tension from the mid-1960s to the early 1970s. Both Washington and Manila concurred that if the Philippine economy was to achieve, in Walt Rostow's words, economic "take-off," the political turmoil of the "parliament of the streets" had to be contained by an expansion of the security capabilities of the military and the police forces.[23] The stakes for successive U.S. administrations included continued access to the Philippine economy and, more important, unhampered use of huge U.S. military installations considered vital to the U.S. defense posture in the Western Pacific. The stakes for Marcos included continued access to foreign loans for development, re-

[21]Stauffer, "The Political Economy of Refeudalization," p. 191; and Walden Bello and Severina Rivera, "The Logistics of Repression," in *The Logistics of Repression and Other Essays: The Role of U.S. Assistance in Consolidating the Martial Law Regime in the Philippines*, ed. Walden Bello and Severina Rivera (Washington, D.C.: Friends of the Filipino People, 1977), pp. 7–48; and David Wurfel, "The Philippines: Intensified Dialogue," *Asian Survey* 7 (January 1967): 46–47.

[22]W. Scott Thompson, *Unequal Partners: Philippine and Thai Relations with the United States, 1965–75* (Lexington, Mass.: Lexington Books, 1975), chaps. 5 and 6, and Table 1-3, p. 15.

[23]Walt W. Rostow, *The Stages of Economic Growth: A Non-Communist Manifesto* (Cambridge: Cambridge University Press, 1962), especially chap. 4.

election in 1969, and, ultimately, the retention of political power beyond the end of a second term.[24]

The nationalist critique, which quickly developed a shrill anti-Marcos and anti-American rhetoric, focused primarily on Philippine economic and military policies. Among those singled out for denunciation with increasing frequency were Marcos' technocrats, whose economic policies were considered too pro-American and, as such, detrimental to indigenous entrepreneurs. From the nationalist perspective, too many of the technocrats prior to entering government service had articulated policies critical of economic nationalism or were former executives of foreign companies. The technocrats' belief in orthodox, neoclassical economic theory and espousal of free enterprise policies, which relied on increasing foreign investment and foreign borrowing, therefore, were anathema to nationalists and were opposed with some success prior to martial law.[25] Likewise, the growing influence of the AFP, through an expansion of civic action programs and an increase in coercive capabilities, was of concern not only to radical nationalists but also to the traditional elites. Both groups, although representing opposite extremes of the nationalist movement, viewed the armed forces as a potential political threat and agreed on the need to reduce the military's power.[26]

The Background of Martial Law

Although the Philippine Congress passed an Investment Incentive Act in 1967 and an Export Incentives Act in 1970 to stimulate capital accumulation and to encourage (and regulate) both domestic and foreign investments, the rising tide of nationalism in the Congress, the Filipino business community, and society generally encouraged the reappearance of protectionism. Coupled with uncertainty over the termination of the Laurel-Langley Agreement in 1974, protectionism contributed to an adverse climate for foreign business and investment. Similarly, nationalist proposals before the 1971 Constitutional Convention restricting foreign participation in the economy and the 1972 Quasha and Luzon Stevedoring Corporation

[24]Stauffer, "The Political Economy of Refeudalization," pp. 188–189.

[25]Alejandro Lichauco, "Imperialism in the Philippines," *Monthly Review* 25 (July–August 1973): 59–67; Stauffer, "The Political Economy of Refeudalization," p. 190; and Charles W. Lindsey, "The Philippine State and Transnational Investment," paper presented at the annual meeting of the American Political Science Association, Washington, D.C., August 30–September 2, 1984, pp. 39–41.

[26]Frank H. Golay, "Some Costs of Philippine Politics," *Asia* no. 23 (Autumn 1971): 57; and Stauffer, "The Political Economy of Refeudalization," p. 192.

decisions of the Supreme Court, which limited foreign ownership of property and foreign participation in the management of companies in sectors reserved for Filipinos, created further uncertainty within the foreign business community in the Philippines and among potential foreign investors.[27] The attempts by nationalists to "filipinize" the economy further were consistently opposed by the American Chamber of Commerce of the Philippines.[28] Although President Marcos and the technocrats sought to reassure foreign investors,[29] U.S. government publications continued to stress the Philippines' uncertain economic and political climate.[30] The net effect was a reduction in investment from abroad and in the growth of export industries. While the economy continued to expand at the aggregate level (measured in terms of GNP), foreign investment between 1968 and 1972 dropped to just one-third of what it had been in the preceding five years. Industries with export potential grew at only an 8 percent annual rate in the 1968–73 period as compared to an 11 percent annual rate in the 1960–67 period.[31]

Also included within the nationalist critique in the late 1960s and early 1970s were government economic programs, endorsed by the United States and the World Bank, that emphasized agricultural development over industrialization.[32] Nationalists saw the "agriculture first" policies as helping to

[27]*Business International*, 12 May 1972, p. 150; *Far Eastern Economic Review*, 19 August 1972, investment focus, p. 60; and *Journal of the American Chamber of Commerce of the Philippines*, September 1972, pp. 4–5, 10, 12.

[28]See, for example, *Journal of the American Chamber of Commerce of the Philippines*, July 1967, pp. 6, 23; August 1967, p. 3; February 1972, pp. 4, 10, 12; March 1972, pp. 4, 41; and April 1972, p. 3.

[29]Ferdinand E. Marcos, "The Philippines and Foreign Investment," speech before the Philippine-American Chamber of Commerce and the Far East American Council and Asia Society, New York City, 20 September 1966, reproduced in Ferdinand E. Marcos, *Presidential Speeches*, vol. 1 (n.p.: Ferdinand E. Marcos, 1978), pp. 143–155; Wurfel, "Intensified Dialogue," p. 47; and Cesar A. Virata, "Philippine Industrialization Strategy and Foreign Investment Policy," *Asia* no. 23 (Autumn 1971): 76.

[30]U.S. Department of Commerce, Bureau of International Commerce, *Overseas Business Reports*, OBR 68–74, August 1968, pp. 16–17; and U.S. Department of Commerce, Bureau of International Commerce, *Economic Trends and Their Implications for the United States*, ET 72–021, March 1972, pp. 4, 9, 11–12, and ET 72–100, September 1972, pp. 7–11.

[31]Charles W. Lindsey, "In Search of Dynamism: Foreign Investment in the Philippines under Martial Law," *Pacific Affairs* 56 (Fall 1983): Table 1, p. 482; and Robert E. Baldwin, *Foreign Trade Regimes and Economic Development: The Philippines*, a special conference series on foreign trade regimes and economic development, vol. 5 (New York: National Bureau of Economic Research, 1975), p. 6.

[32]Edberto M. Villegas, "Debt Peonage and the New Society," in *Mortgaging the Future: The World Bank and IMF in the Philippines*, ed. Vivencio R. Jose (Quezon City: Foundation for Nationalist Studies, 1982), p. 60; and Stauffer, "The Political Economy of a Coup," p. 168.

preserve the rural nature of the Philippine economy and as serving to undermine Philippine industrial development. This view was reinforced by American aid programs which provided greater assistance to the agricultural sector than to the industrial sector and which required large Philippine counterpart funds. One nationalist spokesman, Alejandro Lichauco, charged that American assistance, by encouraging Philippine economic priorities in the direction of "perpetual agriculturalization and ruralization," was condemning Filipinos to "the idiocy of rural life," while Hilarion Henares, another spokesman, maintained that the preeminence given to agricultural development contributed significantly to Philippine dependency and underdevelopment.[33]

Government agricultural policies stressed the need for raising food production through the application of scientific farming methods, for improving incomes and employment through an increase in agricultural exports, and for redistributing wealth through the implementation of land reform.[34] Yet agricultural growth from 1960 to 1971 lagged.[35] Although rice and corn production increased in the decade before martial law, the Philippines did not become self-sufficient in rice production until 1976, and exports failed to offset imports by a wide margin from 1960 to 1972. Moreover, the land reform proposals of the Marcos government were repeatedly blocked or diluted in Congress, and once legislation was passed its full implementation was thwarted in the courts and the bureaucracy by landowning elites.

Much to the frustration of Marcos and the technocrats, presidential initiatives and economic programs aimed at stimulating the economy were regularly stalled in the House of Representatives and the Senate in an endless series of hearings only to be abandoned without action when Congress adjourned. Often programs were tied up until the administration agreed, according to one technocrat, "to every concession and appointment" demanded by powerful members of Congress.[36] Other executive

[33]Lichauco, "Imperialism in the Philippines," pp. 92–94; and Hilarion M. Henares, Jr., "Colonial Strategy against Full Scale Industrialization," in *The Role of Nationalism in Economic Development and Social Justice*, Report No. 20, Institute of Economic Studies and Social Action, Araneta University, Manila, October 1968, p. 42.

[34]Philippines (Republic), *Four Year Economic Program for the Philippines, Fiscal Years 1967–1970* (Manila, 1966), pp. 45–53; Philippines (Republic), National Economic Council, *Socio-Economic Development Program for FY 1966–67 to FY 1969–70*, Part I (Manila, May 1966), pp. 156–162 and 193–194; and Arturo R. Tanco, Jr., "Philippine Demographic Realities, Agricultural Development and Social Stability," *Asia* no. 23 (Autumn 1971): 108–112.

[35]Baldwin, *Foreign Trade Regimes and Economic Development*, Table 1-1, p. 3.

[36]As quoted in Beth Day, *The Philippines: Shattered Showcase of Democracy in Asia* (New York: M. Evans, 1974), pp. 42–43.

agreements, such as the Treaty of Amity, Commerce, and Navigation with Japan, which was necessary to secure more Japanese participation in the economy, and legislative proposals, such as the 1971 petroleum bill encouraging greater foreign participation in oil exploration, were blocked outright as a result of nationalist sentiment in Congress.[37]

By the end of the 1960s vexation over nationalist unrest, an obstructionist Congress, and a sluggish economy contributed to Marcos' willingness to use paramilitary and police forces against his opponents in the name of national security, political stability, and economic development. This was underscored by the president's reaction to the student demonstrations in Manila in early 1970, which resulted in the death of six students and the injury of hundreds of others, and to the grenade attack on opposition Liberal Party candidates in Plaza Miranda in late 1971, which claimed nine lives and injured scores, including eight Liberal Party senatorial candidates. In response to the student demonstrations, Marcos cracked down on the militant *Kabataang Makabayan* ([K.M.] Nationalist Youth), arresting its chairman, Nilo Tayag, on charges of subversion, negotiated an agreement with the opposition mayor of Manila, Antonio Villegas, allowing the Philippine Constabulary (PC) to operate in the city, and delayed the opening of classes. In response to the Plaza Miranda bombing, Marcos immediately suspended habeas corpus and blamed the incident on the communists.

Senators Jose Diokno and Benigno Aquino, Jr., both questioned the government's handling of the student unrest and scoffed at Marcos' explanations about the grenade attack. Diokno accused the president of using the Communist issue to mask the real problems of the country and together with Aquino, who was Marcos' political archrival, suggested in alarm that the president might use the Communist scare to perpetuate his grasp on power. Marcos reacted intransigently, and let it be known that he would do anything necessary, including running his wife Imelda for the presidency in 1973, to block Aquino from becoming president.[38]

Marcos also revealed little hesitation in using the powers of the presidency to outmaneuver his political opponents, as he had done in doling out

[37]Corporate Information Center for the National Council of Churches of Christ in the U.S.A., *The Philippines: American Corporations, Martial Law, and Underdevelopment* (New York: IDOC-North American, 1973), p. 59 (hereafter cited as *American Corporations, Martial Law*); and Shalom, *United States and the Philippines*, p. 168.

[38]Robert O. Tilman, "The Philippines in 1970: A Difficult Decade Begins," *Asian Survey* 11 (February 1971): 141–144; and John H. Adkins, "Philippines 1971: Events of a Year, Trends of the Future," *Asian Survey* 12 (January 1972): 81.

large amounts of government pork-barrel funds in his successful reelection campaign against Sergio Osmeña in 1969. The president personally saw that every barrio captain in the country received ₱4,000 in checks during the campaign, and he distributed large amounts of money from private sources to friendly candidates from both parties.[39] That the expenditures were clearly contributing to an economic crisis that would require a financial bailout from the IMF in early 1970 were of little concern to the president in the heat of the campaign. Similarly, in June 1972 Marcos dispensed money and patronage to overturn a September 1971 vote in the Constitutional Convention barring him or a member of his family from holding the position of head of government or chief of state regardless of the type of regime decided upon by the convention. While 161 delegates voted for the original "ban Marcos" provision, Marcos won the reversal by a vote of 155 to 31.[40]

The exercise of executive authority during the events of 1970–71 and early 1972 foreshadowed the declaration of martial law in September 1972, and demonstrated Marcos' political virtuosity in pursuit of his goals. But Marcos' decision to employ authoritarian methods was not arrived at solely within the context of domestic Philippine politics. The dynamics of the export-oriented development model that he and his technocrats adopted required political stability as a sine qua non for securing more foreign investment and more foreign loans to accelerate economic development—particularly in the export sector—to pay for the additional borrowing. Unfortunately for the president and the technocrats, however, the political turmoil in the late 1960s and early 1970s, characterized by the "parliament of the streets" in Manila and resurgent nationalism in the Philippine Congress, presented a picture of political instability and growing antiforeign sentiment that frightened away potential foreign investors and undoubtedly contributed to some divestment.[41]

Amid what appeared to be a climate of political chaos Marcos declared martial law on 21 September 1972, under Article VII of the 1935 Constitution. The official justifications for martial law, formally set forth in Proclamation 1081, focused on perceived threats to the republic from a variety of sources, including rebellion by the Communists, secessionist demands by

[39]Jose V. Abueva, "The Philippines: Political Tradition and Change," *Asian Survey* 10 (January 1970): 62.

[40]Shalom, *United States and the Philippines*, p. 163. See also Primitivo Mijares, *The Conjugal Dictatorship of Ferdinand and Imelda Marcos I* (San Francisco: Union Square, 1976), pp. 53–54 and 137.

[41]*American Corporations, Martial Law*, p. 20.

Muslim dissidents, coup d'état and assassination plots by rightist oligarchs, the growth of private armies and criminal syndicates, and increased urban unrest among students, workers, and the poor.[42] To eliminate "anarchy" and maintain "peace and order," Marcos ordered the military to arrest thousands, including opposition politicians and eleven delegates to the Constitutional Convention critical of the government, members of the mass media and student, labor, and peasant organizations, and "oligarchical" political opponents accused of conspiracy. The military also disbanded the private armies of many provincial politicians, and within weeks had collected an estimated 500,000 firearms from the citizenry. Congress was closed, foreign travel was curtailed, the activities of labor organizations were restricted, and a curfew was imposed.[43]

The day after the declaration, the president issued a decree setting forth a government reorganization plan that included the decentralization of government, the upgrading of the civil service, and the streamlining of government organizations. The centerpiece of the plan was the creation of the National Economic and Development Authority (NEDA) to oversee the regime's development programs, and, in conjunction with other development agencies such as the Board of Investment (BOI), to set the nation's development goals, including domestic and foreign investment priorities.[44] The restructuring of the government, along with the expansion of the role of the military, presented an image to the world of governmental control and stability and set the stage for the emergence of a new technocratic and military elite.

Marcos also moved quickly in the early days of martial rule to reassure foreign business interests that their investments were safe and to encourage additional investments from abroad. The president expressed an interest "in all forms of foreign capital," and stated emphatically that incentives and protection would be offered to foreign investment. He likewise said there would be "no confiscation" of foreign assets during his presidency and that "the amortization of investment, retirement of capital and transmittal of profits [would be] guaranteed."[45] These verbal assurances were bolstered by a number of political and administrative decisions beneficial to

[42]*Proclamation 1081: Proclaiming a State of Martial Law in the Philippines*, 21 September 1972; and Ferdinand E. Marcos, *Notes on the New Society of the Philippines* (n.p.: Ferdinand E. Marcos, 1973).

[43]John H. Adkins, "Philippines 1972: We'll Wait and See," *Asian Survey* 13 (February 1973): 140–150; Lela G. Noble, "Emergency Politics in the Philippines," *Asian Survey* 18 (April 1978): 350–362; and Mijares, *The Conjugal Dictatorship*, chap. 3.

[44]Day, *Shattered Showcase of Democracy*, pp. 163–164.

[45]*U.S. News and World Report*, 16 October 1972, p. 38.

foreign companies. For example, the nationalist proposals before the Constitutional Convention were omitted from the final draft of the new charter; the effects of the Quasha and Luzon Stevedoring decisions of the Supreme Court were negated; and decrees favorable to foreign investment were issued. And in December 1973 the regime ratified the Treaty of Amity, Commerce and Navigation with Japan in order to clear the way for more Japanese investment.[46]

The reaction of foreign investors to the new sense of security created by the military and to the opening up of the economy was overwhelmingly favorable. The American Chamber of Commerce of the Philippines sent a telegram to the president on 27 September 1972, wishing him "every success" in the restoration of "peace and order, business confidence, economic growth, and the well-being of the Filipino people and nation" and assuring him of the chamber's "confidence and cooperation in achieving these objectives."[47] Expressions of optimism about the improved business climate were also forthcoming from individual foreign corporate executives and from publications assessing business prospects under the Marcos regime, and were matched by an increase in capital inflow and foreign investment. While capital outflow exceeded capital inflow by $52 million from 1968 to 1972, capital inflow showed a net gain of $515 million from 1973 to 1977.[48] Similarly, foreign investment jumped from $21 million in the 1968–72 period to $484 million in the first five years of martial law.[49] Vincente Paterno, chairman of the BOI, stated flatly that "the country needed martial law . . . to attract such investment."[50]

Rather than view the political turmoil of the years prior to martial law as a positive, if difficult and unavoidable, aspect of democratic change, Marcos and the technocrats saw only a condition of advancing political instability and decay that was providing the enemies of the republic—both from the left and from the right—with opportunities for revolution or a coup d'état. Furthermore, the turmoil was frightening away the foreign

[46]*American Corporations, Martial Law*, p. 30; Civil Liberties Union of the Philippines, *The State of the Nation after Three Years of Martial Law* (Makati: Civil Liberties Union of the Philippines, 21 September 1975), pp. 13–14; and Claude A. Buss, *The United States and the Philippines: Background for Policy*, AEI-Hoover Policy Studies (Washington, D.C.: American Enterprise Institute for Public Policy Research, 1977), p. 84.

[47]As quoted in *American Corporations, Martial Law*, p. 32.

[48]Computed from Philippines (Republic), National Economic and Development Authority (NEDA), *1980 Philippine Statistical Yearbook* (Manila: NEDA, 1980), Table 12.2, pp. 502–503.

[49]Computed from Lindsey, "In Search of Dynamism," Table 1, p. 482.

[50]Vincente Paterno, "The BOI: Its Role in the Philippine Industrial Development," *Philippines Quarterly* 1 (June 1973): 29.

investment necessary for the realization of the government's export-oriented industrialization development program. Marcos' solution was the establishment of a constitutional authoritarian system of government. Only through authoritarianism, he argued, was it possible "to carry forth the mass consent and to exercise the authority necessary to introduce and implement new values, measures, and sacrifices."[51] The technocrats and the military agreed with the president, and Cesar Virata, the minister of finance, maintained that, although "Filipinos cherished the ideals of democracy," the nation did "not have time for the slow democratic processes." Instead, what the Philippines needed was "a 'push' to get going."[52]

Beyond the elimination of the "threat of a violent overthrow of [the] Republic" and the restoration of peace and order, Marcos made a commitment to reform the country's "social, economic and political institutions" and to accelerate the "systematic development" of the economy.[53] The president envisioned the creation of a "New Society" to eradicate economic inequities and social injustices and to arrest the "drift and decay of national life."[54] The mechanism for realizing the New Society was constitutional authoritarianism. Intellectually, Marcos justified the need for greater executive powers by referring to the work of Samuel Huntington, and in so doing, placed the development strategy of the Philippines within the mainstream of those advocating bureaucratic authoritarianism for rapid economic and political development in Third World nations.[55] The curtailment of individual liberties and democratic political participation in the name of political order and institution building were viewed by the president and the technocrats as necessary costs of development.[56]

[51]Ferdinand E. Marcos, *The Third World Alternatives* (Manila: National Media Production Center, 1980), p. 25.

[52]As quoted in Day, *Shattered Showcase of Democracy*, p. 187.

[53]"Statement of the President on the Proclamation of Martial Law in the Philippines," 23 September 1972, reproduced in Isabelo T. Crisostomo, *Marcos the Revolutionary* (Quezon City: J. Kriz Publishing Enterprises, 1973), p. 245.

[54]Ferdinand E. Marcos, *Five Years of the New Society* (n.p.: Ferdinand E. Marcos, 1978), pp. 10–11.

[55]Ferdinand E. Marcos, *The Democratic Revolution in the Philippines* (Englewood Cliffs, N.J.: Prentice Hall International, 1974), p. 64. The first section of the book is the American edition of Marcos' 1971 book, *Today's Revolution: Democracy,* in which he argues for stronger executive powers.

[56]Onofre D. Corpus, *Liberty and Government in the New Society: An Intellectual Perspective on Contemporary Philippine Politics* (n.p., 1974?).

The Economy under Martial Law[57]

The imposition of martial rule allowed Marcos and the technocrats to direct the economy without opposition from nationalists in the Congress and elsewhere in Philippine society. The trend toward economic liberalization and deficit financing through foreign borrowing, evident during Marcos' first term as president, was accelerated after 1972. As a consequence, the Philippines' external debt rose steadily from just over $1 billion at the time martial law was declared to nearly $26 billion in 1984.[58] The accumulation of a rapidly increasing foreign debt in the late 1970s and early 1980s compelled Marcos and the technocrats to agree to IMF and World Bank guidelines for restructuring entire segments of the Philippine economy, including industry, finance, agriculture, and energy, to promote the Fund's and Bank's export-oriented industrialization program.[59]

Soaring foreign indebtedness was justified as necessary for promoting economic development, while at the same time paying for oil price increases in 1973 and 1978 and weathering recessions in the developed economies in 1974–75 and in 1980–81. Clearly the oil price increases and the recessions adversely affected the Philippine economy. Yet in comparison to other Southeast Asian nations the Philippine economy grew at a much slower rate between 1970 and 1980. Whereas the Philippine per capita gross domestic product growth rate averaged 3.4 percent per year between 1970 and 1980, the average growth rates of Indonesia, Malaysia, Thailand, and Singapore for the same period were all above 5 percent per year.[60]

The lower average Philippine growth rate was due in large measure not to external factors but to domestic economic and political policies of the Marcos regime. The increasing influence of technocrats who advocated liberal economic policies, including programs for monetary and fiscal expansion, set the stage for increased foreign borrowing. During martial

[57]See Chapter 7 for an analysis of the reaction of the Philippine churches to Marcos' martial law economic policies.

[58]Philippines (Republic), Central Bank of the Philippines, Department of Economic Research, *Twenty Five Years of Economic and Financial Statistics in the Philippines, Public Finance & Prices*, vol. 4 (Manila: Central Bank of the Philippines, 1974), Table 89, p. 978; Guy Sacerdoti, "Politics of Expediency," *Far Eastern Economic Review*, 21 June 1984, p. 80; and Stauffer, "The Political Economy of a Coup," p. 168.

[59]Broad, *Unequal Alliance*, chaps. 4–8.

[60]Harry T. Oshima, "Sector Sources of Philippine Postwar Economic Growth: The Over-All Record in Comparative Perspective," *Journal of Philippine Development* 10 (1st semester, 1983): Table 1, p. 5.

law, for instance, technocrats dominated agencies such as the NEDA, the Ministry of Finance, the Ministry of Trade and Development, the Ministry of Agriculture, the Development Academy of the Philippines (DAP), and, after the retirement of Gregorio Licaros in January 1981, the Central Bank of the Philippines.[61]

The most influential technocrats agreed with the IMF's and the World Bank's export-led industrialization model for development in the Philippines, and used the IMF/World Bank relationship to promote the nation's further integration into the world capitalist system. The level of cooperation, while not without intermittent irritations, was high. The shared outlook of Filipino technocrats and IMF and World Bank officials facilitated the steady flow of foreign loans for development—even when the conditions of the loans went unmet—and contributed to the Philippines' selection as a "country of concentration" by the Bank. Domestically, the close relationship with the Fund and the Bank helped transnationalist technocrats outflank nationalists in the bureaucracy and their allies among the ranks of the nationalist entrepreneurs, both of whom opposed the economic policies of the Marcos government. By 1982, according to Robin Broad, transnationalist technocrats held a hegemonic position in economic decision making within the government.[62]

Transnationalist Filipino technocrats, Stauffer points out, increasingly "shared a developmental vision for the Philippines in consonance with those of the foreign advisors," as well as "agreed on the continuing need to rely on outside experts and external monitoring of development programs."[63] The degree of agreement is underscored by the rise in funds from abroad after 1972 and by the favorable reaction to martial law from Washington and from the IMF and World Bank. Increases in American economic assistance (including funds from U.S. government corporations) to the Philippines from $663.5 million in FY 1969–72 to $1,424.2 million in FYs 1973–76 were accompanied by a rise in assistance from multilateral lending agencies during the same periods from $377.7 million to $1,497.3 million.[64] Moreover, officials in Washington and the U.S. embassy in the

[61]Stauffer, "Philippine Authoritarianism," pp. 371–372; and Broad, *Unequal Alliance*, pp. 89–90. Following the 1978 National Assembly elections, departments became ministries and secretaries became ministers. For purposes of continuity, the terms *ministry* and *minister* are used throughout the book.

[62]Broad, *Unequal Alliance*, p. 177.

[63]Stauffer, "Philippine Authoritarianism," pp. 372–373.

[64]Computed from Walden Bello, "The Contours of U.S. Economic Aid," in *The Logistics of Repression and Other Essays: The Role of U.S. Assistance in Consolidating the Martial Law Regime in the Philippines*, ed. Walden Bello and Severina Rivera (Washington, D.C.: Friends of the Filipino People, 1977), Table 1, pp. 50–51.

Philippines generally viewed the expansion of President Marcos' authority as contributing to stability, pointing out that the loss of civil liberties was unlikely to affect American interests and that, in any case, U.S. military interests in the Philippines were "more important than the preservation of democratic institutions."[65] Officials of the IMF and World Bank were equally sanguine, seeing martial law as an opportunity to help Filipino technocrats achieve development objectives endorsed by the Bank.[66]

Hand in hand with the rise in foreign borrowing during the martial law years was a dramatic increase in Philippine government spending and a sharp rise in the overall deficit of the central government. Much of the deficit was attributable to enormous expenditures on government construction projects. In the second half of the 1970s, for instance, expenditures on both government and private construction, a large portion of which was financed with government money from government financial institutions, quadrupled without a concomitant increase in domestic savings. Unfortunately a majority of the construction projects "both in the private and public sectors," according to De Dios et al., "were not very productive and many were outrightly wasteful."[67]

Government construction projects and private ventures undertaken with government guaranteed loans were not only unproductive and wasteful but were often simply vehicles for private gain. Two examples underscore this point. A primary motive of Marcos in the construction of the Bataan nuclear power plant was an alleged $80 million payoff from the Westinghouse Corporation.[68] Similarly, the expansion of sugar milling capacity during martial law was justified not entirely by increases in sugar cane production but instead by the fact that government backed loans allowed private investors to pocket millions in kickbacks from Japanese corporations without regard to the profitability of the new sugar centrals.[69]

Further aggravating the economic situation was a tripling of the money supply and a doubling of the consumer price index between 1970 and 1980. During the same period, the inflation rate surpassed that of the Philippines' major trading partners, the United States and Japan, while the rate of foreign exchange remained relatively unchanged. The net effect was an overvalued peso which hurt the regime's export-oriented development

[65]Senate Staff Report, 1972, p. 45.

[66]Broad, *Unequal Alliance*, p. 63.

[67]Emmanuel S. De Dios et al., *An Analysis of the Philippine Economic Crisis: A Workshop Report* (Quezon City: University of the Philippines Press, 1984), p. 14.

[68]Aquino, *The Politics of Plunder*, p. 60.

[69]See Appendix F, "Kickbacks," in ICL Research Team, *A Report on Tribal Minorities in Mindanao* (Manila: Regal Printing, 1979).

strategy and encouraged the import of nonessential consumer goods. The regime's unwillingness to devalue the peso to reflect international economic realities resulted in Filipinos having to endure a lower standard of living without the prospect of greater prosperity in the future resulting from increased exports.[70]

Apart from government construction projects of dubious productivity and high inflation, Marcos issued scores of presidential decrees following the declaration of martial law that benefitted his relatives and close business associates; between 1981 and 1983 the most important capital expenditure of the government was corporate equity investment in failing businesses enterprises, often corporations owned by Marcos cronies.

Among the best-known presidential relatives who profited spectacularly during the Marcos years was Herminio Disini, a frequent golfing partner of the president and the husband of Imelda Marcos' cousin, Inday Escolin, who also served as one of the First Lady's private physicians.[71] In 1973 Marcos gave Disini a virtual monopoly over the Philippine cigarette filter industry by issuing a presidential decree that required Disini's chief competitor, Filtrona Philippines, an American- and British-owned company, to pay a 100 percent tariff on imported raw materials in contrast to a 10 percent tariff for Disini's company, Philippine Tobacco Filters Corporation. Other presidential decrees gave Cellophil Resources Corporation, a Disini-controlled company, an exclusive timber concession on the ancestral lands of the Tingguians in the Province of Abra (see Chapter 5). In 1978 reports surfaced that Disini, whose companies were involved in various aspects of the Bataan nuclear power plant, received part of the alleged $80 million Westinghouse payoff as a "commission" for facilitating the deal.[72] By 1980, the Disini conglomerate (Herdis) numbered more than thirty companies, and Disini's personal wealth was estimated at $200 million.

[70]De Dios, et al., *An Analysis of the Philippine Economic Crisis*, pp. 13–14.

[71]The following discussion of relatives and cronies who have profited under Marcos draws heavily on Jovito R. Salonga, "The Marcos Dictatorship and a Program for the Future" (unpublished manuscript, 1984), pp. 35–50; and Reuben R. Canoy, *The Counterfeit Revolution: Martial Law in the Philippines* (Manila, 1980), chap. 10. See also John F. Doherty, "Who Controls the Philippine Economy: Some Need Not Try as Hard as Others," in *Cronies and Enemies: The Current Philippine Scene*, ed. Belinda A. Aquino, Philippine Studies Occasional Paper no. 5, Philippine Studies Program, Center for Asian and Pacific Studies, University of Hawaii (Honolulu, 1982), pp. 7–35; Fred Poole and Max Vanzi, *Revolution in the Philippines: The United States in a Hall of Cracked Mirrors* (New York: McGraw-Hill, 1984), 244–267; and Mijares, *The Conjugal Dictatorship*, pp. 187–210.

[72]See, for instance, *Wall Street Journal*, 12 January 1978, pp. 1, 18; *New York Times*, 14 January 1978, pp. A1, A6; 20 January 1978, p. A3; *Philippine Times,* 15–21 June 1978, pp. 1, 3; and "Uranium and the Third World," a Friends of the Earth Broadsheet (1977), p. 2.

Similarly, with help from President Marcos, Roberto Benedicto and Eduardo Cojuangco set up monopolies in the mid-1970s, respectively, in the Philippine sugar and coconut industries, which together affect the livelihood of nearly 40 percent of the nation's population of fifty-four million. Benedicto established a monopoly in the sugar industry by gaining control of the Philippine Sugar Commission (PHILSUCOM) and the National Sugar Trading Corporation (NASUTRA), while Cojuangco set up a coconut cartel by gaining control of the Philippine Coconut Authority (PCA), the United Coconut Planters' Bank (UCPB), United Coconut Mills, Incorporated (UNICOM), and the coconut farmers' federation. Consolidation of these two industries into monopolies was done ostensibly to make them more efficient and competitive, but just the opposite resulted. By 1985 the sugar and coconut sectors of the economy were in disarray. Because of poor policy decisions, corruption, and inefficiency at home, as well as protectionism, increased regional competition, and the use of substitutes abroad, revenue from sugar and coconuts dropped from 25 percent of all exports to 19 percent in 1984. Translated into human terms the decline of sugar and coconuts resulted in mass unemployment in the cane fields and markedly lower incomes for small coconut producers. At the same time, Benedicto and Cojuangco pocketed huge sums of money.

Marcos' economic policies also represented a change in the priority of budgetary allocations away from social services, such as education, housing, and health. Education, which accounted for approximately one-third of the budget in the two decades preceding martial law, received an average of 12 percent of the budget from 1975 to 1981. Health and housing, which traditionally received small allocations, fared little better in the 1970s and early 1980s. Budgetary allocations for social services in 1982 were roughly half of what they were in 1965: 23.36 percent versus 44.24 percent.[73]

The advancement of a privileged elite with close ties to Marcos and the deterioration of the economy was accompanied by a rapid expansion of the Philippine armed forces. Military expenditures jumped from 15 percent of the national budget in 1970 to nearly 23 percent in 1977 before dropping off. During roughly the same period U.S. military assistance of all kinds (excluding ship transfers) increased from $105.7 million in the period 1968–72 to $261.7 million in the period 1973–77. The nearly $55 and $23 million increases, respectively, in the Foreign Military Sales (FMS) and the Commercial Arms Export (CAE) categories in the 1973–1977 period over the previous half-decade were particularly significant, because they under-

[73]De Dios et al., *An Analysis of the Philippine Economic Crisis*, pp. 35–36.

scored Washington's willingness to provide a variety of arms—including 46,615 M-16s, the basic counterinsurgency weapon of the AFP—to assist the Marcos regime in maintaining internal stability.[74] The result was a rise in social tensions as Marcos, invoking national security, increasingly relied on the military to maintain himself in power and to foster the political and economic interests of his relatives and cronies.

Although the economy steadily deteriorated and military abuses increased during the last decade of Marcos' rule, initially the declaration of martial law and the establishment of a New Society received a mixed reaction from individuals and groups within the Catholic and Protestant churches of the Philippines. Many clergy accepted Marcos' analysis about threats to the republic from the Communists, and supported the elimination of private armies, the confiscation of illegal firearms, the eradication of government inefficiency and corruption as well as the implementation of land reform, and the reorganization of government to encourage development. Yet doubts persisted about the president's motives in jailing political opponents, taking control of the mass media, and detaining large numbers of citizens, estimated to have totaled more than 70,000 by the end of martial rule in 1981.

Similar to the response of most Filipinos, the initial reaction of the Catholic and Protestant hierarchies was one of "wait and see." Most church leaders welcomed New Society reforms that promised improvements in the general welfare, while only a minority openly deplored human rights violations and the loss of civil liberties. With the arrests of priests, nuns, pastors, and layworkers engaged in social justice activities of the churches and revelations about abuses of power by government officials and the military, however, more church leaders gradually became more critical of Marcos' authoritarian rule, producing heightened church-state conflict from the late 1970s until Marcos' fall from power in February 1986.

The context within which the church leaders increasingly questioned the goals and accomplishments of the New Society and, since 1981, the "New Republic" is examined in the next two chapters. Chapter 3 outlines the ideology of the New Society contained within Marcos' "revolution from the center" and explores a number of the major institutional changes the Marcos government made in the name of development and social justice.

[74]Computed from Jim Zwick, "Militarism and Repression in the Philippines," McGill University, Center for Developing-Area Studies, Working Paper Series no. 31 (Montreal, 1982), Table 4, pp. 20–21. See also Bello and Rivera, "The Logistics of Repression," Table 5, p. 21.

3

"Ideology," Structure, and Opposition in the New Society

The inauguration of the New Society in tandem with the issuance of Proclamation 1081 was a clear signal that the objectives of the declaration of martial law went far beyond the provisions of Article VII of the 1935 Constitution. Basically, President Marcos reasoned that while the government (and military) was capable of handling the immediate threats to the republic, a New Society was needed to address a number of problems of Philippine society, namely, to arrest social and political decay, to reduce social injustices and economic inequities, and to implement the regime's development plans, especially the export-oriented industrialization program opposed by economic nationalists. To enhance the regime's capacity to impose political order and to extract resources for the achievement of the goals of the New Society, however, a major overhaul of existing social, political, and economic structures, including the inculcation of new values of discipline and self-sacrifice, was required.[1]

The reinvigoration of national life, according to Marcos, demanded nothing less than a total social revolution. But in calling for the "radicalization" of Philippine society, the president rejected established ideologies both of the left and the right, arguing, for instance, that Marxism-Leninism was out of step with Filipino culture and that American-style libertarianism

[1]See Ferdinand E. Marcos, *The Democratic Revolution in the Philippines* (Englewood Cliffs, N.J.: Prentice Hall International, 1974). Many of Marcos' prescriptions for the ills of Philippine society were in agreement with Samuel P. Huntington, *Political Order in Changing Societies* (New Haven: Yale University Press, 1968).

was insensitive to the needs and yearnings of poor Filipinos.[2] Instead, Marcos advanced the notion of a "revolution from the center" to be initiated and directed by the government and that was neither to the left or the right nor above or below the people, but rather at the center of society. The uniqueness of such a "centerist" revolution, according to the president, was the ability of the government—the only institution in society with the moral authority to act on behalf of all the people—to bring about radical change without violence. No sector of society was to benefit at the expense of another: the rich were not to be threatened with expropriation and disenfranchisement, yet the promise of social justice and economic equality was to be held out to the dispossessed and marginalized poor.[3]

An analysis of the ideology of the "revolution from the center" as well as an examination of some of the major developmental accomplishments of the New Society are important for understanding the nature of church-state relations in the Philippines. Although the rhetoric of the "revolution from the center" is similar to the stress given to social justice and human development by the Catholic and Protestant churches since Vatican II in 1965, the means by which the Marcos regime and church progressives chose to improve the quality of life for Filipinos often led to church-state conflict. The first section of this chapter presents the ideological underpinnings of the "revolution from the center," as articulated in the major writings of President Marcos and in selected documents of the New Society. It focuses on the regime's stated commitment to eradicating social injustice and improving conditions for the poor. The second section examines the methods by which the regime attempted to realize "the revolution from the center." Here the analysis focuses on Marcos' emphasis on the necessity for greater political order by expanding the role of the military, by taking control of the mass media, by reorganizing local government into the *barangay* system (the basic unit of government), and by exercising more comprehensive supervision of the electoral process.

The Ideology of the "Revolution from the Center"

A common theme in much of Marcos' writings after September 1972 was the commitment of the New Society to the improvement of conditions

[2]Ferdinand E. Marcos, *Towards a Filipino Ideology* (n.p., Ferdinand E. Marcos, 1979), p. 7.

[3]Ferdinand E. Marcos, *An Ideology for Filipinos* (n.p., Ferdinand E. Marcos, 1980), p. 29.

for the poor. A sample of excerpts from the president's books clearly underscores this point:

> The dominant characteristic of our society which demands radical change is the economic gap between the rich and the poor.[4]
>
> The conquest of mass poverty is our fundamental goal. Progress shall not be measured merely by the cold, impersonal statistics of the gross national product, but by the individually meaningful and tangible improvement of everyone's well being.[5]
>
> Government must exist for one purpose, and one purpose alone: to develop the mechanisms and the bases for the achievement of that society for which the poor—the overwhelming majority of the population—have been historically clamoring.[6]
>
> Into the year 2000 we expect every Filipino family to be assured of easy access to basic amenities in life like food, clothing, shelter, education and health services. At this stage, much is left to the direct intervention of government, which, as we have repeatedly said, takes the side of the poor.[7]
>
> Even as it is a constitutional imperative, therefore, the promotion of social justice is also a historical and political imperative. Perhaps it is even more particularly imperative in our day and age, characterized by what I have termed "the rebellion of the poor." It is to meet the demands of this rebellion that all of our efforts to promote social justice are addressed.[8]

Moreover, President Marcos stated boldly that the "rebellion of the poor" was thc major reason for the establishment of the New Society: "The rebellion of the poor reverses the traditional situation, in which society sits in judgment of the poor: now the poor sit in judgment of society."[9] To fulfill the aspirations of the poor, Marcos advocated a nonviolent, yet radical restructuring of Philippine society that included the democratization of wealth, more meaningful political participation, greater social justice, improved economic development, and more equality.[10] In his *Five Years of the New Society*, social justice and equality were combined as one of seven

[4]Marcos, *Democratic Revolution*, pp. 78–79.

[5]Ferdinand E. Marcos, *Notes on the New Society of the Philippines* (n.p., Ferdinand E. Marcos, 1973), p. 150.

[6]Marcos, *Five Years of the New Society* (n.p., Ferdinand E. Marcos, 1978), p. 158.

[7]Marcos, *Towards a Filipino Ideology,* pp. 37–38.

[8]Marcos, *Ideology for Filipinos,* p. 61.

[9]Marcos, *Notes on the New Society*, pp. 55–56.

[10]Ferdinand E. Marcos, *Notes on the New Society of the Philippines II: The Rebellion of the Poor* (n.p., Ferdinand E. Marcos, 1976), pp. 1–16.

moral postulates of the regime, while equality itself was portrayed as the ideological cornerstone of the New Society.[11]

The major mechanism for attaining social justice and equality was the "revolution from the center" whereby the government was to become the instrument for the "radicalization" of Philippine society. This was necessary because "built-in constraints" intrinsic in the pre-martial law system favored the privileged and wealthy, and because the "central political authority," as representative of all the people, was the only institution able to "equalize opportunities and alleviate the poor and the downtrodden."[12] But while the government was to function as the catalyst for, and guiding hand behind, the restructuring of socioeconomic, political, and cultural relationships, the president singled out other nongovernment institutions expected to play significant roles in the New Society. Prominent among these institutions was the business community. Marcos viewed the government as engaging in economic ventures too risky for private enterprise and acting as the "guardian and implementor" of programs serving the interests of everyone. He saw the free enterprise system, on the other hand, as the "principal engine for economic growth and prosperity," for only private enterprise had the "creative imagination" necessary for achieving "the full flowering of economic development" for the country.[13]

Actions taken at the declaration of martial law to establish a more comprehensive political order converged with the imperative to improve the lot of the poor in justifying a New Society hierarchy of human rights priorities. Freedom of the press, of speech, of assembly, and competitive elections, for example, were viewed as subordinate to economic rights, which Marcos considered primordial. Rhetorically the president claimed that the New Society was unwilling to exchange essential political rights simply for a guarantee of basic sustenance, but he nevertheless emphasized that the "credibility" of the regime rested less on press freedom and regular elections than on employment and social programs benefiting the poor. Marcos justified the regime's priorities by claiming that the masses were alienated from the political process of the Old Society because of its irrelevance to their basic needs and aspirations, which were primarily economic. Critics of the new priorities were disposed of as disgruntled oligarchs and effete intellectuals who feared the evaporation of their priv-

[11]Marcos, *Five Years of the New Society*, pp. 173–174.
[12]Ibid., p. 174.
[13]Marcos, *Ideology for Filipinos*, p. 27.

ileged positions with the institutionalization of the "revolution from the center."[14]

The preeminence accorded social justice in the New Society was etched in the Declaration of Principles and State Policies of the 1973 Constitution wherein the state was enjoined to "promote social justice to ensure the dignity, welfare and security of all the people" and to "regulate the acquisition, ownership, use, enjoyment and disposition of private property and equitably diffuse property ownership and profits."[15] The president emphasized that this constitutional commitment to social justice was not only based on numerous historical and judicial precedents, but also was stronger than a similar provision in the 1935 Constitution. Marcos "humbly" associated himself with the social justice tradition exemplified by Filipino revolutionary leaders like Emilo Jacinto and Apolinario Mabini and by famous Filipino jurists like Jose P. Laurel in averring that his own contribution lay primarily with the "fusion of social justice and economic development" as exemplified in Philippine development plans since 1972.[16]

Nowhere was President Marcos' stated commitment to social justice more explicit than in his speech on signing Presidential Decree 1200 approving the 1978–82 Philippine Development Plan. In the address, Marcos eschewed measuring economic progress only in terms of GNP and per capita income; instead, he advocated the "substantiation of the true meaning of social justice" by "democratizing . . . social and economic opportunities" in order to improve the "well-being of the broad masses" of society.[17] Marcos went on to say:

> At the heart of the Plans is the concern for social justice. The preparation of these Plans has been guided by one objective: "No Filipino will be without sustenance."
>
> We have therefore set our Development Plans toward a direct and purposeful attack against poverty by: focusing on the poorest of our society, planning to meet their basic nutritional needs, reducing if not entirely eliminating illiteracy, expanding employment opportunities, improving access to basic social services, equalizing opportunities, sharing the fruits of development equitably, and introducing the requisite institutional changes.

[14]Marcos, *Towards a Filipino Ideology*, pp. 16–18; and *Ideology for Filipinos*, pp. 15–20.

[15]*Philippine Constitution, 1973*, Article II, Sec. 6.

[16]Marcos, *Ideology for Filipinos*, chap. 5.

[17]Philippines (Republic), *Summary of the Five-Year Philippine Development Plan, 1978–1982 (including the Ten-Year Development Plan, 1978–1987)* (Manila: National Economic and Development Authority, 1977), p. xvi.

> We will pursue economic development for social justice. We will engage the initiative and resources of our people, according all citizens a rightful share in benefits and obligations. As both the source and object of development, our people will be provided with adequate economic opportunities and social amenities to attain a dignified existence.[18]

The president repeatedly emphasized the link between economic development and social justice in the speech, whereas the Plan itself included a section stating that the "underlying concern . . . of development in the next decade" was social justice.[19] The relegation of economic development to a position secondary to social development and social justice in the 1978–82 Plan represented a departure from development plans dating back to 1955.[20] So too Marcos' rhetoric about the best methods for achieving greater social justice and economic equity was a departure from the past. The president argued that the best way to realize the promises of the "revolution from the center," which he maintained would transform Philippine society, was to establish a constitutional authoritarian system of government that allowed for the imposition of political order from above.[21]

The Search for Political Order in the New Society

The Expansion of the Military

In the quest for political order, which was viewed as essential to the success of the New Society and the achievement of greater social justice, Marcos turned to the military at the commencement of martial law, believing that social discipline was a necessary (but lacking) element in Philippine national development. Not only did a number of senior officers (popularly known as the twelve disciples) participate in the decision to place the country under martial rule, but many other officers, long accustomed to the discipline associated with military hierarchy, also responded favorably to

[18]Ibid., p. xviii.

[19]Ibid., p. 14.

[20]Ledivina V. Cariño, "Some Problems in the Pursuit of Social Development in the Philippines," paper presented at a symposium on "The Philippines in the Third World: Perspectives in the Social Sciences," University of the Philippines Alumni Center, 9 December 1978, p. 5.

[21]Whether Marcos was sincere in maintaining that social justice and economic equity could best be achieved through constitutional authoritarianism is questionable given his use of the presidency, especially after 1972, to further enrich himself, his relatives, and close associates.

the establishment of what the president called the "Command Society."[22] The quid pro quo for the loyalty of the officer corps in the implementation of martial law and the consolidation of the New Society, however, included a substantial increase in material and psychological rewards for the Armed Forces of the Philippines (AFP) as well as an expansion of the military into judicial, administrative, and economic functions previously performed by civilians.

The initial successes of the military came easily. At the outset of martial law the military jailed political opponents and critics of the regime, including members of Congress, the 1971 Constitutional Convention, and the media. Within months it had collected over a half-million loose firearms and disbanded approximately two hundred private armies. Such measures, according to the president, were necessary to arrest the drift towards anarchy and to restore public order.[23] But the role of the military went beyond the mere maintenance of peace and order: Under various presidential letters of instruction, the Ministry of Defense took control of the mass media, major public utilities, and a number of vital industries, namely, the Elizalde Rolling Mills, Inc. and the Jacinto group of companies, which included the Iligan Integrated Steel Mill, Inc. The military was further designated to perform other functions, such as enforcing land reform, removing squatters from public lands, monitoring price controls, and preventing backsliding and inefficiency in government.[24] In addition, Marcos called on the armed forces to "participate in the more immediate and vital defense of the nation against poverty, ignorance, disease and injustice."[25] The result was a significant expansion of the role of the military in Philippine society.

The Defense Ministry's relinquishment of formal control over the mass media and the public utilities (except for the airlines) in May 1973, how-

[22]Harold W. Maynard, "A Comparison of Military Elite Role Perceptions in Indonesia and the Philippines" (Ph.D. diss., American University, 1976), pp. 374–379; and Carolina G. Hernandez, "The Extent of Civilian Control of the Military in the Philippines: 1946–1976" (Ph.D. diss., State University of New York at Buffalo, 1979), pp. 217–218.

[23]Ferdinand E. Marcos, *Progress and Martial Law* (Manila: Ferdinand E. Marcos, 1981), pp. 49–50.

[24]See, for example, *Letters of Instructions, 1 and 2*, 22 September 1972, *No. 27*, 14 October 1972, and *No. 35*, 28 October 1972; and Maynard, "A Comparison of Military Elite Role Perceptions," pp. 350–351. Maynard (p. 353) and Hernandez ("Civilian Control of the Military," p. 232) also reported that the military worked for the First Lady on a diversity of projects ranging from helping with the Miss Universe Contest in 1975 to assisting in the clean-up of the Pasig River and clogged canals in Manila.

[25]Ferdinand E. Marcos, as quoted in Jose M. Crisol, *The Armed Forces and Martial Law* (Makati: Agro Printing & Publishing House, 1980), p. vi.

ever, did not harbinger a reduction in the power and influence of the armed forces in the New Society.[26] Quite the contrary was the case: The military was the major instrument for the implementation of martial law, and as such was charged with the responsibility of eliminating the threats to the republic posed by the Communists, Muslims dissidents, and rightist oligarchs.[27] Moreover, through the creation of military tribunals with the authority to try both civilian and military cases and the establishment of a nationwide system of detention centers to hold suspected "subversives," the armed forces' political power was enhanced at the expense of the civilian judicial system.[28] Initially, the tribunals consisted of twenty military commissions, composed of five members each, and forty-eight single-officer provost courts, but in 1978 were replaced by ten military commissions. The tribunals handled cases involving military officers as well as cases with penalties of more than six years in prison, including cases against persons suspected of rebellion, subversion, and illegal possession of firearms and explosives, while the provost courts handled lesser offenses. Final decision on appeals of tribunal judgments rested with Juan Ponce Enrile, the minister of national defense, and the president.[29] Although the regime committed itself by mid-1977 to phasing out the military tribunals and Marcos promised to dismantle both the military courts and the detention centers following the termination of martial law in January 1981, the military continued to arrest and detain persons suspected of antigovernment activities.

Contributing to the military's high political profile in the New Society was the creation in 1975 of an Integrated National Police (INP) force, composed of the Philippine Constabulary (PC) and local law enforcement agencies, under the jurisdiction of the Ministry of National Defense.[30] The establishment of the INP was hailed by General Jose Crisol, deputy minister for home defense, as "the most significant development in the history of law enforcement" since the passage of the Police Act of 1966. The INP force was considered a significant asset in the nationwide campaign against crime and lawlessness during the early years of martial law.[31] The police

[26] *Presidential Decree 191*, 11 May 1973; and *Letter of Instruction 84*, 29 May 1973.

[27] *Proclamation 1081*, 21 September 1972.

[28] *General Order 8*, 27 September 1972; and *Presidential Decree 39*, 7 November 1972.

[29] Maynard, "A Comparison of Military Elite Role Perceptions," pp. 376–378; and Hernandez, "Civilian Control of the Military," pp. 220–222.

[30] *Philippine Constitution, 1973*, Article 15, Sec. 2; and *Presidential Decree 765*, 8 August 1975.

[31] Crisol, *Armed Forces and Martial Law*, p. 24.

integration program, however, relegated local police agencies into a secondary role vis-à-vis the army and the PC, and resulted in an unprecedented centralization of political intelligence and security information gathering in the armed forces. All major security agencies, such as the National Intelligence and Security Authority (NISA), the Constabulary Security Unit (CSU), the integrated Intelligence Service of the Armed Forces of the Philippines (ISAFP), the Central Intelligence Service Agency (CISA), and the Constabulary Anti-Narcotics Unit (CANU), were henceforth dominated by the military.

At the inception of the integration program, the combined law enforcement strength of the country rose to 74,000 with a concomitant improvement in the police-to-population ratio (assuming a population of 43 million) from 1:1,050 to 1:528. That the police-to-population ratio was still considered unsatisfactory was offset somewhat by the flexibility of the integration program, which allowed the deployment of INP forces regionally according to security needs. Also assisting the INP were *barangay* officials, who were required by law to inform the police about criminal activity and the presence of suspicious persons in local neighborhoods, and Police Advisory Council members, who advised the INP at all levels of government on questions of peace and order and public safety.[32]

The military's growing political influence was additionally bolstered during martial law by the AFP's home defense program, which was revised in June 1978, and by the deployment of the Integrated Civilian Home Defense Force (ICHDF). The home defense forces included both unarmed and armed civilian units; although some units performed civic action functions, the primary objective of the ICHDF was to defend the local community, in Jose Crisol's words, "against lawless elements and to assist law-enforcement agencies in restoring peace and order."[33] The ICHDF was organized into standard military units, and fell under the supervision of regular PC or AFP commands. The military, in consultation with local officials, was responsible for the selection and appointment of members of the armed ICHDF units as well as for overseeing their training in the maintenance of local security.

The military's organizational expansion after 1972 was initially matched by a similar increase in size and budget, as Tables 1 and 2 demonstrate. Regular troop strength nearly tripled during martial law, jumping from 58,100 in 1971 to 158,300 in 1982, while local defense forces grew from a

[32]Ibid., pp. 26–31.
[33]Ibid., p. 46.

Table 1. Personnel of the Armed Forces of the Philippines, 1971 and 1982

Regular Forces	*1971*	*1982*
Army	17,600	70,000
Navy/Coast Guad	8,000	28,000
Air Force	9,000	16,800
Constabulary	23,500	43,500
TOTAL	58,100	158,300
Irregular Forces		
Civilian Home Defense Force	(400 Armed Units)	65,000
Reserves	—	124,000

Sources: The Military Balance, 1971–1972 (London: International Institute for Strategic Studies, 1971), p. 50, and *1982–1983* (London, 1982), pp. 92–93.

few hundred armed units to a force of 65,000 during the same period.[34] Defense expenditures also went up dramatically, rising from ₱879 million in FY 1972 to ₱5,243 in FY 1981, representing nearly 20 percent of total government expenditures in the 1975–77 period. In individual terms, the Philippine government spent nearly $1,500 more per soldier in 1979 than in 1972.[35] In addition, from 1973 to 1977, arms imports, primarily from the United States, were double what they were from 1968 to 1972. Washington agreed in 1979 and in 1983 to pay Manila $500 million and $900 million, respectively, in military and economic assistance for continued access to military bases in the Philippines through 1989.[36]

The growth of the armed forces was likewise accompanied by accelerated promotions for senior officers (especially those considered politically loyal to President Marcos) and by significant pay increases, resulting in salaries that jumped by 150 percent immediately after the imposing of

[34]The PC is included in the "regular forces" category because, although it performs the police function of the armed forces and as such is considered a paramilitary force, it shifted away from only a small unit police function after 1972 to a role that included ten mobile battalions equipped and deployed similarly to AFP battalions. See Maynard, "A Comparison of Military Elite Role Perceptions," pp. 463–464.

[35]Ruth L. Sivard, *World Military and Social Expenditures, 1974* (New York: Institute of World Order, 1974), Table 3, p. 25; and Ruth L. Sivard, *World Military and Social Expenditures*, 1982 (Leesburg, Va.: World Priorities, 1982), Table 3, p. 32. See also Filipe B. Miranda, "The Military," in *The Philippines after Marcos*, ed. R. J. May and Francisco Nemenzo (London: Croom Helm, 1985), pp. 94–95.

[36]Jim Zwick, "Militarism and Repression in the Philippines," McGill University Center for Developing-Area Studies, Working Paper Series no. 31 (Montreal, 1982), Table 3, p. 19; and Larry A. Niksch and Marjorie Niehaus, "The Internal Situation in the Philippines: Current Trends and Future Prospects," Congressional Research Service, Library of Congress, Report no. 81–21 F, 20 January 1981, pp. 118–119.

Table 2. Philippine defense expenditures, 1972–82

Year	*Defense expenditures (millions of dollars)*[a]	*Defense expenditures as percentage of government expenditures*
1972	136	22.1
1973	172	22.6
1974	312	24.2
1975	407	19.3
1976	410	18.0[b]
1977	420[b]	18.0[b]
1978	794	17.9
1979	766	18.9
1980	962	13.0
1981	832	13.7
1982	910	14.8

Sources:

[a]Figures are from *The Military Balance, 1975–1976,* p. 77, *1976–1977,* p. 79, *1981–1982,* p. 113, *1983–1984,* p. 127, and *1984–1985,* p. 141 (London: International Institute for Strategic Studies, 1975, 1976, 1981, 1983, and 1984).

[b]Figures from Carolina G. Hernandez, "The Extent of Civilian Control of the Military in the Philippines: 1946–1976" (Ph.D. diss., State University of New York at Buffalo, 1979), Table 6, p. 234.

martial law and increased by another 100 percent for some ranks in 1976.[37] Other material gains by the military included improved retirement and separation benefits, special group insurance rates, subsidized commissary privileges, better educational opportunities for armed forces personnel and for dependents of military men killed in action, and advantages in appointments as directors of government corporations.[38]

With the promulgation of martial rule not only were some high-ranking officers retained beyond normal retirement age,[39] but military personnel also became more active in the economy. Apart from the military's management of the Elizalde steel complex and the Jacinto group of companies, Marcos created the Philippine Veterans Investment Development Company (PVIDC) and the Philippine Expeditionary Force to Korea Investment and

[37]Maynard, "A Comparison of Military Elite Role Perceptions," p. 348; Hernandez, "Civilian Control of the Military," p. 246; and Walden Bello and Severina Rivera, "The Logistics of Repression," in *The Logistics of Repression and Other Essays: The Role of U.S. Assistance in Consolidating the Martial Law Regime in the Philippines*, ed. Walden Bello and Severina Rivera (Washington, D.C.: Friends of the Filipino People, 1977), p. 42.

[38]Hernandez, "Civilian Control of the Military," p. 246. See also Miranda, "The Military," note 1, p. 107.

[39]Ibid., p. 218.

Development Corporation (PEFTOK-IDC) in July 1973 to provide employment and investment opportunities for retired military personnel. The corporations were created as rewards for the military's loyalty under martial law, and both were initially capitalized at over $500,000. Six months later, the president declared PVIDC a tax-free corporation, increased the government's subscription to $10 million, and in early 1974 opened its investments and benefits to members of the armed forces on active duty. The economic activities of the corporations have been varied, ranging from janitorial services in government organizations to agribusinesses in Mindanao.[40]

Perhaps more important than the military's participation in corporate management was the expansion of the political role of the armed forces in the New Society. While most military officers stressed the subordination of the armed forces to civilian control—most specifically that of the president—and often appeared uncomfortable engaging in political discussions, the fact remains that a significant number of retired generals were appointed to important governmental positions and to ambassadorial posts abroad. And, as Harold Maynard points out:

> Congressmen have been replaced by military officers dispensing favors. Both civilians and military personnel now regularly call upon senior officers to plead for assistance in getting jobs, solving family problems, processing applications, securing community development projects, or replacing inept government officials. Military patrons are sought out to help cut all forms of government red tape; traditional patron-client relationships have simply moved to a new arena under martial law.[41]

Although senior officers eschewed the notion of themselves as "modern-day politicians," the military's presence nevertheless continued to loom large politically. The armed forces routinely participated at the national and local level in discussions with civilian groups on problems of peace and order. In many rural areas, especially regions of high unrest, the military was often the dominant political voice.[42] And in the politics of economic development the role of the military was also boosted under martial law.

[40]*Presidential Decree 243*, 12 July 1973, *257*, 31 July 1973, and *353*, 26 December 1973. See also Maynard, "A Comparison of Military Elite Role Perceptions," pp. 407–408; and Hernandez, "Civilian Control of the Military," pp. 224–225.

[41]Harold W. Maynard, "Views of the Indonesian and Philippine Military Elites," in *The Military and Security in the Third World: Domestic and International Impacts*, ed. Sheldon W. Simon (Boulder, Colo.: Westview Press, 1978), p. 131.

[42]Hernandez, "Civilian Control of the Military," pp. 226–227.

The president declared in 1974, for example, that in addition to guaranteeing the security of the country, the military was in the process of becoming a full "partner in progress" and "national development."[43] Increasingly after the declaration of martial law, therefore, the armed forces were used to build roads, airfields, port facilities, and irrigation networks; by 1978, military officers composed 50 percent of the president's regional officers for development (PRODs).[44] As PRODs, Maynard tells us, the officers supervised all development projects in their military command areas, and, in some cases, had the power to intervene "in any ministry and at any echelon to ensure project completion."[45] Such authority put PROD officers at least on a par politically with provincial governors.

The extensive powers of the military PRODs, along with the reorganization of the four Philippine Constabulary (PC) zones into thirteen regional commands in 1978, increased the influence of the military in local administration,[46] and was, according to Kit Machado, part of the regime's program to centralize control and "weaken the local influence of old provincial leaders" in order to achieve the political order and development goals of the New Society.[47] The process of centralization in the military, Rodney Tasker writes, continued with the introduction in 1983 of "a 'regional unified command' structure" that placed all of the armed forces in a region (or group of provinces) under a single commander.[48]

Control of the Mass Media

Perhaps the earliest manifestation of the Marcos regime's move toward centralized control was the takeover upon the declaration of martial law of the country's mass media and the detention of prominent newspaper publishers, editors, and journalists and many employed in the radio and television industry. The president immediately closed all but one of Manila's sixteen daily newspapers, shut down six of the city's seven television stations, and allowed only the continuation of radio broadcasts by the Voice

[43]Ferdinand E. Marcos, "The Military and National Development," speech delivered at the Graduation Exercises of the 6th Regular Course, CGSC, 23 May 1974, as quoted in Hernandez, "Civilian Control of the Military," p. 225.

[44]Hernandez, "Civilian Control of the Military," pp. 223, 226.

[45]Maynard, "A Comparison of Military Elite Role Perceptions," p. 398.

[46]Hernandez, "Civilian Control of the Military," pp. 227–228.

[47]Kit G. Machado, "The Philippines 1978: Authoritarian Consolidation Continues," *Asian Survey* 19 (February 1979): 135.

[48]Rodney Tasker, "Rivalry in the Ranks," *Far Eastern Economic Review*, 8 March 1984, p. 40; and *Philippine News*, 20–26 February 1985, p. 4.

of the Philippines and the Far East Broadcasting Company.[49] Strict censorship was imposed on all news and the Ministry of Public Information issued guidelines requiring newspapers and radio and television stations to print and broadcast only "accurate" news that reflected positively on the government and the military.

President Marcos initially stated that control of the media was necessary because the press and radio were "infiltrated by Communist propagandists" and were "guilty of distorted, tendentious reporting" that "weakened resistance to Communism,"[50] but later he claimed that continued restrictions were needed to prevent rightist oligarchs from using the media to undermine the goals of the New Society. Thus the media empires of the Lopez, Soriano, Elizalde, and Roces families were dismantled and turned over to close associates and relatives of President Marcos and his wife, Imelda.[51] The result was the creation of six major media combines headquartered in Manila that were directly or indirectly controlled by the Marcoses. The largest was the Philippine Daily Express Company (*Daily Express*, *Filipino Express*, *Expressweek*, and *Sportsexpress*), reportedly owned by Marcos through Roberto Benedicto, former ambassador to Japan, and financed in part by presidential discretionary funds. The second and third largest dailies, *Bulletin Today* and *Balita ng Maynila*, and a group of vernacular magazines, including *Liwayway*, *Hiligaynon*, and *Bannawag*, were among the publications controlled by the late Hans Menzi, a former military aid to the president, while the *Times Journal* and the *Manila Journal* (for circulation in the United States) and two monthly magazines, *Women's Journal* and *People's Journal* were published by Benjamin Romualdez, Marcos' brother-in-law and governor of Leyte Province.

An organization publishing the *Evening Post*, *Focus Philippines*, and the *Orient Express* was owned by Juan Tuvera, a presidential assistant, and his wife, Kerima Polotan, the official biographer of Imelda Marcos. The

[49]*New York Times*, 25 September 1972, p. 3, and 26 September 1972, pp. 1, 10; and *Washington Post*, 26 September 1972, p. A20. For a slightly different and more extensive account, see Primitivo Mijares, *The Conjugal Dictatorship of Ferdinand and Imelda Marcos I* (San Francisco: Union Square 1976), pp. 327–329.

[50]*New York Times*, 27 September 1972, p. 3.

[51]The following discussion draws extensively on an article and paper by John Lent, "Underground Press Fills the Gaps in the Philippines," *Philippine News*, 30 January–5 February 1975, p. 9, and "Philippine Mass Media Thirty Years after Independence: Not Very Independent," paper presented at the Asian Studies on the Pacific Coast conference, Pacific Grove, California, June 11–13, 1976; C. R. Bryant, "The Philippine Press under Martial Law," *Cormosea Newsletter* 6 (June 1973): 1–6; and Mijares, *The Conjugal Dictatorship*, pp. 329–339.

United Daily News, a merger of the *Kong-Li-Po News* and the *Great China Press*, was published by a Kuomingtang group headed by Ralph Nubla, a supporter of Marcos in the Chinese community. The *Weekly Examiner* was owned and published by Leon O. Ty, a Marcos appointee to the governorship of the Development Bank of the Philippines. Added to these were a plethora of government publications, including the *Republic*, *Philippine Prospect*, *Philippines Today*, *Foreign Affairs Monthly*, *National Security Review*, and *Government Report* as well as numerous periodicals, such as *Fina*, *Game*, and *Sunday Observe*, that were issued by supporters of the president. With the exception of the *Daily Express* and a few provincial newspapers, all of these newspapers and magazines commenced publication after the imposition of martial rule.

Marcos also exercised considerable influence over the broadcast media. He controlled the Kanlaon Broadcasting System (KBS), which by 1975 ran at least fifteen radio stations and two television channels and allowed a third network, Barangay Broadcasting Corporation, to use the KBS Broadcasting Center. Marcos also had access to at least nineteen other radio stations operated by the government and the military. John Lent tells us that the television stations of the Banashaw Broadcasting Corporation, Radio Philippines Network, and GTV—which included three of the nation's five networks and half of the stations in the country—were managed by KBS's broadcasting management company. The only full-color television channels in the Philippines belonged to KBS. The dominance of KBS was further bolstered by reports that the cost of advertising jumped by as much as 400 percent only a few months after martial law began and remained high.[52]

In the areas of telephone, cable, and satellite communications a similar concentration of power existed, with close associates of the president serving as local partners with transnational telecommications corporations. Ramon Cojuangco, Roberto Benedicto, and Juan Ponce Enrile, all longtime intimates of Marcos, were involved in a multiplicity of telecommunications enterprises—ranging from the Philippine Long Distance Telephone Company (PLDT) and Oceanic Wireless to Domsat and Philcomsat—that had links to multinational corporations such as Siemens Corporation of the Federal Republic of Germany, Cable & Wireless of Great Britain, and the Marubeni Trading Corporation of Japan.[53]

[52]E. San Juan, Jr., "Marcos and the Media," *INDEX on Censorship* 7 (May–June 1978): 40.

[53]Gerald Sussman, "Telecommunications Technology: Transnationalizing the New Philippine Information Order" *Media, Culture and Society* 4 (1982): 381–383.

The regime's control of the mass media was facilitated by a series of presidential orders, decrees, instructions, and appointments after the inauguration of the New Society. The day after the proclamation of martial law Marcos issued Letter of Instruction 1 ordering the press secretary and the minister of national defense jointly "to take over and control . . . all such newspapers, magazines, radio and television facilities and all other media of communications, wherever they are, for the duration of the present national emergency."[54] But, as designated in Letter of Authority 1 dated the same day, the *Daily Express*, the Philippines Broadcasting System, Voice of the Philippines, Radio Philippines Network, and KBS were allowed to remain open. A few days later, on 25 September 1972, Order 1 of the Ministry of Public Information established censorship of the media, requiring all domestic "materials for publication and broadcast" and "foreign dispatches and cables" to be cleared by the ministry, and set forth stringent guidelines for media performance.[55] Pressure from foreign news agencies and foreign correspondents resulted, beginning in October 1972, in a gradual relaxing of the rules on overseas dispatches, but it was not until after the assassination of former Senator Benigno Aquino, Jr., in August 1983 that a modicum of press freedom began to return to the Philippines.

The new owners of the print and telecommunications media received other advantages from the government and from President Marcos. The Benedicto group of companies, for example, successfully negotiated large loans from the Philippine National Bank to expand its Radio Philippines Network (RPN) into all of the country's twelve regions, while a 1978 presidential Letter of Instruction granted Nivico, a Benedicto-owned television manufacturing company, the sole right to import duty-free components from Japan. Similarly, in 1980 Marcos ordered a merger of the Republic Telephone Company (RETELCO), the nation's second largest telephone company, and PLDT; as a result, Ramon Cojuangco became president of a significantly larger communications empire.[56]

Placing the mass media in the hands of the president's relatives and close associates, coupled with the implementation of greater government control over the media, was justified, in part, as a necessary step for the acceleration of national development. Representative of this position was a 1973 statement by Francisco Tatad, Marcos' former minister of public information, that henceforth "the development of media . . . must be solely

[54]*Letter of Instruction 1*, 22 September 1972.

[55]Reprinted in *Bulletin of Concerned Asian Scholars* 5 (July 1973): 58.

[56]Sussman, "Telecommunications Technology," pp. 381–385; and Leo Gonzaga, "Disentangling the Wires," *Far Eastern Economic Review*, 12 December 1980, pp. 56–57.

measured in terms of the advancement of society" and that the "media as an active agent for social change" were required "to help inculcate in the polity such values and attitudes that must precede the transformation of society."[57] The theme of communications for development was reflected in the government's ten-year economic development program (1978–87) in which ₱3.21 billion was earmarked to improve domestic telecommunications in order to stimulate "integrated socio-economic development, especially on the regional level."[58] Little of the projected investment was realized, however, because of budgetary limitations. Instead, control of the media for development translated into increased centralization, censorship, and an emphasis on serving the needs of the foreign investors that the regime was relying upon to accelerate economic development.

The Creation of Barangay *Government*

Expansion of the military and censorship of the mass media were accompanied by other reforms aimed at improving the regime's image and enhancing its political control. Reorganizing the government, attacking graft and corruption, and the holding of referenda and elections were hailed as facilitating economic development, improving social justice, and encouraging responsible participatory democracy; all received praise from the president as martial law achievements. Marcos labeled the establishment of the *Sandiganbayan* and *Tanodbayan*, which were provided for in the 1973 Constitution, "as the people's instrument against corruption in government," and in 1982 boasted that the *Tanodbayan* had received more than thirteen thousand complaints since 1979.[59] Similarly, he hailed the creation of the *barangay* assemblies and the *sanggunian* (council) system as well as the convening of the interim *Batasang Pambansa* (National Assembly) and the two *Sangguniang Pampook* (Regional Assemblies) for the autonomous Muslim areas (regions 9 and 12) as important steps toward the "democratization of political power." Significantly, Marcos also stressed that the

[57]*Business Day*, 7 February 1973, as quoted in Sussman, "Telecommunications Technology," p. 379.

[58]Philippines (Republic), *Annex to the Five-Year Philippine Development Plan, 1978–1982: Profiles of Selected Development Projects* (Manila, 21 September 1977), pp. 177–178.

[59]*Philippine Constitution, 1973*, Article 13, Secs. 5 and 6; *Proclamation 2045*, 17 January 1981, reprinted in *Philippine News*, 21–27 January, pp. 1, A; and Ferdinand E. Marcos, *The New Philippine Republic: A Third World Approach to Democracy* (Manila, 1982), pp. 21–22. The *Sandiganbayan* is an anticorruption court established to try only cases against government officials brought by the *Tanodbayan*, a government ombudsman or special prosecutor.

system of *barangay* assemblies represented a reorientation of Philippine politics toward fuller, more meaningful participation of the masses in contrast to the corruption, apathy, and indifference that characterized the Old Society.[60]

The establishment of the *barangay* assemblies and the *sanggunian* system played an important part in the consolidation of Marcos' power under martial law.[61] The president created the citizen assemblies on 31 December 1972 "to broaden the base of citizen participation in the democratic process and to afford ample opportunities for the citizenry to express their views on important national issues."[62] A week later, on 5 January 1973, he stated that the *barangay* assemblies "shall constitute the base for citizen participation in governmental affairs and their collective views shall be considered in the formulation of national policies or programs and, wherever practicable, shall be translated into concrete and specific decisions."[63] The assemblies were also empowered to vote on the new constitution, the prolongation of martial law, the reconvening of Congress, and the scheduling of elections in November 1973.[64]

Initially the president scheduled a nationwide plebiscite on the new charter, to be preceded by a period of free debate, for 15 January 1973, but within days of the issuance of Presidential Decree 86-A Marcos suspended debate on the constitution, alleging that "enemies of the state" were abusing freedom of speech by sowing discord and confusion among the electorate. He postponed the vote until after a "national consultation" with the *barangay* assemblies between 10 and 15 January 1973.[65] By a show of hands, *barangay* members fifteen years of age or older endorsed the new constitution, which established a parliamentary system of government, and approved the continuation of martial rule; they rejected the reopening of

[60]Marcos, *Notes on the New Society II*, pp. 151–164; and Marcos, *Five Years of the New Society*, pp. 162–167. See also Leonardo B. Perez, "Barangay Democracy and the New Society," *Fookien Times Yearbook, 1975*, pp. 268, 270–271, 359–360; and Jose Roño, "The Sangguniang Bayan: A Great Leap toward Genuine Participatory Democracy," *Fookien Times Yearbook, 1976*, pp. 288, 302.

[61]On some of the political uses of these organizations, see Blondie Po, *Rural Organizations and Rural Development in the Philippines: A Documentary Study*, Final report submitted to the Asian Center for Development Administration by the Institute of Philippine Culture (Quezon City: Institute of Philippine Culture, Ateneo de Manila University, 1977), pp. 97–110; and Robert B. Stauffer, "Philippine Corporatism: A Note on the 'New Society,'" *Asian Survey* 17 (April 1977): 393–407.

[62]*Presidential Decree 86*, 31 December 1972.

[63]*Presidential Decree 86-A*, 5 January 1973.

[64]Ibid.

[65]*New York Times*, 2 December 1972, p. 9; 8 January 1973, p. 3; and 9 January 1973, p. 2.

Congress and the holding of elections in November 1973. They also affirmed several other questions favorable to the regime.[66]

Emboldened by an overwhelming mandate from the citizen assemblies, Marcos convened a Peoples' Congress composed of approximately 4,600 *barangay* representatives where, on 17 January 1973, he signed three decrees affirming the ratification of the new constitution, the abolition of the interim National Assembly provided for in the constitution's transitory provisions, and the indefinite continuation of martial law.[67] A week later the Supreme Court dismissed ten petitions challenging the suspension of the 15 January plebiscite, and on 2 April 1973, the court again upheld the president on the new constitution in a long and complex decision.[68] Although the justices felt that the constitution was improperly ratified (based on referenda procedures in the 1935 Constitution), they nevertheless recognized that, lacking the necessary six votes for an outright declaration of unconstitutionality, the new charter was de facto in force.[69]

The Supreme Court's decision in *Javellana vs. The Executive Secretary, et al.*, while controversial, was a political victory for the president. With the elimination of Congress and the interim National Assembly, which was to include members of the old Congress who opted to serve in the assembly as well as members of the 1971 Constitutional Convention who voted in favor of the 1973 Constitution, Marcos acquired vast powers guaranteed in the new constitution's transitory provisions, including the retention of all the "powers and prerogatives" of the president under the 1935 Constitution plus presidential and prime ministerial powers under the new charter. He could replace government officials, including members of the judiciary, at will, and all his decrees, orders, and instructions automatically became "part of the law of the land." Similarly, treaties, executive agreements, and contracts approved by Marcos were immediately "recognized as legal, valid, and binding."[70]

Several additional referenda were held prior to the end of martial law. In July 1973, Marcos asked the citizen assemblies for an extension of his term beyond the December 1973 deadline set by provisions of the 1935 Constitution; although martial law restrictions were relaxed for a few days to

[66]*New York Times*, 11 January 1973, p. 5.

[67]Jean Grossholtz, "Philippines 1973: Whither Marcos?" *Asian Survey* 14 (January 1974): 103; and *Proclamations 1102, 1103, and 1104*, 17 January 1973.

[68]*New York Times*, 24 January 1973, p. 2; and 3 April 1973, p. 3.

[69]Rolando V. del Carmen, "Constitutionality and Judicial Politics," in *Marcos and Martial Law in the Philippines*, ed. David A. Rosenberg (Ithaca: Cornell University Press, 1979), p. 96.

[70]*Philippine Constitution, 1973*, Article 17, Secs. 3, 10, and 12.

allow "free debate," little organized opposition materialized.[71] Generally government officials, including *barangay* leaders, urged support of the measure, as did the controlled media; Marcos warned that anyone failing to vote was subject to a trial, with a penalty of up to six month in jail. The Commission on Elections (COMELEC), newly reorganized and headed by former senator Leonardo Perez, a close associate of Marcos, announced a 90 percent "yes" vote, and revealed a "consensus" among *barangay* officials that the president appoint an advisory council to assist in formulating and implementing government policies and programs.[72]

Again in February 1975, Marcos asked the *barangay* assemblies for an endorsement of martial law and the reforms of the New Society; in a move to strengthen his political control at the grass roots, he included a question on whether local officials should be elected or appointed (clearly signaling he wanted a mandate to appoint). A three-week period of "open debate" on the referendum failed to produce significant support for a "no" vote in public rallies and in the media, as permits for public meetings and the media were firmly under the control of the regime, but the opposition did organize a boycott movement and petitioned the Supreme Court against martial law and the referendum. The justices upheld Marcos on the grounds that, according to the transitory provisions of the constitution and as a result of "overwhelming endorsement from the people" in the first two referenda, "he was President in fact as well as by law."[73] The president campaigned vigorously in favor of the referendum measures, and, predictably, COMELEC announced another 90 percent victory. Only in Cebu did a majority ask that local officials be elected.[74]

Flushed with reinforced appointive powers following the third referendum, Marcos restructured local and regional governments with four major proclamations issued between November 1975 and April 1976, and created a legislative advisory body, the *Batasang Bayan*, at the national level in September 1976. In November 1975, the president reorganized government in greater Manila and established the *sanggunian* system to replace the old local government edifice in the nation's towns, cities, and provinces.[75] Under the new setup, the four cities and thirteen municipalities

[71]*New York Times*, 8 July 1973, p. 17.

[72]*New York Times*, 25 July 1973, p. 5; 26 July 1973, p. 6; 27 July 1973, p. 6; 28 July 1973, p. 3; and 1 August 1973, p. 5.

[73]*New York Times*, 2 February 1975, p. 12; and 27 February 1975, p. 2.

[74]*New York Times*, 1 March 1975, p. 8; and 3 March 1975, p. 7.

[75]The discussion of the *sanggunian* system draws extensively on two papers by Belinda A. Aquino: "Politics in the New Society: *Barangay* 'Democracy,'" paper presented at the annual meeting of the Association for Asian Studies, New York City, 25–27 March 1977,

composing greater Manila were placed under the Metropolitan Manila Commission with Imelda Marcos as governor. Nationwide, the *sangguniang bayan* or *sangguniang pambayan* replaced the municipal council, the *sangguniang panglungsod* replaced the city council, and the *sangguniang panlalawigan* replaced the provincial board.[76] The *sangguniang bayan* were subsequently organized into a national body called the *Katipunan ng mga Sanggunian* (National Federation of Councils) in January 1976, and the city and provincial *sangguniang bayan* were, in turn, grouped into regional federations known as the *Pampook na Katipunan ng mga Sanggunian* (Federation of Regional Councils) the following April.[77]

The *sanggunian* structure, while essentially retaining the powers and functions of the pre-martial law municipal, city, and provincial governments, was created ostensibly to provide greater citizen participation at the local level, whereas the *Katipunan ng mga Sanggunian* and the *Pampook na Katipunan ng mga Sanggunian* were established to provide local officials with a broader perspective on policy considerations at the national and regional level. Accordingly, the size of the *sangguniang bayan* was significantly greater (some had as many as fifty members) than that of the old local government bodies. Not only previous local government officials such as mayors, governors, and councilors served but representatives from capital, labor, and the professions—the so-called "sectoral representatives"—were included as were *barangay* captains and representatives from the *Katipunan ng mga Kabataang Barangay*, the national youth organization. Appointment to and/or retention in the various *sangguniang bayan* was at the pleasure of the president, which clearly increased his control over local politics.[78]

Once the *sanggunian* structure was in place, President Marcos revealed, on 10 September 1976, the appointment of members to the *Batasang Bayan*, a national legislative advisory body made up of cabinet officers and representatives from the Association of Local and Provincial Assemblies;

---

and "The Philippine *Barangays* as Instruments of Central Control," *Proceedings of the Fourth International Symposium on Asian Studies, 1982* (Hong Kong: Asian Research Service, 1982), pp. 365–374.

[76]*Presidential Decree 824*, 7 November 1975, and *826*, 14 November 1975; and Lela G. Noble, "The Philippines 1975: Consolidating the Regime" *Asian Survey* 16 (February 1976): 179.

[77]*Presidential Decree 877*, 21 January 1976, and *925*, 24 April 1976; and Antonio Orendain, *Local Governments in a New Setting: An Annotated Compilation of Presidential Decrees Affecting Local Governments*, vol. 2 (Manila: Alpha Omega Publications, 1972), p. 47.

[78]Aquino, "Politics in the New Society," p. 25.

almost simultaneously he announced another referendum for 16 October 1976, to consider nine amendments to the new constitution.[79] The constitutional changes, while including the creation of an Interim *Batasang Pambansa* ([IBP] Interim National Assembly), provided for Marcos to continue using the powers contained in the transitory provisions even after the IBP's convening. The president was also authorized to exercise legislative powers until the termination of martial law, and was given sweeping emergency powers to act through "decrees, orders, or letters of instruction," when in his judgment the nation faced a threat not adequately handled by the IBP or regular National Assembly. The amendments also legitimized the establishment of the *barangay* assemblies and the *sanggunian* bodies, though anytime they could be altered, and referenda could be used "to ascertain the will of the people" on important policy matters. In keeping with the pattern of past referenda, despite calls for a boycott by opponents, Marcos again won nearly 90 percent of the vote, and ten days later, on 27 October, declared the amendments, "in full force and effect."[80]

With local, provincial, and regional government firmly under the control of the regime, the next step politically in the president's "revolution from the center" was the holding of elections aimed at moving the Philippines from a presidential to a parliamentary system in accordance with the 1973 Constitution and returning the country to normalcy through increased, although closely controlled, political participation. Ever cautious, however, Marcos first tested the political waters with yet another referendum on 17 December 1977, which asked: "Do you vote that President Ferdinand E. Marcos continue in office as incumbent President and be prime minister after the organization of the interim *Batasang Pambansa* as provided for in Amendment 3 of the 1976 amendments to the Constitution?" Beyond making sure of his popularity, some thought the president called the referendum to demonstrate (especially to Washington) the regime's overwhelming popular support amid heightened criticism of human rights violations. Although the political opposition boycotted, labeling the exercise as a "brazen mockery" of democracy given martial law restrictions, Marcos achieved another sweeping (89.5 percent) victory.[81]

[79]*New York Times*, 11 September 1976, p. 7; and 3 October 1976, p. 3.

[80]*Philippine Constitution, 1973*, Amendments 1–9; *Proclamation 1595*, 27 October 1976; and Lela G. Noble, "The Philippines 1976: The Contrast between Shrine and Shanty," *Asian Survey* 17 (February 1977): 133–134.

[81]Rodney Tasker, "The Choice according to Marcos," *Far Eastern Economic Review*, 11 November 1977, pp. 17–19; Rodney Tasker, "The President's Persuasive Leadership," *Far Eastern Economic Review*, 30 December 1977, pp. 10–11; and Kit G. Machado, "The Philippines in 1977: Beginning a 'Return to Normalcy'?" *Asian Survey* 18 (February 1978): 204.

Immediately after the referendum, IBP elections were scheduled for 7 April 1978. Taking no chances on the outcome, the *Batasang Bayan*, with Marcos' approval, issued a new election code containing a controversial provision for block voting, which allowed voters to select an entire slate of candidates by simply indicating a preferred party. The president created a new political party, the *Kilusang Bagong Lipunan* ([KBL] New Society Movement), composed of prominent national and local government officials, to contest the election. Although a forty-five-day campaign period free of some martial law restrictions was declared, many opponents of the regime were dubious about Marcos' willingness to conduct a fair election. The Liberal Party (LP), citing the lack of freedom of the press and assembly and criticizing the block voting scheme as inherently unfair, chose to boycott, while other Marcos opponents formed new organizations, such as *Lakas ng Bayan* ([LABAN=fight] People's Strength), and *Pusyon Bisaya* (Visayas Merger), and the Mindanao Alliance, to run against the KBL under the premise that "the election offered an opportunity to criticize the regime and the possibility of securing a regular platform for 'fiscalizing'."[82]

The election was intensely contested in metro-Manila where the KBL slate was headed by Imelda Marcos and the LABAN ticket was headed by former Senator Benigno Aquino, Jr., Marcos' archrival. Aquino, who, at the time, was appealing a conviction for murder, subversion, and illegal possession of firearms, was denied, ostensibly for security reasons, a temporary release from Fort Bonifacio to campaign, but he was allowed a ninety-minute television interview. Aquino's appearance, however, came only after several days of negotiations between his sister, film director Lupita Concio, and the government's National Media Production Company. Although none of Aquino's remarks was edited, he likewise refrained from criticizing the Marcoses. LABAN campaigned against government corruption and the negative aspects of martial law, while the KBL emphasized the political and economic accomplishments of the New Society and attacked LABAN both as a tool of the Communists and of the United States.[83]

Many observers thought that some LABAN candidates—especially

[82]Rodney Tasker, "Opposition Rejects the Rules," *Far Eastern Economic Review*, 10 February 1978, pp. 20–21; and Machado, "The Philippines 1978," pp. 131–134. The act of "fiscalizing" in the Philippines denotes watching for wrongdoing in government, particularly with respect to charges of graft and corruption, and comes from the term *fiscal*, a Spanish official who functioned as an inquisitor, public defender, and district attorney.

[83]Machado, "The Philippines 1978," p. 133; Rodney Tasker, "A Political Star Is Reborn," *Far Eastern Economic Review*, 24 March 1978, pp. 10–11; and *Christian Science Monitor*, 4 April 1978, p. 6.

Aquino, who handled himself well on television—might win, but all twenty-one seats in metro-Manila went to the KBL, with Governor Marcos garnering the most votes. Not only did the president control COMELEC, the mass media, and local government down to the *barangay* assemblies, but he also improved the KBL's chances by increasing the salaries and benefits of government employees, including public school teachers, who supervised the balloting, and increased the funding for public works projects over the objections of the opposition.[84] Furthermore, as Kit Machado pointed out, numerous "irregular steps," such as the "intimidation of government employees, manipulation of registration and voting procedures to permit large-scale movement of transient voters into Manila and 'flying voters' to cast multiple ballots, and plain ballot box stuffing," were employed to guarantee victory in Manila. Only in areas outside of the capital were a few seats won by the opposition, namely the triumph (after a protest) of thirteen *Pusyon Bisaya* candidates in the Central Visayas and the success of Reuben Canoy, former Mayor of Cagayan de Oro City in Mindanao, who ran as an independent.[85]

A three-hour noise barrage on election eve and a postelection demonstration over alleged election fraud resulted in the reimposition of restrictions on freedom of speech and assembly and the arrest of nearly six hundred persons, including former Senator Lorenzo Tañada and several other opposition figures, among whom was Fr. Romeo Intengan, an important Social Democrat (Soc-Dem) organizer and ideologue.[86] The president averred that there would be no accommodation to "anarchists, radicals and terrorists," and he warned that the midnight-to-dawn curfew might be restored.[87] Most of the demonstrators were soon released, and although the distrubance over the election had dissipated by the time the IBP was convened on 12 June, Independence Day, it was clear to critics of the regime that the president had no intention, despite protestations to the contrary, of sharing political power or of nurturing a loyal opposition in the British parliamentary tradition.

That Marcos' power remained undiminished, as guaranteed by the 1976 constitutional amendments, was underscored in the opening of the National

[84]*New York Times*, 7 April 1978, pp. 1, A7; United States Foreign Broadcast Information Service (FBIS), *Daily Reports*, vol. 4, Asia & Pacific, 2 February 1978, p. P1, and 30 March 1978, p. P1.

[85]Machado, "The Philippines 1978," pp. 133–134; and *Philippine Times*, 22–28 June 1978, p. 3.

[86]See Chapter 4 for a discussion of the Soc-Dems.

[87]Rodney Tasker, "Marcos Ends a Fleeting Taste of Freedom," *Far Eastern Economic Review*, 21 April 1978, pp. 10–13.

Assembly. The president, who concurrently assumed the position of prime minister, continued to rule by decree even though law-making under the 1973 Constitution was a function of the National Assembly. Nonelected cabinet ministers (thirteen) were decreed IBP members, and Imelda Marcos was appointed to head the newly created Ministry of Ecology and Human Settlements. Assembly committee chairmanships were reserved for ministers, and the consideration of parliamentary acts required prior cabinet approval. The period for questioning government ministers was limited to a single hour once a month, thereby limiting interpolation, and the interrogatives had to be submitted in writing to the speaker of the National Assembly a week in advance.[88] With an overwhelming KBL majority and presidential loyalists in control, the IBP unerringly supported the policies and programs of the New Society; in contrast, the parliamentary opposition remained divided and largely ineffective.

The remaining major political achievements of the regime prior to the termination of martial law were the holding of Muslim autonomous area (regions 9 and 12) elections on 7 May 1979, following the 1976 Tripoli Agreement with the Moro National Liberation Front (MNLF) and the holding of local elections on 30 January 1980.[89] The leadership of the MNLF factions based in the Middle East and North Africa denounced the *Sangguniang Pampook* elections of the autonomous regions as a violation of the Tripoli Agreement, and refused to participate. Although some individual Muslims—including some identified as MNLF members—ran under the KBL umbrella, the traditional opposition, still irked over the massive rigging of the previous year's IBP election, also boycotted. Only a few independents and a smattering of regional parties ran against the KBL. In at least one instance, much to the consternation of COMELEC, the Concerned Citizens Aggrupation, headed by former Zamboanga City mayor Cesar Climaco, fielded a local "crackpot" as a protest, saying: "We would rather have a crank than a crook" for a *Sangguniang Pampook* representative.[90] As expected, however, all the assembly seats were won by KBL or KBL-affiliated candidates, and as Marcos appointed the entire membership of the two *Lupong Tagapagpaganap ng Pook* (Regional Ex-

[88]Machado, "The Philippines 1978," p. 134; and *Philippine Times*, 15–21 July 1978, p. 5.

[89]Philippines (Republic), Ministry of Foreign Affairs, *The Southwestern Philippines Question*, 3d ed. (Manila: Ministry of Foreign Affairs, 1980).

[90]*Asiaweek*, 11 May 1979, p. 12, and 18 May 1979, pp. 14–15; and Sheilah Ocampo, "Why the 'Water Banker' Stood," *Far Eastern Economic Review*, 18 May 1979, pp. 16, 21–22.

ecutive Council), "Muslim autonomy" remained firmly under the control of the regime.[91]

Of much more importance were the January 1980 local elections for provincial, city, and municipal officials. The Liberal Party and LABAN, disputing the thirty-day campaign period as unconstitutional, protesting last-minute election code changes that specifically barred Benigno Aquino from running, and disagreeing with the continuation of martial law controls, again boycotted.[92] Other oppositionists ran against the regime under various banners, including the Nacionalista Party, the Mindanao Alliance, the National Union for Liberation (NUL), *Bicol Saro*, (United Bicol), and *Pusyon Bisaya*, with only spotty success.[93] That Marcos was determined to retain control at the local level was evident in the revamping of the KBL, the fielding of New Society candidates nationwide, and the use of government resources to insure victory. Prior to the election, for example, the president promised *barangay* leaders ₱5,000 apiece for neighborhood development schemes, and in a move reminiscent of previous Old Society campaigns, the regime dispersed large sums of "pork barrel" money to *barangay* officials for local infrastructure projects, such as road and bridge construction.[94] COMELEC also denied the NUL accreditation to participate in the election as an official party in a decision upheld by the Supreme Court. Marcos also challenged the credentials of the Nacionalista Party, as many of its candidates had run under the KBL umbrella in 1978. Although the Nacionalista petition for accreditation was eventually sustained both by COMELEC and the Supreme Court, the ensuing confusion over the party's status worked to the advantage of the KBL.[95] Similarly, the mass media were manipulated so that the activities of President Marcos and the First Lady were covered extensively, while those of the opposition were either ignored or only mentioned briefly. Not a single speech of major opposition figures was aired in the controlled media, and LABAN was unable to purchase newspaper space to publish the party's justifications for boycotting

[91]Sheilah Ocampo, "Marcos Still Calls the Shots," *Far Eastern Economic Review*, 10 August 1979, pp. 26–27; and Clark D. Neher, "The Philippines 1979: Cracks in the Fortress," *Asian Survey* 20 (February 1980): 159–160.

[92]*Bulletin Today*, 19 December 1979, pp. 1, 14.

[93]*Bulletin Today*, 30 December 1979, pp. 1, 8.

[94]Sheilah Ocampo, "Preparing for Election Weather," *Far Eastern Economic Review* 21 December 1979, p. 10; Sheilah Ocampo, "The One-Party Election Show," *Far Eastern Economic Review*, 11 January 1980, pp. 15–16; and Sheilah Ocampo, "Marcos Wins on All Fronts," *Far Eastern Economic Review*, 15 February 1980, pp. 13–14.

[95]*Bulletin Today*, 5 January 1980, p. 1; 17 January 1980, pp. 1, 5; 26 January 1980, pp. 1, 8; and 30 January 1980, pp. 1, 9; and *Asiaweek*, 15 February 1980, p. 20.

the election. In contrast, the entire platform of the KBL was reproduced in the Manila press.[96]

Although the election was marred by violence, resulting in a number of deaths, and by the usual charges of fraud, the KBL romped to victory, winning sixty-nine of seventy-three governorships and all but a few of the 1,560 mayoral contests. In Ilocos Norte, Elizabeth Roca, Marcos' sister, was reelected governor, and Ferdinand "Bongbong" Marcos, Jr., after an election code change lowering the age requirement from twenty three to twenty-one, ran unopposed for vice-governor. Jose Laurel V, a Nacionalista, won the governorship of Batangas in an acrimonious campaign, and several candidates of the Mindanao Alliance, the NUL, and the Concerned Citizens Aggrupation triumphed in gubernatorial and mayoral races elsewhere in the country. *Pusyon Bisaya* and other opposition groups, plagued by factionalism and lack of resources, were less successful against the Marcos juggernaut.[97]

Marcos' formula for success at the polls proved equally potent after the lifting of martial rule. The voters approved several constitutional amendments in a 7 April 1981 referendum. The first amendment established a presidential-parliamentary system similar to that of the French Fifth Republic. Under the new structure, the president, who was elected for a six-year, renewable term, functioned as chief executive and head of state. The president also appointed the prime minister and, until its abolition in 1984, a fourteen-member executive committee to assist in running the government. The prime minister was removable by a no-confidence vote in the National Assembly, but he also served, as did the members of the executive committee, at the pleasure of the president. Another feature of the first amendment was a provision granting Marcos and others immunity from suit for official acts during the president's term of office and protecting government and military officials from prosecution for carrying out presidential orders during martial law. The other two amendments established new procedures governing political party membership, accreditation, and participation on electoral boards, and granted natural-born Filipinos who were foreign citizens the right to purchase limited amounts of property in the Philippines. Although the United Democratic Opposition (UNIDO) and

[96]*Bulletin Today*, 15 January 1980, p. 15; and *Philippine Times*, 4 February 1980, pp. 1, 15.

[97]*Bulletin Today*, 19 February 1980, pp. 1, 14; 3 March 1980, pp. 1, 14; FBIS, 18 January 1980, p. P1; Ocampo, "Marcos Wins on All Fronts," pp. 13–14; and Clark D. Neher, "The Philippines in 1980: The Gathering Storm," *Asian Survey* 21 (February 1981): 261–263.

other groups waged a spirited boycott, the amendments passed by a comfortable margin, receiving an affirmative vote of 79 percent.[98]

Immediately following the referendum, Marcos announced a presidential election for 16 June 1981. Just as in the 7 April referendum, UNIDO refused to participate when Marcos rejected its demands for (1) extending the campaign period from 55 days to 120 days; (2) purging the voters' lists of unqualified voters; (3) providing the opposition equal access to the media; and (4) reorganizing COMELEC to guarantee impartiality in supervising the election.[99] Although twelve candidates eventually ran against the president, none was a serious threat. Nevertheless, concerned over the boycott movement, which included not only UNIDO but also a more radical coalition called the People's Movements for Independence, Nationalism and Democracy (People's MIND), Marcos campaigned vigorously, releasing "pork barrel" funds for development projects and distributing as much as ₱6,000 to *barangay* chairmen. In addition, he threatened nonvoters in the 7 April referendum with legal action unless they went to the polls on 16 June.[100] As an added inducement to increase voter turnout, the president put a popular referendum question on the ballot about the desirability of holding *barangay* elections in the near future. As a result, voter turnout was high (85 percent), and Marcos, with 88 percent of the vote, ran away with the election.[101]

In keeping with the voter's wishes, *barangay* elections at the grass roots were held on 17 May 1982, for the first time in a decade in the country's 42,000 neighborhood organizations. Although nonremunerative, the positions were a source of prestige and influence in the local community; *barangay* leaders were expected to play a pivotal role, which they did, in the 1984 *Batasang Pambansa* elections and in other elections Marcos had scheduled for 1986 and 1987. Knowing that the overwhelming majority (perhaps 90 percent) of *barangay* officials supported the government, Marcos declared the elections nonpartisan. The moderate democratic opposition, still groping for unity, protested the president's declaration. The Social Democratic Party (SDP) claimed the decision undercut the "development of a real party system in the country," while UNIDO accused pro-Marcos governors and mayors of intimidating candidates and of dictating the vote. Although the opposition catalogued numerous polling irreg-

[98]*Philippines Daily Express*, 6 February 1981, pp. 1, 6; and *Filipino Reporter*, 6–12 March 1981, pp. 1–2.

[99]*Asiaweek*, 15 May 1981, pp. 42–49.

[100]*Asiaweek*, 26 June 1981, pp. 12–13.

[101]Robert L. Youngblood, "The Philippines in 1981: From 'New Society' to 'New Republic,'" *Asian Survey* 22 (February 1982): 226–228.

ularities, voter turnout was nearly 90 percent, and Marcos was again credited with skillfully jockeying the KBL to a galloping success.[102]

The ability of Marcos and the KBL to run roughshod over the opposition at the polls, however, was considerably weakened as a result of anger and revulsion, especially among elites who previously supported the regime, over the circumstances of the murder of Benigno Aquino on 21 August 1983, upon his return from three years of political exile in the United States. Thousands waited hours to view the body at the Aquino home in Quezon City in the immediate aftermath of the assassination, and ten days later a crowd estimated at two million lined the funeral cortege route, with many chanting slogans in defiance of the government. During the mass in memory of Aquino at the Santo Domingo Church, Cardinal Sin denounced the climate of tyranny and oppression pervading the Philippines, and called for the restoration of freedom and justice.[103] Few believed the official version of the assassination that Aquino, while in the custody of the military, surrounded by heavy security at Manila International Airport, was killed by a lone gunman with alleged links to the Communists. The credibility of the government was further eroded because the only reliable, comprehensive source of information on the murder and its aftermath was from Veritas, the radio station of the Roman Catholic church.[104] Moreover, Sin and several other prominent Filipinos refused appointments to a board of inquiry into the assassination. Within weeks middle-class Filipinos repeatedly marched and demonstrated against the regime in Makati, the financial center of the Philippines. By the end of September, clashes between protesters and the police in Manila turned violent, resulting in death and injury, prompting Marcos to hint at the reimposition of martial law.[105]

Despite the president's harsh rhetoric, opposition to the regime continued. Marcos was forced to abolish the executive committee and reinstate the office of vice president, which was approved in a January 1984 referendum, and to make electoral reforms, such as the abolition of block voting, the easing of a ban on political turncoatism, and the purging of fraudulent voter registration lists, prior to the May 1984 National Assembly elections. Although the moderate democratic opposition remained divided over the

[102]Sheilah Ocampo, " . . . and the Village Voice," *Far Eastern Economic Review*, 21 May 1982, pp. 14–15; *Asiaweek*, 21 May 1982, p. 15; and *Philippine News*, 26 May–1 June 1982, pp. 1, 8.

[103]*Wall Street Journal*, 1 September 1983, p. 26.

[104]Felix B. Bautista, *Cardinal Sin and the Miracle of Asia* (Manila: Vera-Reyes, 1987), chap. 10.

[105]G. Sidney Silliman, "The Philippines in 1983: Authoritarianism Beleaguered," *Asian Survey* 24 (February 1984): 154–157; and *Washington Post*, 22 September 1983, pp. 1, A36.

question of participation in the *Batasang Pambansa* elections, UNIDO, a coalition of the Philippine Democratic Party (PDP) and LABAN, the SDP, and factions of the Nacionalista and Liberal parties (NP and LP) all fielded candidates, while a group of citizens, headed by businessman Jose Concepcion and supported by powerful elements within the Roman Catholic church, organized the National Citizen's Movement for Free Elections (NAMFREL) to oversee the polling and the canvassing of the ballots. Only massive spending by the regime (estimated at more than ₱2 billion)[106] and considerable electoral fraud prevented the defeat of the KBL. Under the circumstances, the fact that the opposition parties won morc than 70 seats was viewed by many as an electoral victory, although the KBL, with 108 seats, still controlled the *Batasang Pambansa*.[107]

The strong showing of the moderate democratic opposition in the 1984 National Assembly election was a portent of the February 1986 snap presidential election that resulted in Marcos' being forced into political exile in the United States and in Corazon "Cory" Aquino becoming president of the Philippines. The Aquino assassination in 1983 and the collapse of the Philippine economy in 1984, coupled with the dramatic growth of the Communist New People's Army (NPA) since the late 1970s and rising dissatisfaction within the military over graft and corruption and favoritism, were all manifestations of the failure of Marcos' "revolution from the center." Marcos' "revolutionary" prescription for the country, with its concentration on bureaucratic authoritarianism, reliance on the military, and emphasis on an export-led development program based upon heavy foreign borrowing, not only failed to raise standards of living, except for the wealthy and those with close ties to the First Family, but resulted in economic bankruptcy and in widespread abuses of human rights, which, as indicated at the end of Chapter 2, contributed to heightened church-state conflict from the late 1970s until Aquino assumed power in February 1986. Much of the acrimony revolved around the emphasis by many church leaders on social justice activities that conflicted with government policies and programs. The shift toward stress on social justice and liberation as an integral part of preaching the gospel within the Philippine churches, especially the Roman Catholic church, is discussed in Chapter 4.

[106]Charles W. Lindsey, "Economic Crisis in the Philippines," *Asian Survey* 24 (December 1984): 1198.

[107]Richard J. Kessler, "Politics Philippine Style, circa 1984," *Asian Survey* 24 (December 1984): 1209–1228. A more conservative estimate of opposition strength in the *Batasang Pambansa* was fifty-nine, as some of the non-KBL candidates ran with the support of President Marcos.

4

From Social Action to Liberation

Much of the rhetoric of Marcos' "revolution from the center" mirrored the emphasis given to human development and to social justice by popes John XXIII and Paul VI and by Vatican II as well as by various Protestant denominations; like liberation theology, it also called for significant changes in secular society. Yet any similarities between the stated goals of the Marcos government and the social action of the Catholic and Protestant churches in the 1960s and the 1970s were overshadowed after 1972 by periodic military raids on church institutions, the jailing of priests and pastors engaged in social justice work, and the deportation of foreign missionaries ministering to the needs of the poor. The elimination of subversion, the protection of national security, and the achievement of the goals of the New Society (1972–81) and the New Republic (1981–86) were the major justifications by the Marcos regime for the crackdowns against church activists. But the causes of church-state conflict were complex and were rooted, in part, in the development model the Marcos regime chose to achieve socioeconomic and political modernization. Thus it is important to compare and contrast the ideological basis and the nature of the commitment of the Marcos government to greater social justice with the programs of the Catholic and Protestant churches to understand why, with seemingly identical goals of uplifting the poor (without persecuting the rich), conflict between the regime and the churches steadily intensified after 1972. I examine in this chapter (1) social action in the Catholic and Protestant churches since 1965 and its development within the Asian and

Philippine context; (2) the influence of Latin American liberation theology in a shift from social action projects to a commitment to total human liberation; and (3) the increasing emphasis on creating Basic Christian Communities (BCCs) as the best means for achieving social justice.

Vatican II and Asian Christians

Catholics and Protestants engaged in the social action work of the churches in the Philippines often point out that much of Christ's ministry was directed toward rectifying social injustices and nurturing the poor. Yet emphasis given to social justice by the Roman Catholic church and a number of major Protestant denominations (most notably those associated with the World Council of Churches) is of recent historical origins, dating back only to the late nineteenth and early twentieth centuries. Intensified interest in promoting social justice as an integral part of the gospel message is largely a post–World War II phenomenon linked with decolonization and the rising expectations of Third World nations in Asia, Africa, and Latin America burdened with widespread, deeply rooted poverty and violence. Theologically, the reevaluation marks a shift away from the purely spiritual aspects of Christianity to greater stress on the social justice features of the gospel; politically, it represents a reaction to the failures of liberal democracy and developmentalism and to the appearance of repressive regimes in much of the Third World. Considerable support for eradicating unjust social structures and evangelizing among the poor in the Philippines comes from recent papal encyclicals, documents from the Asian Bishops' conferences and various Catholic organizations in the Philippines, and, to a lesser extent, from statements of Asian and Filipino Protestants and Protestant organizations. Of importance also are the writings of Latin American theologians of liberation such as Paulo Freire, Gustavo Gutierrez, Jose Bonino, and Leonardo Boff,[1] and the examples of activist church officials and laymen at home and abroad such as Fr. Edicio de la Torre of the

[1]Paulo Freire, *Pedagogy for the Oppressed* (New York: Herder and Herder, 1970); Gustavo Gutierrez, *A Theology of Liberation*, trans. and ed. Caridad Inda and John Eagleson (Maryknoll, N.Y.: Orbis Books, 1973); Jose M. Bonino, *Doing Theology in a Revolutionary Situation* (Philadelphia: Fortress Press, 1975); Leonardo Boff, *Jesus Christ Liberator: A Critical Christology for Our Time*, trans. Patrick Hughes (Maryknoll, N.Y.: Orbis Books, 1978), and *Church: Charism and Power*, trans. John W. Diercksmeier (New York: Crossroad, 1986).

Philippines, the late Fr. Camilo Torres of Colombia, and Bishop Daniel Chi and Kim Chi-ha, the poet, in South Korea.[2]

Although the current debate within the Roman Catholic church started with Pope Leo XIII's *Rerum Novarum* (1891) and Pope Pius XI's *Quadragesimo Anno* (1931), it was not until Pope John XXIII's *Mater et Magistra* (1961) and *Pacem in Terris* (1963) and the Second Vatican Council's *Gaudium et Spes* (1965) that the church began to address on a broad scale the problem of social injustice in the world. In 1971 the Synod of Bishops stated unequivocally in *Justice in the World* that "action on behalf of justice and participation in the transformation of the world" is "a constitutive dimension of preaching the Gospel."[3] Pope Paul VI spoke of structural injustices within and between nations in *Populorum Progressio* (1967) and of the need for liberating the poor in *Evangelii Nuntiandi* (1975). But even as Paul VI expressed the need for reform, he warned against the "recourse to violence" as a means of rectifying "wrongs to human dignity," adding: "We know . . . that a revolutionary uprising—save where there is manifest, long-standing tyranny which would do great damage to fundamental personal rights and dangerous harm to the common good of the country—produces new injustices, throws more elements out of balance and brings on new disasters. A real evil should not be fought against at the cost of greater misery."[4]

Pope John Paul II likewise cautioned, in separate visits to Latin America in 1979 and the Philippines in 1981, against the resort to "socio-political radicalism" and "an exaggerated interest in the wide field of temporal problems" in the name of the gospel. But he rejected conditions of "subjection and dependence" and "any violation of the fundamental dignity of the human person or the basic rights that safeguard this dignity."[5]

[2]Edicio de la Torre, "Some Notes for a Theology of Social Reform," *Philippine Priests' Forum* 1 (September 1969): 20–26; "The Challenge of Maoism and the Filipino Christian," in *Challenges for the Filipino: Lenten Lectures 1971*, Theology Series no. 2, ed. Raul J. Bonoan (Quezon City: Ateneo de Manila University, 1971), pp. 16–31; and "Christians in the Struggle for National Liberation," *Impact*, September 1971, pp. 29–32; Camilo Torres, *Revolutionary Priest: The Complete Writings and Messages of Camilo Torres*, ed. John Geressi (New York: Random House, 1977); James P. Sinnot, "Silence—A Dictator's Friend," *Maryknoll*, November 1977, pp. 15–19; and "Imperialism and Repression: The Case of South Korea," *Bulletin of Concerned Asian Scholars* 9 (April–June 1977): 2–41; and John C. England, "Kim Chi Ha and the Poetry of Christian Dissent," *Ching Feng* 21, no. 3 (1978): 126–151.

[3]Joseph Gremillion, *The Gospel of Peace and Justice: Catholic Social Teaching since Pope John* (Maryknoll, N.Y.: Orbis Books, 1976), p. 514.

[4]Ibid., p. 396.

[5]Pedro S. de Achútegui, ed., *Journey to Puebla: The Speeches of John Paul II* (Quezon

The social justice thrust of the last three papacies is mirrored in numerous meetings, documents, and statements of the Asian Catholic churches. Between 1967 and 1970, four pan-Asian conferences underscored the importance of the church becoming the "voice of the voiceless."[6] At a meeting in the Philippines with Pope Paul VI in 1970, the Asian bishops emphasized a determination "to eradicate entrenched injustice and replace oppressive structures" as well as avoid "compromising entanglements with the rich and powerful" in responding to the aspirations of the poor.[7] The bishops also approved guidelines for what became the Federation of Asian Bishops' Conferences (FABC) in 1972 to continue the work of Vatican II. An Office for Human Development was established in Manila to coordinate the FABC's social justice work. In 1974 the bishops again committed themselves to uplifting the poor and to destroying unjust structures at the FABC's first assembly in Taipei; in 1978 they reaffirmed a "solidarity with the poor and the powerless, the marginalized and oppressed" at the federation's second assembly in Calcutta.[8] The FABC has also sponsored a number of Bishops' Institutes for Social Action (BISA) since 1974 to acquaint the prelates with "the latest thinking on social analysis and action," and the OHD publishes a monthly newsletter, *Info on Human Development*, to keep the bishops abreast of Asian social concerns and development problems.[9]

The Philippine Catholic bishops have likewise spoken out in favor of the powerless and disadvantaged in a series of pastoral letters since the late

---

City: Cardinal Bea Institute, Loyola School of Theology, Ateneo de Manila University, 1979), pp. 29 and 127; "Faith amid Politics," *Asiaweek*, 27 February 1981, p. 30; and *Papal Speeches on Social Issues in the Philippines* (Manila: Office for Human Development of the Federation of Asian Bishops Conferences, 1981), p. 6.

[6]Vitaliano R. Gorospe, "To the Pan Asian Bishops: Listen to the People," *Impact*, November 1970, pp. 4–10.

[7]Vitaliano R. Gorospe, *The Four Faces of Asia: A Summary Report on the Asian Bishops' Meeting*, Manila, 23–29 November 1970, Theology Series, no. 1 (Quezon City: Ateneo de Manila University, 1971), pp. 65–67.

[8]"Asian Bishops' Conference," *Impact*, January 1971, pp. 30–35; "Statutes of the Federation of Asian Bishops' Conferences," *Impact*, March 1973, pp. 101–105, 107; FABC, *Evangelization in Modern Day Asia*, First Plenary Assembly of the Federation of Asian Bishops' Conferences, 22–27 April 1974, Taipei, Republic of China, Book 2 (Quezon City: Cardinal Bea Institute, Loyola School of Theology, Ateneo de Manila University, 1976); and FABC, *Prayer—The Life of the Church of Asia*, the Second Plenary Assembly of the Federation of Asian Bishops' Conferences, 19–25 November 1978, Calcutta, India (Quezon City: Cardinal Bea Institute, Loyola School of Theology, Ateneo de Manila University, 1979), p. 49.

[9]Julio X. Labayen, ed., *The Bishops' Institutes for Social Action of the Federation of Asian Bishops' Conferences*, FABC Papers no. 6 (Hong Kong: FABC, 1977).

1960s on various aspects of social justice. In 1971, for example, the bishops cited the need for more social responsibility in helping the "economically deprived and politically . . . powerless" poor. They issued major pastoral letters on social justice and development (1973) and education for social justice (1978). The bishops returned to the theme of social justice in two blunt pastoral letters in 1983 and 1984 that addressed the high level of poverty and violence in Philippine society.[10] Even stronger statements and actions in support of social justice were issued and carried out by individual bishops working alone or in cooperation with other activist bishops.[11]

The Association of Major Religious Superiors of the Philippines (AMRSP), representing over three thousand priests and brothers and over seven thousand nuns, and, prior to martial law, the Philippine Priests Incorporated (PPI), composed of over fourteen hundred secular and religious priests, were just as outspoken as the bishops in support of the poor and were more active than the bishops in attempting to bring about greater social justice.[12] The same can be said for the National Secretariat for Social Action, Justice and Peace (NASSA), the social action arm of the Catholic bishops, along with affiliated groups, such as the Share and Care Apostolate for Poor Settlers (SCAPS). Concern for social justice has also been expressed on numerous occasions at various meetings and synods, and by the pastoral conferences, especially the one serving Mindanao and Sulu, of the Catholic church.

Protestant social action activities were given a boost in 1966 by a call from the World Council of Churches (WCC) for the implementation of a more significant social ministry among the member churches. Although the response was not immediate in Asia and the Philippines, advocates of the new orientation of the WCC eventually began to be heard as the old evangelical and social orientations fell short in the struggle to reverse institutionalized social inequities. Increasingly from the late 1960s, the Protestant Christian Conference of Asia (CCA), the National Council of Churches in the Philippines (NCCP), and individual Protestant churches have issued documents and established programs aimed at eradicating unjust social structures and improving conditions for the dispossessed and

[10]Richard P. Hardy, ed., *The Bishops Speak (1968–1983)* (Quezon City: Maryhill School of Theology, 1984), pp. 36–40, 52–77, 173–200, 232–238; and CBCP, "Let There be Life," Tagaytay City, 11 July 1984 (mimeographed).

[11]See, for example, "Statement of Seventeen Bishops *Ut Omnes Unum Sint*," in Felix Casalmo (pseud.), *The Vision of a New Society* (Manila, 1980), pp. 271–278.

[12]Pedro S. de Achútegui, "The Catholic Church in the Philippines: A Statistical Overview," *Philippine Studies* 32 (First Quarter 1984): 82, 95–96; and *Philippine Priests' Forum*, 12 (September 1980): 41.

marginalized members of Philippine society.[13] The Wednesday Fellowship of the Protestant churches, organized after the imposition of martial rule, provided an arena for the discussion of social justice issues. Moreover, progressive Protestants have readily cooperated with Catholics inside and outside of the Philippines in the area of social action, frequently attending ecumenical meetings and coordinating efforts on behalf of the poor.[14]

The influence of liberation theology and the political activities of Christians abroad, especially Asian Christians, are manifest in the Philippines. Materials on liberation theology and the deliberations of the Latin American Episcopal Conference (CELAM) are available in mimeographed publications circulated by activist Christians as well as in academic journals and books. The Influence of Latin American liberation theology is evident in the writings of Filipino theologians and religious leaders.[15] Additionally, references to the struggle of Latin American guerrilla priest Camilo Torres appear in the writings of Father Edicio de la Torre, and the persecution of Bishop Daniel Chi and Kim Chi-ha in South Korea drew rebukes from members of the Philippine Catholic hierarchy and received widespread publicity among activist Christians in the Philippines.[16]

Concern with social justice, especially within the context of liberation, reflects a shift within the Roman Catholic church and the major Protestant denominations from viewing sin as a purely private matter to accepting the idea that social injustice represents a form of "structural sin" or, more emphatically, "structural violence" permeating society's institutional relationships. Accordingly, the low wages paid Filipino migrant laborers (*sakadas*), the alienation of tribal minorities from ancestral lands, and the insecurity of squatters in urban slums are less the result of individual

[13]Philippine Ecumenical Writing Group, *Moving Heaven and Earth: An Account of Filipinos Struggling to Change Their Lives and Society* (Manila: Commission on the Churches' Participation in Development [CCPD], World Council of Churches [WCC], 1982), pp. 26–34; CCA, Office of Development and Service, "On the Development of Peoples and Societies," *Tugon* 1 (May 1980): 66–76; and Henry B. Aguilan, comp., "Development: NCCP, CDSC Concerns and Involvement" (Quezon City: Commission on Development and Social Concerns [CDSC], National Council of Churches in the Philippines [NCCP], 1979) (mimeographed).

[14]Cirilo A. Rigos, "The Prophetic Ministry of the Church in the Philippines under Martial Law" (D.M. diss., San Francisco Theological Seminary, 1976).

[15]See, for example, Rodrigo D. Tano, *Theology in the Philippine Setting: A Case Study in the Contextualization of Theology* (Quezon City: New Day, 1981), chap. 4; and the entire issue of *Witness* 4 (July 1985).

[16]Edicio de la Torre, "The Role of the Priest in Social Reform," *Philippine Priests' Forum* 2 (September 1970): 29–38; *Signs of the Times*, 10 October 1975, pp. 3–6; 17 October 1975, pp. 3–8; 16 April 1976, pp. 13–14; 7 August 1976, pp. 24–25; and *Ichthys*, 13 July 1979, special issue on human rights in Korea, 1978.

sinfulness (and sloth) than the consequence of "structural injustices" inherent in liberal capitalism. Under such circumstances, argues Antonio Lambino, a moral theologian at Ateneo de Manila University's Loyola School of Theology, "effective Christian love" must be "manifested in solidarity with the poor and the oppressed" as they "struggle to liberate themselves from the unjust structures of society."[17] Man's secular needs for sustenance and human development in the present are stressed in this "activist" interpretation of the gospel equally with the promise of eternal salvation in a life hereafter. In concrete terms, this conceptualization of the gospel has led, on the one hand, to a questioning of the structural basis of social, political, and economic inequities extant in Philippine society, and, on the other hand, to attempts both at national and local levels to create new institutional structures emphasizing social justice, equality, and human development.[18]

Divisions within the Philippine Churches

The move of Vatican II toward making the church more relevant in the modern world by becoming involved in man's struggle to liberate himself from unjust social and political structures clashes with an older ecclesiological orientation in the church that, in Brian Smith's words, "sanctions the distinction of planes between sacred and secular, and underscores the necessity for the official church to avoid interference in temporal affairs." From the "distinction of planes" perspective, "faith and religious commitment are seen in more personal and individualistic terms," in contrast to a social imperative to work for justice and liberation in the world, while the church is viewed as a "haven or sanctuary for those seeking refuge from the problems and cares of secular society" rather than

[17]Antonio B. Lambino, "Justice and Evangelization: A Theological Perspective," in *On Faith and Justice: Contemporary Issues for Filipino Christians*, Loyola Papers 5, ed. Pedro S. de Achútegui (Quezon City: Loyola School of Theology, Ateneo de Manila University, 1976), pp. 31–32.

[18]See also Carlos H. Abesamis, *Salvation: Historical and Total* (Quezon City: JMC Press, 1978); and Catalino G. Arevalo, "The Task of the Church: Liberation and Development," in *The Filipino in the Seventies*, ed. Vitaliano R. Gorospe and Richard L. Deats (Quezon City: New Day, 1973), pp. 233–283, and "Notes for a Theology of Development," *Philippine Studies* 19 (January 1971), reprinted in Douglas J. Elwood, ed., *What Asian Christians Are Thinking: A Theological Source Book* (Quezon City: New Day, 1976), pp. 398–424. Abesamis and Arevalo, like Lambino, advocate liberation without supporting a particular political ideology.

as an institution for mobilization against oppressive social and political structures.[19]

Differences in ecclesiology are not only manifested in disagreement over the proper role of the church today, but are also reflected in the internal and external structural relationships of the church. Thus, as Smith points out, bishops "opting for the 'distinction of planes' model are usually closely associated with the established social order and comfortable with the benefits accruing to the Church from this relationship," while bishops "proposing the model of the Church as a 'community of liberation' are frequently more directly involved with the problems of the poor and want the Church to present a more critical challenge at every level against the repressive aspects of existing regimes."[20]

The contrasts within the Philippine Catholic church, especially among bishops, in terms of the "distinctions of planes" and "community of liberation" models, were palpable during much of the martial law period, and the basis of major factional alignments. Similar differences were also observable within and among Philippine Protestant denominations.

Among the major organizations of the Roman Catholic church are the Catholic Bishops' Conference of the Philippines (CBCP), numbering ninety-four active bishops in 1983, and the AMRSP and the PPI. Of the three organizations, the CBCP is considered the most conservative, yet even within the Bishops' Conference, conservative, moderate, and progressive divisions have been identified, based on their attitudes toward the government and the church's role in the modern world. According to 1979 data, the conservatives numbered forty-six bishops (58 percent of the CBCP) and followed in outlook the late Julio Cardinal Rosales of Cebu.[21] The conservatives generally supported the Marcos regime; if they criticized the government at all, they did so in moderate terms, and only on matters of specific church interests. They disagreed, for example, with such proposals

[19]Brian H. Smith, "Religion and Social Change: Classical Theories and New Formulations in the Context of Recent Developments in Latin America," *Latin American Research Review* 10 (2): 12–13.

[20]Ibid., p. 13.

[21]For a detailed explanation of how the bishops were classified, see Robert L. Youngblood, "Structural Imperialism: An Analysis of the Catholic Bishops' Conference of the Philippines," *Comparative Political Studies* 15 (April 1982): 29–56. Other classifications are contained in Benjamin McCloskey (pseud.), "Church, State and Conflict in the Philippines," in *In the Philippines Today: Christian Faith, Ideologies . . . Marxism*, Loyola Papers 10, ed. Catalino G. Arevalo, Antonio B. Lambino, and Francisco F. Claver (Quezon City: Loyola School of Theology, Ateneo de Manila University, 1978), pp. 103–111; and Mil Roekaerts, "The Philippines: Five Years of Martial Law," *Ichthys*, special issue, no. 8, 14 July 1978.

as the taxation of parochial schools and the legalization of divorce, and with such programs as family planning. Their ecclesiological outlook stressed the sacred mission of the church in providing a refuge for the fulfillment of religious needs and an avoidance of involvement in temporal affairs, beyond, of course, engaging in charitable works.

The moderates in the CBCP, eighteen bishops in all (23 percent), also criticized government programs that threatened vital church interests, but, in contrast to the conservatives, they reserved the right to criticize specific injustice, while not going to the extent of attacking the legitimacy of the regime. Moderate opposition was denoted by what Jaime Cardinal Sin, archbishop of Manila, termed "critical collaboration."[22] The ecclesiology of the moderates was similar to that of the conservatives. However, because of the influence of Vatican II and recent social encyclicals, coupled with gross inequities in Philippine society, the moderates recognized, with reservations, that the church must become more responsive to the needs and demands of contemporary society. The conservatives and the moderates, both of whom tended to be older and to occupy the highest positions in the hierarchy, typically controlled the CBCP and its executive board.

A third group of fifteen bishops (19 percent of the CBCP), identified with Bishop Francisco Claver and considered progressive or activist, joined with conservatives and moderates in defending vital church interests against undesirable government programs, but differed from the other two groups by repeatedly speaking out against a wide array of reported governmental and military abuses as well as by condemning the Marcos regime as immoral and without legitimacy. The progressives typically adhered to the "community of liberation" model of the church and in general were younger than the conservatives or moderates, held none of the church's highest offices, and often administered bishoprics in frontier areas of the country.

Homogeneity of outlook was also absent in other Catholic organizations, yet the AMRSP, along with the individual religious orders, such as the Society of Jesus (SJ), the Society of St. Columban (SSC), the Maryknoll Fathers (MM), and the Missionary Sisters of the Immaculate Heart of Mary (ICM), was viewed as more progressive than the CBCP. Not only did the Major Superiors take less traditional positions on issues such as family planning, but, as indicated previously, they were also more active in

[22]The notion of "critical collaboration" is defined in "Statements and Interviews by Jaime L. Card. Sin of Manila," *IDOC Bulletin*, nos. 8, 9, 10 (August, September, October 1980), p. 5.

support of the poor and during the Marcos years were less inhibited about criticizing government programs and military abuses.[23] In return, religious order priests and nuns and foreign missionaries often bore the brunt of government crackdowns, which included jailings, deportations, and the closing of Catholic newspapers and radio stations (see Chapter 5). Similarly, in the years prior to martial law, the PPI, through its publication, the *Philippine Priests' Forum*, called for reforms and an end to injustices. As a result of government intimidation under martial law, however, articles in the *Forum* became more circumspect after 1972, and in 1982 the journal's name was changed to *Life Forum*. Although the PPI remained committed to reforms both inside and outside the church, the association's tone of dissent ultimately gave way, in the words of one activist, "to more sober themes" and to "more constructive dialogues."[24]

Organizationally, the major division among Protestants was between denominations belonging to the National Council of Churches in the Philippines (NCCP) and a large number of nonecumenical Christian sects (at one time numbering more than two hundred) that were considered conservative on social justice issues. But even among (and within) NCCP-affiliated denominations a conservative-progressive dichotomy was present, resulting in a generally low social action profile of most Philippine Protestants. While there were exceptions, such as the programs of the Commission on Development and Social Concerns (CDSC) of the NCCP, the Wednesday Fellowship, the Philippine Ecumenical Action for Community Development (PEACE), and the activities of certain activist pastors and laymen, the efforts of Protestants in the area of social justice and support for the poor often were obscured by the activities of activist Catholics. Part of the lower visibility of the Protestants no doubt was due to their smaller numbers and desire to work in an ecumenical context. Perhaps more important, most Protestant denominations in the Philippines were founded by American missionaries, and as a result, acquired the religious practices and social orientations of the mother churches.

Theologically for many Protestants, stress is placed on personal salvation: the attainment of individual purity rather than involvement "in the

[23]H. Monte Hill, "Catholic Interest Groups and Philippine Family Planning Policy under Martial Law," paper presented at the First International Philippine Studies Conference, Western Michigan University, 29–31 May 1980.

[24]Interview with former religious activist, PPI Office, 18 July 1979; "The Philippines under Martial Law," *Pro Mundi Vita*, special note 32, December 1973, reprinted in *Various Reports*, 8 November 1974, p. 13; and Aimee M. Ramirez, "Editorial," *Life Forum* 14 (March 1982): 3.

struggles of overcoming evil in the world."[25] Thus, according to the Filipino Protestant theologian Emerito Nacpil:

> To be a good Christian one must be active in the internal affairs of the church, helping the pastor in his work and coming to church services and meetings regularly and supporting generously the financial responsibilities of the church. He is a good layman who is active in the church as a religious fellowship and not as a member of the people of God who must live out the Gospel in the world.[26]

Such a spiritual orientation inhibits active involvement in the world beyond being personally charitable and an exemplary Christian. Few Protestants were in the forefront of those demanding fundamental structural changes in the Philippines, because much of what they found wrong with Philippine society only required an end to the Marcos regime and a return to a liberal democratic system of government. Just as had been reported for Latin American Protestants, Filipino Protestants when confronted with economic and political problems tended to identify with developmentalism and reformism in contrast to radical solutions.[27]

The lack of radicalism among Protestants in the Philippines was reflected in Protestant theological writings, and was attributable in part to the class backgrounds and education of Filipino theologians and pastors.[28] Many Filipino Protestant pastors came from the country's small middle class, and most attended theological schools run or funded by American missionaries or, in some cases, received advanced training in the United States. While a few activist Protestant pastors and laymen had affiliations with (or sympathies for) groups considered subversive by the government, most Protestants opposed to the Marcos regime were classifiable as politically moderate. Nevertheless, a few prominent Protestants, such as Senator Jovito Salonga, consistently spoke out, often defiantly, against government and military abuses. By the late 1970s and early 1980s there were some indications suggesting that activist Protestants were becoming more recep-

[25]Emerito P. Nacpil, "The Philippines," in *Asian Voices in Christian Theology*, ed. Gerald H. Anderson (Maryknoll, N.Y.: Orbis Books, 1976), p. 119.

[26]Ibid.

[27]Beatriz M. Couch, "New Visions of the Church in Latin America: A Protestant View," in *The Emergent Gospel: Theology from the Underside of History*, Papers from the Ecumenical Dialogue of Third World Theologians, Dar es Salaam, 5–12 August 1976, ed. Sergio Torres and Virginia Fabella (Maryknoll, N.Y.: Orbis Books, 1978), pp. 193–226.

[28]Elwood, *What Asian Christians Are Thinking*; and Emerito P. Nacpil and Douglas J. Elwood, eds., *The Human and the Holy: Asian Perspectives in Christian Theology* (Quezon City: New Day, 1978).

tive to the arguments of liberation theology, which favored changing unjust social, economic, and political structures as frustrations with the Marcos regime accumulated.[29]

Social Justice and Christian Liberation

The Commitment to Social Action

Although there was a continuing debate among Catholics and Protestants (both inside and outside of the churches) over the proper sociopolitical role of the churches in Philippine society, efforts were made just before the conclusion of the Second Vatican Council to respond to the social action challenges set forth in *Gaudium et Spes*. The new emphasis on social action in the Catholic church prompted a monthlong Priests' Institute for Social Action (PISA) held in Hong Kong in August 1965 that was attended by thirty-one priests and a bishop from the Philippines.[30] PISA was followed in 1966 by the publication of a newsletter, *Impact*, which later became a monthly magazine specializing in Asian human development problems. Also at this time, the National Secretariat for Social Action, Justice and Peace (NASSA), was established, under the jurisdiction of the Episcopal Commission on Social Action, with the goal of placing a social action center in each diocese in the country to initiate and implement social action projects and to encourage the development of similar centers at the parish level.[31] A justice and peace function was added to NASSA's charge in 1969, and between 1969 and 1974, three regional units—the Mindanao-Sulu Secretariat of Social Action (MISSSA), the Visayas Secretariat of Social Action (VISSA), and the Luzon Secretariat of Social Action (LUSSA)—were created to assist in coordinating church social action programs. By 1981 there were sixty-eight diocesan social action centers around the country.

The church in Mindanao and Sulu was at the forefront of promoting social action and social justice. MISSSA was the first of the regional units

[29]Interviews with Protestant church activists, 13 and 15 July 1979; Philippine Ecumenical Writing Group, *Moving Heaven and Earth*, pp. 27–37; and "Towards a Theology of the Struggle," *Kilusan* 3, nos. 1–2 (1984): 33.

[30]"Philippines: Vision and Frustration," *Impact*, December 1970, p. 11.

[31]"Church Girds for Social Action," *Impact*, September 1966, p. 2; and "Philippines: Proposals of the Episcopal Commission on Social Action, 1967," *Impact*, June 1967, pp. 9–10.

to be formed, and served as a model for the organization of VISSA and LUSSA. MISSSA pioneered in fostering collaboration, cooperation, and integration of the social action programs of the regional centers, and in functioning as a communications hub and clearinghouse for social action information emanating from within the region and from NASSA's headquarters in Manila. The commitment to social action within the Mindanao church was underscored additionally by the establishment of the Mindanao Development Center in 1969. Among the services and programs sponsored by the center were leadership training seminars, the use of applied research for analyzing problems of development, the organization of farmers and laborers, and the promotion of development and liberation through Christian reflection.[32]

Following the creation of NASSA, the bishops sponsored a "National Congress for Rural Development" in 1967, aimed at alleviating what Marcos called the nation's "social volcano" which, he stated further, was threatening to "erupt any day with, or even without, the benefit of communist prodding."[33] A year later the Catholic prelates joined the president in proclaiming 1968–69 "National Social Action and Economic Development Year."[34] Both occasions were preceded by pastoral letters from the Catholic hierarchy that stressed the plight of the poor (especially farmers, agricultural workers, and fishermen), the need for land reform, and the educational role of the church in teaching social justice and, at the same time, that called on the rich to continue supporting charitable works.[35] Although many parish priests were dubious about the importance of the rural congress, by 1969 approximately two thousand church-sponsored social action projects had been started, nearly 90 percent of the church's dioceses had at least part-time social action directors, and about four hundred priests had received some training in social action work. Yet most social action directors admitted spending little time on social action activities at the diocesan level; most of the training seminars were less than

[32]Pasquale T. Giordano, "A Theological Analysis of the Changing Understanding of the Social Mission in the Philippine Church after Vatican II: 1965–81" (Ph.D. diss., Catholic University of America, 1983), p. 41.

[33]Ferdinand E. Marcos, *Presidential Speeches*, vol. 1 (n.p., Ferdinand E. Marcos, 1978), p. 274.

[34]*Impact*, September 1968, p. 10.

[35]"The Call to Action," *Impact*, March 1967, pp. 2–3; "The Philippine Catholic Hierarchy on Social Awareness," *Impact*, September 1968, pp. 14–19; and Domingo Diel, "The Confrontation of the Roman Catholic Church with the Economic and Social Development in the Philippines in Relation to the Influence of the Socio-Theological Position of the II Vatican Council" (Ph.D. diss., University of Hamburg, 1974), pp. 115–123.

ten days in duration; and few priests and nuns were engaged full-time in social action endeavors.[36]

Initially, the social action emphasis of the church focused on self-help programs such as organizing credit unions, agricultural projects, cooperative associations, farmers' unions, health and sanitation projects, and cottage industries. Although these programs were an advance over earlier social welfare and relief activities, it soon became obvious that self-help projects tended to benefit only the upper-lower class or the lower-middle class, while companion community development projects tended to founder once change agents departed, leaving the vast majority of the poor unaffected. Moreover, the technology required on many of the projects was often oversophisticated and thus inappropriate in the absence of skilled personnel. And throughout the country there was no uniform plan of projects, as support for social action was up to each bishop individually.

The self-help and community development approach of the church in the late 1960s and early 1970s suffered from several weaknesses: (1) the approach worked to the disadvantage of the poor by neglecting inequities in community power structures and by stressing compromise and harmonious community relations, resulting in unchallenged elite structures and unresolved conflicts between groups with fundamental differences, such as landowners and tenants, agribusinesses and workers, land developers and tribal minorities; (2) the approach ignored people's participation in project formulation, often allowing programs to serve the needs and interests of outside groups; and (3) the approach, as Dette Abrera et al. emphasize further, stressed management training "over membership training so that project continuity" and success hinged on the leadership, further contributing to membership dependency.[37]

The National Congress for Rural Development and National Social Action and Economic Development Year represented the high-water mark of church-government cooperation in social action; nonetheless, although initial press reaction to the rural congress was favorable, dissatisfaction with church reforms and social action efforts soon surfaced.[38] Two years after the rural congress, for example, the Laymen's Association for Post–Vatican II Reforms (LAPVIIR) questioned the bishops' commitment to the

[36]"What Happened after the Rural Congress?" *Impact*, February 1969, pp. 4–5. See also "Projects Started after the Rural Congress" *Impact*, March 1968, p. 11; and "Evaluation of the Rural Congress," *Impact*, March 1968, p. 12.

[37]Dette L. Abrera, Sophie L. Bodegon, and Ralph C. Salazar, "Servant of Humanity: Church Social Action in the Philippines (1966–1980)," *NASSA News*, January 1981, p. 26.

[38]"Reaction to the Congress," *Impact*, March 1967, p. 8.

poor, and, in an April 1969 demonstration against Rufino J. Cardinal Santos, archbishop of Manila (1953–73), LAPVIIR demanded a financial accounting by the church of its income and expenditures.[39] LAPVIIR's challenge to the hierarchy's record on reforms and social action was echoed by the PPI. The role of the priest on behalf of the poor was not only a central theme of the first three annual PPI conventions, but a shift from merely supporting "existing social reform organizations" to emphasizing identification "with the poor in the struggle for liberation" also took place between the 1970 and 1972 conventions. By 1972 the PPI advocated teaching liberation theology and becoming "more fully aware of the major forces of oppression" such as "*foreign imperialism . . . , local landlordism* and *bureaucrat-capitalism*."[40] In a major address to the priests, Fr. Edicio de la Torre recommended both using Communist ideology for analyzing the ills of Philippine society and employing revolution to achieve liberation.[41]

In the late 1960s and early 1970s, the rhetoric of liberation for solving the problems of social injustice was matched by action in some cases as individual clergy affiliated with mass organizations, such as the Federation of Free Farmers (FFF), the Federation of Free Workers (FFW), and youth groups, such as *Kilusang Khi Rho ng Pilipinas* ([KKRP] Khi Rho Movement of the Philippines), *Kilusang Kristiyano ng Kabataang Pilipino* ([KKKP] Christian Youth Movement of the Philippines), *Kapulungan ng mga Sandigan ng Pilipinas* ([KASAPI] Assembly of Persons upon whom the Philippines Rely), and the Young Christian Socialists of the Philippines (YCSP). Other clergy helped establish mass organizations. Frs. Edmundo Garcia and Edicio de la Torre, for example, were among the founders, respectively, of *Lakasdiwa* (Strength of Spirit) and the Christians for National Liberation (CNL). The FFF and its youth organization, Khi Rho, attracted the largest number of clergy, and by 1972 claimed thirty-eight chaplains and thirty nun advisers nationwide in addition to numerous sympathizers within the church.[42] The FFF, along with other reformist groups linked to

[39]"A Plea for Reforms within the Church," *Philippine Priests' Forum* 1 (June 1969): 29–31; Edward R. Kiunisala, "Questions for the Cardinal," *Philippines Free Press*, 12 April 1969, pp. 4, 69; Henry Lim and Manny Gabriel, "Youth's Response to the Church," *Philippines Free Press*, 22 November 1969, p. 57; and "How Rich Is the Philippine Church," *Philippines Free Press*, 28 November 1970, pp. 10, 42, 44.

[40]For resolutions of the first three PPI conventions, consult *Philippine Priests' Forum* 2 (March 1970): 30–36; 3 (March 1971): 51–54; and 4 (June 1972): 33–35.

[41]Edicio de la Torre, "Church and Liberation in the Philippines," *Philippine Priests' Forum* 4 (June 1972): 11–15.

[42]Rolando Yu and Mario Bolasco, *Church-State Relations* (Manila: St. Scholastica's College, 1981), pp. 69–71; and *Toward a Filipino Ideology* (Quezon City: R. P. Garcia, 1972), p. 98.

the Catholic and Protestant churches, also became more militant, participating in a series of sit-ins, pickets, and demonstrations from 1967 until the declaration of martial law.[43] The result was, naturally, heightened church-state tension. The Jesuits, particularly Fr. Jose Blanco, were reportedly singled out in March 1970 by Marcos for "revolutionary" activities, and Fr. Garcia, advisor to *Lakasdiwa*, was jailed in October 1970 for protest activities. Moreover, just after the 1969 presidential election seven bishops wrote Marcos outlining the kind of "deeply moral" leader the nation needed. The government responded the following November in a publication that labeled the church "the single biggest obstacle to progress" in the Philippines. Although Malacañang denied that the president either accused the Jesuits of subversion or authorized the antichurch publications, neither official explanations nor apologies were ever issued.[44]

Inability to effect significant socioeconomic and political changes through the use of traditional political methods and the employment of moral suasion caused rifts within many moderate reformist organizations and influenced a number of clergy to move to the left. Among the organizations with close church affiliations that underwent a split in the early 1970s was the Jesuit-inspired Federation of Free Farmers (FFF) headed by Jeremias Montemayor.[45] The success of landlords and political elites in blocking reforms and in subverting peasant organizations sponsored by the FFF contributed to the heightened militancy of many of the younger members of the federation in the late 1960s. The young militants, who were increasingly unhappy with the FFF's legalistic and reformist methods and centralized decision making structure, staged a fifty-eight-day demonstration at the Bureau of Agriculture in 1969.[46] The demonstration—known popularly as the Agrifina Circle affair—caused considerable internal dissention within the FFF, and resulted in Montemayor's and the older leadership's imposing ideological censorship and "expelling members identified with radical ideas."[47] The conflict was intensified after September 1972 by

[43]*Toward a Filipino Ideology*, p. 101; and Ramon de la Llana et al., eds., *Free My People: Commitment to Liberation* (n.p.: Tambuli Press, 1972), passim.

[44]"Message to the President," *Philippines Free Press*, 10 January 1970, pp. 1, 28A; Teodoro L. Locsin, Jr., "That 'Revolutionary' Talk," *Philippines Free Press*, 14 March 1970, pp. 12, 59; Quijano de Manila, (pseud.) "Tiro al Blanco," *Philippines Free Press*, 19 May 1970, pp. 2–3, 54–55; Teodoro L. Locsin, Jr., "Malacañang Paper Attacks the Church," *Philippines Free Press*, 21 November 1970, pp. 2–3, 12, 43; and Yu and Bolasco, *Church-State Relations*, pp. 74–77.

[45]Giordano, "A Theological Analysis," p. 43.

[46]V. J. D. Quiazon, "Catholic Philippines: 1969—An Assessment," *Contemporary Studies* 7 (April 1970): 43–44.

[47]Blondie Po, *Rural Organizations and Rural Development in the Philippines: A Docu-*

Montemayor's support of martial law. At the National Policy Board meeting in 1973 on the island of Leyte, seven militant leaders, including Fr. Zacarias Agatep, were arrested by the military on allegations of conspiring to assassinate President Marcos. Montemayor quickly "assumed full emergency powers" and purged twenty members, including those detained by the military, "to cleanse the FFF of all subversion of the left and of the right." Many suspected Montemayor of betraying the militant leaders in order to avoid confrontation with the government, and, no doubt, to maintain control over the federation.[48]

Amid the conflicts within the FFF and other moderate reformist associations a small number of Catholic and Protestant priests, nuns, pastors, seminarians, and young Christians, many of whom were affiliated with the KKRP and the KKKP, met in 1971 to discuss the question of Christian-Marxist cooperation and the participation of Christians in the "national democratic struggle" spearheaded by the Communist Party of the Philippines ([CPP] Marxism-Lenism-Mao Zedong Thought). The outcome of the 1971 meetings was the establishment of the Christians for National Liberation (CNL) in February 1972 and the organization of the CNL's first National Assembly in August 1972.[49] With the arrest of numerous CNL-affiliated Christians after the declaration of martial law, the association was forced underground, and in April 1973, joined with other groups and individuals, collectively known as the National Democrats (Nat-Dems), to found the National Democratic Front (NDF), the major front organization of the CPP. Initially, in 1973, the CNL put out a journal entitled *Pilipinas*, but discontinued it after several issues to join in the publication of *Liberation*, the official organ of the NDF. As a member of the Preparatory Commission of the NDF, the CNL supported both the objectives, expressed

---

mentary Study, Final report submitted to the Asian Center for Development Administration by the Institute of Philippine Culture (Quezon City: Institute of Philippine Culture, Ateneo de Manila University, 1977), pp. 77–78; and Mario Bolasco, "Marxism and Christianity in the Philippines: 1930–1983," in *Marxism in the Philippines: Marx Centennial Lectures*, ed. Third World Studies Center (Quezon City: Third World Studies Center, University of the Philippines, 1984), pp. 117–119.

[48]*Pro Mundi Vita*, "The Philippines under Martial Law," pp. 19–20; and Yu and Bolasco, *Church-State Relations*, p. 106. Fr. Agatep later died a violent death. The military maintained he was killed as a member of the NPA in a hostile engagement, a claim disputed by his friends. He is revered as a martyr by the "Christian Left."

[49]Edicio de la Torre, "The Passion, Death and Resurrection of the Petty-Bourgeoisie Christian," *Asian-Philippine Leader*, 31 March 1972, reprinted in "The Philippines: The Church and Martial Law," *International Documentation Project on the Future of the Missionary Enterprise*, Dossier no. 5 (Rome: IDOC International, 1973), pp. 22–26; and Simeon G. Del Rosario, *Surfacing the Underground: The Church and State Today* (Quezon City: Manlapaz, 1975), pp. 35–37.

in the NDF's ten-point program, and the methods of the CPP, including the armed struggle, for "liberating" the Philippines from the status quo.[50] By late 1985, according to Ross Munro, the CNL consisted of approximately twelve hundred Catholic priests and nuns distributed throughout the Catholic church in secret cells and counted among its members a number of Catholic lay workers and some Protestants.[51]

Not all clergy who were dissatisfied with the approach of the moderate reformist associations and who shifted to the left in the late 1960s and early 1970s joined the CNL, subscribed to the programs of the NDF, or embraced Marxism. On the contrary, priests, nuns, seminarians, and young Christians affiliated with such groups as *Lakasdiwa*, KASAPI, the National Union of Students of the Philippines (NUSP), and the Young Christian Socialists of the Philippines, rejected Communism in favor of a kind of democratic socialism popular in Western Europe.[52] The *Katipunan ng Demokratikong Sosyalista ng Pilipinas* ([KDSP] Association of Democratic Socialists of the Philippines) and its successor, the *Nagkakaisang Partido Demokratikong Sosyalista ng Pilipinas* ([NPDSP] United Democratic Socialist Party of the Philippines), were organized to propagate the policies of the Social Democrats (Soc-Dems) and to counter the appeals of the Nat-Dems. Fr. Romeo Intengan, a medical doctor and a Jesuit priest, was active in establishing both the KDSP and NPDSP.[53]

The Soc-Dems and Nat-Dems articulated similar views about the problems of Philippine society and utilized nearly identical techniques for

[50]Leon Fortaleza, "Giving Flesh and Blood to Christianity," *Liberation*, January 1982, pp. 5–6; "The Christians for National Liberation (CNL)," *Kilusan* 3, nos. 1–2 (1984): 39–42; and *Christians for National Liberation: 2d National Congress Documents* (n.p., n.d.). The 2d National Congress was held in the Southern Tagalog region during the last three months of 1981.

[51]Ross H. Munro, "The New Khmer Rouge," *Commentary*, December 1985, p. 26. It should be emphasized that Munro cites no sources for his figures, and much of the substance of his article, particularly as it applies to the Philippine churches, has been disputed. See, for example, Sr. Mariani Dimaranan, "Task Force Detainees of the Philippines on Ross H. Munro's Article," 28 January 1986 (typewritten); and Fidel V. Agcaoili, "Munro Misrepresented Himself to Me," *Philippine Daily Inquirer*, 21 December 1985, p. 5.

[52]Interview with a ranking Soc-Dem theoretician, Quezon City, Philippines, 25 July 1979, who indicated that the Soc-Dems originated with a group of students taught by Fr. Jose Blanco in the late 1960s; and "Obscurantism and Reformism—The Historical Record of Clerico-Fascism," *Philippine Resistance* 1, no. 2 (1980): 9–12. Many of the original members of the Nat-Dems and Soc-Dems belonged to the same organizations in the late 1960s and early 1970s, but later disagreed on the best way to change Philippine society.

[53]Sheilah Ocampo, "Seeking Integrity for Stability," *Far Eastern Economic Review*, 27 April 1979, p. 23. See also Norberto B. Gonzales and Romeo Intengan, Jr., *The Philippines: Crisis and Commitment* (n.p., n.d.) for an account of some of the early ideas of the Soc-Dems.

organizing at the grass roots. Both groups accepted the necessity of the armed struggle to rid the Philippines of Marcos and the influences of foreign imperialism, namely, that of the United States. Yet their differences led to an intense rivalry. The major differences between the two groups, according to the late former Senator Jose Diokno, lay in the fact that the Soc-Dems were adamantly anti-Communist and advocated the use of elections to achieve their goals once the Marcos regime was toppled. The Nat-Dems, while also supporting "a democratic government composed of representatives of different sectors of society who . . . opposed martial law and imperialism," remained ambiguous about how the sectoral representatives were to be chosen.[54] Another difference was the fact that the Soc-Dems were both less critical of the institutional churches than the Nat-Dems and were viewed, particularly by Nat-Dems, as linked to the Jesuits. Neither group, however, was sanctioned officially by the hierarchies of the Catholic and Protestant churches.[55]

Although the Soc-Dems and the Nat-Dems were considered subversive by the Marcos government, most estimates suggest that the Nat-Dems, both within the clergy and society generally, were by far the more numerous; as a result, given their support of the CPP, they were dealt with more harshly by the regime than the Soc-Dems.[56] Nevertheless, the Soc-Dems were not totally overlooked, especially the leadership. Fr. Intengan, for example, was arrested for alleged subversion after the Interim *Batasang Pambansa* ([IBP] Interim National Assembly) elections in 1978; in 1981, while underground as a fugitive, he was accused by Defense Minister Juan Ponce Enrile, along with other Soc-Dem activists, of planning "terroristic activities" against the Philippines.[57]

The Movement toward Basic Christian Communities

The declaration of martial law coincided with the reevaluation of the church's social action program—evident in additional calls from church activists for liberation of the poor—and contributed to two policy shifts in

[54]Jose W. Diokno, "Tasks and Problems of the Filipino People," in Australian Council for Overseas Aid (ACFOA), *Development Dossier* 2 (July 1980): 13.

[55]Ocampo, "Seeking Integrity for Stability," p. 33; and interview with church activist, Quezon City, 4 August 1979.

[56]Interview with ranking Soc-Dem theoretician, Quezon City, Philippines, 25 July 1979; and Diokno, "Tasks and Problems of the Filipino People," p. 13.

[57]*Philippine News*, 18–24 November 1981, p. 8.

NASSA.[58] The first shift, according to Bishop Julio Labayen, was a reinvigoration of NASSA's Justice and Peace program, brought about by the detention of large numbers of political prisoners on allegations of "subversion" (but without charges in many cases) and the loss of civil liberties as a result of martial rule. For instance, NASSA was instrumental in helping to establish the Church-Military Liaison Committee (CMLC) in 1973 to resolve conflicts between the military and church officials and workers, and it helped create Citizens' Committees for Justice and Peace at the diocesan level to monitor human rights violations. The national secretariat continued throughout the martial law period to coordinate documentation on human rights abuses, primarily with AMRSP's Task Force Detainees (TFD), and maintained a legal aid desk that handled thirty-five court cases serving approximately four thousand persons as of January 1981.[59]

The second shift in NASSA policy (occurring simultaneously in other Catholic and Protestant organizations) was the creation of programs that emphasized human development through "conscientization" and the establishment of Basic Christian Community–Community Organization (BCC-CO) structures. The program linked Latin American ideas of consciousness raising (*concientização*), pioneered by Paulo Freire among the poor in Brazil, and the notion of a small Christian community (*Comunidad cristiana de base*, literally, "basic Christian community") with American community organization concepts already in use in the Philippines. The BCC-CO approach added a new dimension to the churches' emphasis on social action whereby persons were encouraged to participate in decisions that affected them directly—both within the church and the community—through a process described by Bishop Francisco Claver in discussing other BCCs as "discernment, involvement, and shared responsibility."[60] The establishment of Christian communities provided a context not only for examining church and community problems in terms of the gospel, but also for engaging in collective action in the search for solutions. The BCC-CO was aimed at breaking the dependency syndrome of the marginalized and dispossessed by assisting them in becoming the agents of their own libera-

[58]Much of the following two sections was originally published in Robert L. Youngblood, "Basic Christian Communities and the Church-State Conflict," *Diliman Review*, 33 (November–December 1985): 43–47.

[59]Julio X. Labayen, "What is NASSA?" keynote homily delivered at the 8th NASSA Annual Convention, 1976; Abrera et al., "Servant of Humanity," pp. 26–27; and "Philippines: NASSA Reorganized," *Impact*, March 1974, pp. 508–509.

[60]Francisco F. Claver, "Who's Afraid of the Basic Christian Communities?" *Solidarity* no. 95 (1983): 26. The BCC-CO is only one type of BCC in the Philippines, and it is sometimes associated with the "Christian Left." BCC-COs of a "Christian Left" persuasion, it should be stressed, are different in structure and orientation from those discussed by Bishop Claver.

tion, and became an important theme, in one form or another, in NASSA's annual conventions after 1975. By 1978 a national board, headed by Bishop Miguel Purugganan of Ilagan, Isabela, was organized at the first BCC-CO national meeting to coordinate BCC-CO activities throughout the country.[61] The AMRSP also began to raise its social action profile by the late 1960s; in 1971 it issued the following statement in support of building Christian communities:

> We, the Major Religious Superiors of the Philippines, recognize the desires of our people to be liberated from the oppressive factors present in our social institutions and structures. We see that the role of the Church in the Philippines today is to intensify every effort to awaken the consciousness of all our people to a full realization of their dignity and equality as persons. In particular we affirm this need in regard to the poor and underprivileged, that they may be aroused to exercise their right as human beings to participate in the decisions that affect their lives as individuals and their destiny as a people. . . . This luminous goal summons all of us to participate in the radical restructuring of the present unjust social order in our country.[62]

The statement went on to underscore the importance of conscientization, both within and without the church, lay leadership training, and the role of people's organizations to the achievement of greater social justice in Philippine society.

The commitment of the Major Superiors to the creation of Christian communities to help the poor and to improve social justice conditions was accelerated by the declaration of martial law. In 1974, as a result of decisions taken at the associations' January 1974 annual meeting, the AMRSP established an Office for Justice and Peace to assist NASSA's Justice and Peace Commission, organized task forces for urban and rural conscientization, and voted to continue financial assistance to a number of people's organizations, including Zone One Tondo Organization (ZOTO), the *Samahan ng Kristiyanong Komunidad* ([SKK] Christian Community Association) and the National Federation of Sugar Workers (NFSW).[63] The Major Superiors also initiated programs to conscientize the "religious so they will better understand and respond to the needs of the poor and oppressed classes" in Philippine society.[64]

[61]Abrera et al., "Servant of Humanity," p. 27; Ted Anana, "Highlights: 7th NASSA Convention," *NASSA News*, August 1975, pp. 2–3; and "BCC-CO Holds First Consultation: Forms National Board," *NASSA News*, November–December 1978, p. 14.

[62]"Statement of Major Religious Superiors, December 1971" (typewritten).

[63]"Main Activities of the AMRSMP, 1971 to 1975," pp. 3–4 (typewritten).

[64]Association of Major Religious Superiors of the Philippines (AMRSP) to the Catholic Bishops' Conference of the Philippines (CBCP), 12 January 1974.

Internal AMRSP documents demonstrate that after 1974 the Major Superiors devoted considerable effort toward conscientization and the creation of Christian communities. Religious priests and nuns already familiar with the problems of the urban poor were recruited for the Task Force on Urban Conscientization (TFUC) to work in Tatalon, an urban poor area in Quezon City, while ousted leaders of the FFF were contacted to assist the Task Force on Rural Conscientization (TFRC) in ten areas nationwide. The AMRSP initially allocated ₱20,000 to the conscientization programs in 1974, but TFUC spent over ₱20,000 in 1975 alone on the Tatalon project. A year later, in 1976, a number of community projects were initiated in Tatalon and the *Ugnayan ng mga Samahan sa Tatalon Estate* ([USTE] Union of the Associations of Tatalon Estates)—an alliance of sixteen local groups with more than one thousand members—was organized to assist in the mobilization of the poor.[65] Efforts by the Major Superiors among the rural poor were also expanded in the late 1970s. Both task forces emphasized people's participation in the identification and resolution of community problems similar to the BCC-CO program of NASSA; In 1978, the AMRSP revealed that among its new ministries were a BCC-CO program and a lay minister and lay missionary program.[66] The AMRSP's Christian community orientation was also reflected in the themes of the congresses of the Southeast Asian Major Superiors' Conference (SEAMS) held between 1976 and 1981. By 1982 the AMRSP's Philippine Lay Missionary Program (PLMP) boasted "36 members distributed among 10 different areas in the Philippines and in two foreign countries."[67]

Protestant social action activities paralleled those of the Catholic church during this period. By the late 1960s individual pastors and some Protestant denominations were already active in community organizations such as the Confederation of Tondo-Foreshore and Community Organization (CTFCO) and its successor the Philippine Ecumenical Council for Community Organizations (PECCO). In a 1972 statement the NCCP characterized the "Philippines social economic conditions as oppressive and exploitative" and called upon member churches "to emphasize those activities which will enhance human development and liberation." Among the rec-

[65]AMRSP, "To All Major Superiors of Men and Women," 25 April 1974 (typewritten); "Task Force on Urban Conscientization: Tatalon," 17 February 1976 (typewritten); and "Task Force Urban Conscientization, Annual Report, 1977" (typewritten).

[66]AMRSP, "Letter to Religious," 30 June 1978 (typewritten).

[67]Editorial: "The 'Asean' in Retrospect," *Witness* 1 (4th Quarter, 1981): 2–3; and Gerald Nagle, "PLMP: Taking the Lay Mission Challenge to Heart," *Witness* 2 (1st quarter, 1982): 7.

ommendations of the National Council was a call for a reevaluation of the "institutional life" of the member churches as well as the NCCP structure itself and for a rechanneling of personnel and funds into "programs and projects that have to do with people's organization for power."[68] Two years later, on the second anniversary of martial law, the National Council proposed a set of priorities for liberation and development that included research and conscientization about unjust structures, community organization development, and equal opportunity projects for the poor, and, as special priority areas, assistance to political detainees and tribal minorities. The strategy for implementing the priorities focused on grass-roots participation and stimulating local initiative. By the end of the decade the NCCP, through its Commission on Development and Social Concerns (CDSC), was heavily committed to the Basic Christian Community concept.[69]

The BCC-CO emphasis of NASSA and the AMRSP was but one manifestation of a general reorientation of the Catholic church since Vatican II toward greater concern with secular problems and more co-responsibility at the local level. In January 1977, the Catholic Bishops' Conference of the Philippines (CBCP) issued a pastoral letter supporting the creation of Basic Christian Communities[70] and the following June stated: "We endorse the resolution of the National Convention of the Lay Apostolate to adopt the formation of Basic Christian Communities as the new thrust of the lay apostolate throughout the country."[71] But increased lay participation and the building of BCCs based on the Latin American experience (endorsed by the Latin American Episcopal Conference [CELAM] in Medellín, Colombia, in 1968), were most vigorously pursued in Mindanao and Sulu. As part of a frontier area with many northern Filipino immigrants and a high percentage of foreign missionaries, Mindanao-Sulu bishoprics tended to be

[68]National Council of Churches in the Philippines (NCCP), Executive Committee, "Statement of Concern of the National Council of Churches in the Philippines," 5 February 1972, in "Project Proposal of the Commission of Development and Social Concerns" (Quezon City: National Council of Churches in the Philippines, 1977), Annex-2A (mimeographed).

[69]Interview with church activist, Quezon City, Philippines, 13 July 1979; Philippine Ecumenical Writing Group, *Moving Heaven and Earth*, p. 34; "Statement on Priority and Strategy on Development—1974," in "Project Proposal of the Commission on Development and Social Concerns" (Quezon City: National Council of Churches in the Philippines, 1977), Annex-2B (mimeographed); and "Project Proposal of the Commission on Development and Social Concerns" (Quezon City: National Council of Churches in the Philippines, 1977) (mimeographed).

[70]The pastoral letter is reprinted in *NASSA News*, January–February 1977, pp. 7–8.

[71]As quoted in Sean Purcell, "Small Christian Communities," in "Selected Readings on Building Basic Christian Communities—Community Organizations" (n.p., n.d.), p. 1 (mimeographed).

less conservative, yet large in size and population relative to the number of priests and religious workers.[72] With one priest for every nine thousand Catholics in Mindanao and Sulu, training lay leaders and increasing lay participation in church decision-making was essential. One of the earliest lay leadership programs for training individuals to serve as a parish *kaabag* (partner or helper) was initiated by the Maryknoll Fathers in the Prelature of Tagum in Davao del Norte and Davao Oriental in the late 1960s. Yet it was not until the establishment of the Mindanao-Sulu Pastoral Conference (MSPC) in 1971 that lay leadership and BCC formation received region-wide endorsement.[73]

Stimulating lay leadership and organizing small Christian communities was a central theme as well as among the priority recommendations of the first four triennial MSPC conferences held between 1971 and 1980, and was clearly linked to improved conditions of social justice. MSPC I in 1971 set the tone by recommending increased lay leadership formation within the context of an open dialogue that encouraged "full community participation" in decisions affecting parishes, such as finances, organizations, and projects. The aim was to create BCCs sensitive to local social development needs and opposed to "all forms of paternalism in the community." The goals of MSPC I were underscored even more forcefully in subsequent pastoral conference meetings. Training lay leaders among the rural poor and building BCCs for "total human development" and "liberation" were noted as top priorities of MSPC II in 1974, while focusing on social justice and human rights problems, particularly among Muslim and tribal minorities, were central concerns of MSPC III in 1977. Continued work in the "conscientization and the organization of the poor" in "building Christian communities," according to Carlos "Karl" Gaspar, outgoing MSPC Secretariat (MSPCS) executive secretary, were among the key objectives of MSPC IV in 1980.[74]

Initially the small Christian community emphasis of the MSPC focused on bringing people together in local *kapilya* (chapels) for Sunday services. Yet, while the liturgical orientation remained paramount, an integral part of

[72]Carlos M. Gaspar, "The Growth and Development of MSPC," *What Is the MSPC* (n.p, n.d.), pp. 14–16.

[73]John Rich, *Life Together in Small Christian Communities: A Leadership Training Course* (Davao City: Maryknoll Fathers, 1977), p. 1. A *kaabag* is a liturgical lay leader from the community who is approved by the local ordinary. *MSPC Communications*, February 1972, contains an account of MSPC's organization and initial emphasis on lay leadership.

[74]For summaries of the first four MSPC conferences, themes, and recommendations, consult *What Is MSPC*, pp. 18–19, 24–39, and *Proceedings MSPC IV* (Davao City: MSPC, 1980?), letter of Carlos Gaspar on the inside cover.

the lay leadership and BCC program seminars also dealt with questions of social justice and liberation of the poor. The leadership training course of the Prelature of Tagum and the conscientization program of the Prelature of Malaybalay, Bukidnon, for example, both included social justice as an important aspect of BCC formation. The Tagum training course not only devoted a separate section to questions of "Freedom and Oppression," but also included examples of social action activities of Christian communities in other sections that emphasized self-reliance and democratic processes in leadership selection and community problem solving.[75] Malaybalay's *Kristohanong Katilingbanong Alagad* (Christian Community Servant) program, a part of the prelature's commitment to conscientization, was primarily concerned with "*increased social awareness*." Just as the *kaabag* in Tagum, the *alagad* were volunteer Catholic laymen, preferably married men twenty-five to forty-five years of age, who served a three-month apprenticeship and attended a training seminar before assuming full *alagad* responsibilities within the BCC. In addition to liturgical duties, such as leading prayer services, *alagad* were expected to be "*agents of analysis*" in helping the BCC identify "social, economic, political and cultural problems in the light of gospel teachings and facilitate the community's *organization* and *planning* aimed at the solution of these problems."[76] Moreover, although *alagad* worked closely with the parish priest, emphasis was placed on democratic participation, open dialogue, and co-responsibility within the BCC rather than blind acquiescence to, or dependence upon, higher church authority.

The link between lay leadership/BCC formation and social action was also evident in other MSPC bishoprics as well as elsewhere in the Philippines. For example, the Cagayan de Oro Archdiocesan Center for Community Action (COACCA), organized in 1972, stated that its "over-all objective" was BCC formation, stressing the importance of social action, conscientization, and community organization. In 1978 Bishop Federico Escaler indicated that conscientization, including "social, economic, cultural and political involvement," was a significant aspect of the BCC program of the Prelature of Kidapawan, North Cotabato. Similarly, the Diocesan Pastoral Center of Tandag, Surigao del Sur emphasized compara-

[75]Rich, *Life Together*, passim.

[76]"Conscientization Program of the Prelature of Malaybalay, Bukidnon, *Kristohanong Katilingbanong Alagad Program*," pp. 1–4 (mimeographed). For a general description of the program, see Robert Cunningham, "Lay Leadership Program," in Francisco F. Claver, "Quinquennial Report Prelature of Malaybalay, 1981," Appendix D, pp. 60–64 (mimeographed).

ble training techniques and social justice goals in its BCC program.[77] In 1977, at the recommendation of MSPC III, the regional secretariats of MISSSA and MSPCS were merged, and by 1980 Christian formation, lay leadership, and social action represented 57 percent of the apostolate activities of the church in Mindanao and Sulu.[78]

Outside of the MSPC, Bishop Ricardo Tancinco, Jr., formerly bishop of the Diocese of Calbayog, Samar, along with other church officials and lay leaders, committed themselves in August 1975 to "building a genuine Christian community through the removal of unjust structures existing inside and outside of the institutional church" by organizing "for people's power" and educating "for justice and human rights." The promotion of "democratic relationships among the clergy" and laity, "the integration of social involvement and spirituality," and the welfare of the poor and oppressed were singled out for emphasis. BCCs in other areas of the Philippines likewise sided with the poor and engaged in social justice work. At the national level, NASSA continued in 1979–80 to promote people's organizations and participation. In January 1982 the CBCP, echoing MSPC II in 1974, reiterated the importance of BCC formation to "liberation" and "total human development."[79]

Although parish statistics were incomplete, lay participation in church affairs, including social justice, increased dramatically in the MSPC after 1971. The number of lay delegates to MSPC conventions, for instance, roughly equaled the number of church delegates; laymen constituted 48 percent of the delegates attending MSPC I–II and IV and were a majority of the 284 delegates attending MSPC III. But perhaps more important, laymen participated fully in the proceedings, and the clergy, including some bishops, listened. This was in sharp contrast to other Philippine pastoral conference meetings where lay representation was as little as 10 percent.[80]

[77]*MSPC Communications*, January 1974, pp. 20–22; Bishop Federico Escaler, "Building the Community in Kidapawan," *MSPC Communications*, July 1978, p. 10; and Igmedio Abogado, "Building the Community in Tandag," *MSPC Communications*, July 1978, pp. 6–9.

[78]"MSPC III Recommendations," *What Is the MSPC*, p. 38; and *Proceedings MSPC IV*, p. 28.

[79]"Church in Samar Speaks for the Poor," *NASSA News*, September 1975, p. 10; Alfred W. McCoy, *Priests on Trial* (Sydney: Penguin Books Australia, 1984); Bruce Stannard, *Poor Man's Priest: The Fr. Brian Gore Story* (Sydney: Collins/Fontana, 1984); Philippine Ecumenical Writing Group, *Moving Heaven and Earth*, pp. 42–50; "At the Bar of History: Christianity through Social Action," *NASSA News*, May 1980, p. 1; "Support for People's Organizations Affirmed," *NASSA News*, June 1980, pp. 1, 20; and "Towards Social Justice: Pastoral Directives and Priorities," *Witness* 2 (1st quarter, 1982): 53.

[80]The percentage of lay delegates to the MSPC conventions was calculated from figures in *MSPC Communications*, September 1973, p. 4; January 1974, p. 2; June 1977, p. 13; and

Another example of lay participation was the establishment by social action workers of the Mindanao-Sulu Social Action Personnel Assembly (MISSACPA) in 1975 to enhance the working conditions and economic security of church lay personnel. MISSACPA became the Church Workers Assembly (CWA) in 1978 with the inclusion of other church personnel. The CWA focused on economic issues and on becoming a more effective bridge between the laity and the clergy by fostering improvement in democratization and collective decision-making within the church.[81] The division of MSPC into six subregions also stimulated lay participation. As an outgrowth of the BCC movement, subregionalization attempted to bring decision-making in the church closer to the local parish; as such, it provided more opportunities (with fewer expenses) for the laity and the clergy to come together to discuss church and community problems. In some dioceses, subregionalization clearly contributed to greater involvement in social justice issues.[82]

Much of the lay participation in the Catholic church was an outgrowth of the implementation of lay leadership programs and the organization of BCCs. Bishop Claver credited the *alagad* program for the "richer involvement of . . . lay people in the work of the Church" in Bukidnon, and in 1981 reported that out of the 1,000 *alagad* who had received training since the inception of the program in the Prelature of Malaybalay 600 remained active and were supported by another 1,000 men and women working in areas such as community organization, family life instruction, and health delivery.[83] Similarly, the Society of St. Columban announced that 660 laymen and laywomen had participated in their Christian community leadership programs in the Philippines between 1975 and 1984, and indicated that lay participation generally had increased in areas with active BCCs.[84]

Lay leadership and BCC formation in the MSPC, as well as elsewhere in the country, were not without problems, even in the most progressive bishoprics. Reliance on foreign financing, insufficient local participation, obsequiousness toward and dependency on church and government offi-

---

Proceedings MSPC IV, p. 79. For indications of the extent of lay participation in the discussions at the conferences, consult *MSPC Communications*, February 1972, pp. 2–5; Jesus Varela, "A Brief History of MSPC," *What Is the MSPC*, pp. 12–13; and "The Question of Delegations to MSPC II," *MSPC Communications*, December 1973, supplement.

[81]Remedios A. Guillena, "Lay Participation in the Church," *MSPC Communications*, January–June 1980, pp. 47–48.

[82]Various aspects of subregionalization are discussed in the October 1980 and April and August 1981 issues of *MSPC Communications*.

[83]Claver, "Quinquennial Report, 1981," pp. 2–3, 8.

[84]"Philippines: Lay Leadership," *Columban Mission*, April 1984, p. 3 and passim.

cials, and lack of program continuity and coordination plagued the Christian community movement from its inception. There was also concern among many Catholic bishops and other church officials that some church organizations closely associated with social justice activities were inordinately influenced by persons sympathetic to the NDF. Such concern resulted in conflict between the bishops of the Mindanao and Sulu region and the lay secretariat and board of the MSPC in the early 1980s. Two issues troubled the bishops. First, the prelates disputed the secretariat's claims of autonomy in the management of church programs, many of which were funded externally, and refused to tolerate the lay body's practice of conducting programs within a diocese without the knowledge or approval of the local bishop. Second, the bishops were concerned about the secretariat's ties to the underground, tolerant attitude toward the use of violence, and the possibility that church funds were being funneled to the CPP/NPA through projects sponsored under the auspices of the MSPC. The conflict culminated in March 1982, when the bishops refused to recognize the secretariat and board and denied them the use of the MSPC title. The secretariat, with the help of other, more sympathetic church organizations, formed a new ecumenical organization called the Mindanao-Sulu Interfaith People's Conference.[85]

Despite the blow-up between the bishops of Mindanao and Sulu and the secretariat and board of the MSPC, the lay leadership and BCC thrust of the Catholic church, particularly in Mindanao and Sulu, contributed significantly toward greater human development and liberation among the poor in a number of dioceses and prelatures. Participants in BCC programs noted that improvements in community education, pride, participation, and peace and order often went hand in hand with heightened community political awareness. Among the results were demands for a larger voice in local planning and decision-making, and greater resistance to harassment and intimidation by local elites, including government and military officials. Accordingly, the BCCs, which numbered in the thousands nationwide, were a step in the direction of helping the poor to become instruments of their own liberation; as such, the Christian communities were potentially formidable agents for change.[86] Given the colonial heritage of the Philippines and continued governmental paternalism, increasing participation in

[85]For an extensive discussion of the dissolution of the MSPC, see Julia Anne Hallward, "Episcopal Power and the Prophetic Church: Ecclesiological Divisions in the Mindanao Sulu Pastoral Conference, 1971–1982, the Philippines" (B.A. honors thesis, Harvard and Radcliffe Colleges, 1988), especially chap. 4.

[86]Claver, "Who's Afraid of the Basic Christian Communities?" pp. 25–27.

local decision-making resulted in tension and conflict between church and lay leaders active in BCC formation and the Marcos government.

The Marcos Regime, Social Justice, and BCCs

The Marcos regime's uneasiness with the endeavors of Catholic and Protestant activists was underscored by two confidential government reports, one by the Ministry of labor in 1975 and the other by the Ministry of National Defense in 1978. The labor study, reportedly written for Blas Ople, the minister of labor, outlined the tenets of liberation theology and conscientization as put forth by Gustavo Gutierrez and Paulo Freire, reviewed the Catholic church's commitment to the poor, and discussed the potential for Central Intelligence Agency (CIA) and Communist manipulation of a "Church-led 'liberation' movement." Although recognizing that it was "doubtful if the deepening involvement of the church in Philippine politics would slow or even be halted," the report concluded with recommendations for undercutting church "activists," including mobilizing the masses while accelerating reforms, restricting aliens while encouraging Filipinization in the church, and separating church and state while stressing church-state dialogue.[87] The defense report—part of which was published in 1979 by Galileo Kintanar—was also concerned with activism in the church; it focused, however, primarily on so-called left and right religious radicals, and singled out the BCC movement as a "dangerous form of threat from the religious radicals" because of its potential as "an infrastructure of political power" on a national scale. In addition to identifying and punishing religious radicals individually on national security grounds, the report recommended a twofold strategy for lessening their influence as a group within the church. On the one hand, the report urged that the government support the "conservative mainstream of the church hierarchy and clergy" and cooperate with the church on social action projects and on moral and civil issues. On the other hand, it advocated that the government suppress religious radicals by sowing dissension and by using public criticism and modern intelligence techniques. The study also suggested that religious personnel be required to obtain government approval before establishing BCCs and initiating social action projects, and recommended that local officials "be directed to report immediately to higher authorities when . . .

[87]Institute of Labor and Manpower Studies, Ministry of Labor, "Liberation Theology," confidential report (n.p., n.d.), pp. 1–30 (photocopied).

religious or non-religious personnel of the BCCs utter denunciations of the government." Furthermore, the report revealed official apprehensions about antigovernment groups, both of the left and the right, using BCCs to subvert the government.[88]

The labor and Kintanar studies were followed in 1983 by another analysis of church-state relations, reportedly authored by a government spokesman, the *Crisis Papers*, which also was critical of the role of the Roman Catholic church in Philippine society. In order to win "the hierarchy—and therefore the institutional Church—over" to the government, the *Crisis Papers* suggested that (1) the vital interests of the church be guaranteed, perhaps with legislation; (2) criticism of the church in the controlled media be curtailed; and (3) ideological differences between the church and state be downplayed while ideological differences within the church be emphasized. The *Crisis Papers* stressed "the positive attitude of certain elements within the Church hierarchy towards present State reform efforts in contrast to the negative attitude of the [Cardinal] Sin Group." The objective was twofold: undercutting criticism of the government by church leaders like Sin and, at the same time, creating an image of church-state amity.[89] Taken together the three reports were reminiscent of the "Banzer Plan," developed by General Hugo Banzer Suarez, former president of Bolivia, in recommending that conservative church leaders be co-opted while progressives church leaders critical of the government be discredited.

Actions of the Marcos regime against the church's Christian community program occurred periodically throughout the country after the declaration of martial law, but government repression of lay leaders and BCCs—especially those engaged in social justice work—was particularly intense and widespread in Mindanao and Sulu. In July 1976, the military obtained a sworn statement from a PANAMIN employee,[90] Lilia Judilla, also reportedly a member of the CPP, alleging relations between the church and the Communist Party and the party's military arm, the New People's Army (NPA). Although the statement dealt generally with the so-called "Christian Left," the church in Mindanao was emphasized. Among those listed as

[88]Galileo C. Kintanar, "Contemporary Religious Radicalism in the Philippines: An Analysis," a reprint from the *Quarterly National Security Review* of the NDCP, June 1979, pp. 1–9 (typewritten).

[89]L. C. Ranida, ed., "Basic Issues in Philippine Church-State Relations," published by the Communication Research Institute for Social and Ideological Studies from a government report, *Crisis Papers*, reprinted in *MSPC Theological Articles*, August–September 1983, pp. 18–20.

[90]PANAMIN, the Presidential Assistant on National Minorities, is a cabinet-level office that oversees and coordinates government policy for Philippine tribal minorities.

members of the "Christian Left" were six bishops (Reginald Arliss, Francisco Claver, Julio Labayen, Antonino Nepomuceno, Felix Perez, and Jesus Varela) and numerous priests and nuns active in the MSPC's lay leadership and BCC program. Bishop Claver was singled out as "the strongest and most powerful prelate in the clerical left," while the Prelature of Tagum was identified as having a majority of priests supportive of leftist ideology. Judilla claimed that the CPP used church leadership programs, newsletters, and radio stations, particularly in Tagum and Malaybalay, for ideological training purposes and that BCCs, by engaging in democratic decision-making when confronting parish and community problems, contributed to the "national struggle" of the CPP. Judilla also stated that the church's conscientization efforts ran "parallel with the National Democratic program," underscoring the fact that the Nat-Dems accepted "violence as a methodology for the take-over of the government." Judilla thus concluded that "*there* [was] *no difference in the ideology supported by the clerical left and the ideology supported by the Party*."[91]

The church dismissed Judilla's accusations, yet the military closed two church radio stations, DXCD in Tagum and DXBB in Malaybalay, and picked up sixty-nine persons in the Prelature of Tagum in November 1976 on charges of subversion and inciting to rebellion. The military claimed the radio stations and those detained had links with the CPP and the NPA. Of the arrested, seven were listed in Judilla's statement as members of the "Christian Left"; many were parish leaders and *kaabag*; and more than half were clearly identifiable as church workers.[92] Bishop Joseph Regan of Tagum and Bishop Claver of Malaybalay swiftly denounced the raids and arrests, as did other bishops in the MSPC, and in a pastoral letter, Bishop Regan said: "I personally know many of these Catholic lay leaders. They have done fine work here in the Prelature of Tagum, and so far no proof has been presented to me which justifies their confinement in the Tagum and Mati Stockades, just as no proof has been given to me for the closing of the radio station DXCD."[93] In a letter to President Marcos, a group of "Concerned Bishops of Mindanao-Sulu" averred that an emphasis on social justice was the "common thread" linking the military raids against DXCD and DXBB and the arrests of lay leaders in Tagum to similar actions against

[91] "Supplementary Information on CPP/NPA Relations with the Church with Emphasis on Mindanao by Lilia Judilla," July 1976, *Informationis Causa* 1, nos. 134–137, pp. 1–15 (typewritten).

[92] "Church Worker-Detainees," *MSPC Communications*, January 1977, p. 18.

[93] Pastoral letter of Bishop Joseph Regan to the people of the Prelature of Tagum, 25 November 1976, reprinted in *MSPC Communications*, January 1977, p. 5.

church institutions and personnel elsewhere. The bishops criticized the "constant equating of Church action *with the poor with support of the NPA*," noting the legitimacy of the church's commitment to "the authentic development of people" through the formation of Christian communities.[94] Although most of those arrested were soon released and none was brought to trial, the military nevertheless refused to allow the radio stations to reopen.

The controversy surrounding the raids in Tagum and Malaybalay only temporarily inhibited (if at all) the military's pressure on church lay leaders and BCCs engaged in social action programs in Mindanao and Sulu. In July 1979, for example, two lay workers in the Prelature of Kidapawan, North Cotabato, were arrested and tortured, while the prelature's basic Christian communities (*Gagmayng Kristohanon Katilingban* [GKK]) were labeled "subversive" by the military. The arrests, according to Bishop Federico Escaler in a letter to Deputy Minister of Defense Carmelo Barbero, highlighted a pattern of intimidation by *barangay* officials and the Philippine Constabulary (PC) against church lay leaders for holding seminars and prayer meetings suspected of being infiltrated by the communists. Yet, Escaler pointed out further, few, if any, alleged "acts of subversion" were ever "substantiated by concrete evidence."[95] In 1981, Orlando Quevedo, the new bishop of Kidapawan, noted that while the reputation for "extreme radicalism" among the prelature's clergy and lay leaders was unfounded, the military continued to harass BCC leaders, instilling fear that resulted in the avoidance of parish responsibilities and, in some cases, the abandonment of homes and farms.[96]

Despite protests from high church officials, including the conservative (progovernment) Antonio Mabutas, archbishop of Davao, and repeated assurances that close cooperation with the church in the area of social justice was paramount to the military, militarization and violence against the general population (71 percent of which was Catholic in 1981) as well as against individual Christian community leaders continued to be a problem for the MSPC.[97] By 1980, in addition to the presence of over 100,000

[94]A group of "Concerned Bishops of Mindanao-Sulu," Davao City, to President Marcos, 20 November 1976, reprinted in *MSPC Communications*, January 1977, pp. 3–4.

[95]See an open letter from a group of "Concerned Christians of the Prelature of Kidapawan" (undated), and Bishop Federico O. Escaler, Kidapawan, North Cotabato, to Carmelo Barbero, deputy minister of defense, 26 August 1979, both reprinted in *MSPC Communications*, October 1979, pp. 28–29.

[96]Beato Tariman interview of Bishop Orlando Quevedo, *MSPC Communications*, August 1981, pp. 24–25, 47.

[97]Pastoral letter of Antonio Ll. Mabutas, archbishop of Davao, 16 August 1979, reprinted in *MSPC Communications*, October 1979, pp. 14–15; and a speech by "Brig. General

police, paramilitary men, and Civilian Home Defense Forces (CHDF), the Mindanao and Sulu region was home for 60 percent of the country's armed forces. According to Bishop Escaler, in a twelve-month period prior to August 1980, 69 military operations in the region led to the documentation of 485 political detentions, 74 "salvagings" (extrajudicial killings), and 79 cases of torture.[98] Additionally, in July 1981, the military inaugurated a "strategic hamlet" program, resulting in substantial population relocations, often far from farms and sources of food, in areas of Mindanao considered infiltrated by the NPA. A number of the communities targeted for "hamletization" had well-established BCCs and active church lay leaders. The effect was that of silencing the people and cowing them into obeying the dictates of the local military commanders. Beyond suppressing the NPA, however, some reports suggested that the "pacification" program was linked to agribusiness expansion by multinational corporations and that elements of the military, in cooperation with local political officials, sought vacated land for rubber and *ipil-ipil* tree plantations.[99] The military claimed that the people relocated voluntarily "to avoid communist harassment," but following investigations by human rights groups, including one organized by the Integrated Bar of the Philippines, Defense Minister Juan Ponce Enrile, who was evidently unaware of the program, ordered it dismantled, stating that "the forcible grouping of people in specified residential villages or centers" was a violation of "constitutional rights."[100]

Enrile's admonition, however, did not stop the practice of hamletization nor did it curtail military repression of critics within the Catholic and Protestant churches. On the contrary, between 1981 and 1984 an estimated 500,000 Filipinos nationwide were forced into strategic hamlets. Following the Enrile memorandum of March 1982, reports indicated that hamlet centers tripled in the Mindanao provinces of Agusan del Sur, Davao del Sur, North Cotabato, and Zamboanga del Norte, resulting in considerable deprivation and suffering, especially among young children.[101]

Federico D. Navarro during the Executive Session of the MND [Ministry of National Defense] Investigating Committee and the Davao Archdiocese—IBP [Interim *Batasang Pambansa*] Panel" (undated), reprinted in *Ichthys*, 30 November 1979, pp. 7–12.

[98]Speech of Bishop Federico Escaler to the Bishops-Businessmen Conference, Makati, 25 September 1981, reprinted in *MSPC Communications*, November 1981, p. 32.

[99]Mindanao Documentation Committee for Refugees, *The Strategic Hamlets of Mindanao* (n.p., n.d.); Sheilah Ocampo, "A Little Vietnam," *Far Eastern Economic Review*, 12 March 1982, pp. 38–40; and "In the Hamlets of San Vicente," *NASSA News*, December 1981, pp. 14–15.

[100]*Asia Record*, March 1982, p. 9; April 1982, p. 10; and August 1982, p. 14.

[101]Virginia Leary et al., *The Philippines: Human Rights after Martial Law* (Geneva: International Commission of Jurists, 1984), pp. 35–39; "An Old Tactic Revived: Strategic

Raids on church institutions and the arrest of priests, nuns, pastors, and church workers suspected of leftist tendencies increased markedly in 1982. From July 1982 until the assassination of former Senator Benigno Aquino, Jr., in August 1983, the government-controlled media ran numerous articles critical of alleged church radicals without allowing clarifications or rebuttals from church officials. Among the activities singled out were church social justice and BCC programs. Perhaps nowhere was this harassment more dramatically underscored than in the case of two Columban missionaries, Frs. Brian Gore, an Australian, and Niall O'Brien, an Irishman, who, along with a Filipino diocesan priest, Vicente Dangan, and six lay leaders, were formally charged in February 1983 with the March 1982 assassination of Pablo Sola, the mayor of Kabankalan, Negros Occidental. Also killed at the time were four of the mayor's associates.[102] Earlier, in September 1982, following a military raid on the parish house in Oringao, a market settlement fifteen kilometers from Kabankalan, Gore had been charged with "illegal possession of explosives and ammunition" and "inciting to rebellion."[103] In November 1982, according to a story in the *Visayan Daily Star*, Gore and O'Brien were accused of having been involved in the assassination despite the fact that a previous military investigation and statements in *Paghimakas* (Struggle), a publication of the NPA in Negros, credited the NPA with the murders.[104]

Although the charges were eventually dismissed in July 1984 following a political settlement, the case represented a microcosm of church-state conflict over the implementation of social justice programs and the establishment of BCCs by church activists committed to the social teachings of Vatican II. At the heart of the case was Gore's antagonism of the local and provincial elite, including sugar czar Roberto Benedicto, by his criticism of their life-style, by his work as the Kabankalan organizer of the FFF, and by

---

Hamleting," *KSP Kilusan* 1, nos. 1–2 (1982): 18–30; Earl Martin, "In the Name of Security: A Philippine Strategic Hamlet," *Southeast Asia Chronicle*, no. 83, April 1982, pp. 16–18; "Are Hamlets a Continuing Nightmare?" *MIPCS Memo*, November 1983, p. 5; and "Laac Yesterday and Today: Hamlets and Land Problems Exposed," *MIPCS Memo*, February 1984, pp. 4–5.

[102]Extensive accounts of the trial and the circumstances surrounding the case are provided by McCoy, *Priests on Trial*; Stannard, *Poor Man's Priest*; and Niall O'Brien, *Seeds of Injustice: Reflections on the Murder Frame-up of the Negros Nine in the Philippines from the Prison Diary of Niall O'Brien* (Dublin: O'Brien Press, 1985); and Niall O'Brien, *Revolution from the Heart* (New York: Oxford University Press, 1987).

[103]*Columban Mission*, January 1983, passim; and *Political Detainees Update*, 15 October 1982, p. 1.

[104]McCoy, *Priests on Trial*, pp. 190–193.

his and O'Brien's successful establishment of BCCs (*Kristianong Katilingban*) among subsistence hill farmers. The participatory and conscientization processes of the BCCs gave the peasants a new sense of solidarity, which allowed for the mobilization of large crowds on political issues, and resulted in the hill farmers no longer being afraid of speaking out against military misconduct and governmental corruption. Rather than embrace the heightened politicization of the peasants as a healthy, even necessary, aspect of democratic development, the local elites, along with the Marcos government, saw it as a loss of political control, equating BCC participation with membership in the CPP/NPA, and responded with military repression.[105]

An emphasis on social justice and the establishment of BCCs was a common thread running through the arrests of priests, nuns, pastors, and layworkers as well as the raids on church institutions after 1972. Much of the church-state conflict following the termination of martial rule in 1981 must be interpreted in this context; as indicated above, the government and military often viewed working with the poor and organizing BCCs as synonymous with supporting the CPP/NPA. To be sure, the CPP was as attracted as the government was worried by the potential the BCCs offered for the creation of an independent political base, and there were indications that some social action programs were manipulated by the CPP through supporters of the NDF within the churches. For example, Fr. Edgardo Kangleon admitted while in military detention that the Catholic Social Action Center he directed in Catbalongan, Samar, had been used by the Communists.[106] It is clear from church documents associated with the 1982 withdrawal of the Mindanao-Sulu bishops from the MSPC that many of the bishops believed that the MSPC Secretariat was unduly influenced by the NDF.[107] Bishop Claver likewise discussed the problems of resisting attempts by the NDF and the Communists to influence lay leadership and BCC programs in the Prelature of Malaybalay.[108] Yet the Marcos regime's simple equating of social action programs and BCC formation with general

[105]Ibid, chaps. 4 and 5.

[106]*Bulletin Today*, 13 December 1982, pp. 1, 20; and *Times Journal*, 31 December 1982, pp. 1, 6.

[107]Carlos "Karl" Gaspar, former executive secretary of the Mindanao-Sulu Pastoral Conference, to Bishop Fernando Capalla, 28 May 1981 (typewritten); Bishop Francisco Claver, Malaybalay, Bukidnon, to Bishop Fernando Capalla, 15 May 1982 (typewritten); Bishop Fernando Capalla, Baguio City, to Bishop Francisco Claver, 8 July 1982 (typewritten); and Ben Verberne, "What Happened to the Mindanao-Sulu Pastoral Conference?" *MSPC Theological Articles*, July 1983, pp. 1–6.

[108]Claver, "Quinquennial Report, 1981," pp. 12–13, 21–23, 33, and 35–36.

subversion, especially in the form of support for the CPP, overlooked the legitimate concern of the Catholic and Protestant churches for the poor. Such a crude link ignored the fact that indiscriminate repression of church activists (and others), particularly in the absence of concrete evidence of wrongdoing, not only exacerbated church-state relations, but also served to increase the ranks of the Communists.

Repression of BCCs suspected of antigovernment activities and church personnel engaged in social justice activities was but a part of a more comprehensive attempt by the Marcos regime, through the military, to control opposition in the name of national security and national development. Chapter 5 examines in greater detail the effect of increased militarization after 1972 on church-state relations.

5

Militarization and the Churches

President Marcos justified the expansion of the armed forces following the imposition of martial law as necessary for the security of the nation and for political stability conducive to rapid economic development. To be sure, the maintenance of political order was essential for attracting foreign investments and loans and, perhaps more important, for perpetuating the president's power. Increased militarization, however, resulted in heightened church-state conflict. Although the Catholic and Protestant church leaders were in agreement with the government on the desirability of helping the poor, the implementation of church social action and social justice programs often conflicted with Marcos' concern for national security and political order. Thus clergy and laypersons ministering to the needs of the poor and engaged in social justice programs were often suspected of "subversion" and antigovernment activities; as a consequence, they were repeatedly the target of government and military crackdowns.

To resolve conflicts, a Church-Military Liaison Committee (CMLC) was established in November 1973. Significantly, the military agreed to prohibit the arrest of religious persons or raids on church establishments "without prior coordination with and in the company of the highest/senior religious superior or his/her representative."[1] Nevertheless, the CMLC

[1]Cable from Maj. Gen. Fidel V. Ramos to all zone, provincial, and other commanders under his authority, 3 December 1973.

agreement was often violated, and church officials, who were initially optimistic about the prospects of a genuine dialogue, became more critical of the military. In January 1983, the Catholic bishops voted to withdraw from the CMLC.

After 1972, the intermittent acrimony that plagued relations between the Philippine churches and the military frequently revolved around the twin issues of military misconduct versus church involvement in politics. In this chapter I examine the effect of increased militarization during the Marcos presidency on church-state relations. I first deal with church-military conflict over the use of the military in fostering the regime's development program. Emphasis is given to the role of the military in supporting the expansion of agri-industrial and natural resource extraction enterprises as well as the implementation of other development projects that led to the displacement of large numbers of poor farmers, tribal minorities, and urban workers and slum-dwellers. I then focus on major church-military clashes between 1974 and 1984 that resulted in the confiscation of church property and the arrest, detention, and deportation of clergy who were engaged in programs aimed at uplifting the poor and, at the same time, were frequently critical of the government and the military. I conclude by juxtaposing the military's mission to maintain law and order as a means for attracting foreign investment and accelerating economic development against the Catholic and Protestant churches' seeking social and economic justice for the poor.

Development and the Military

From the beginning of martial rule, the Marcos regime's espousal of rapid economic development through heavy foreign borrowing, the promotion of exports, and the attraction of foreign investments conflicted with a number of Catholic and Protestant church programs among the poor. Government projects, such as agribusiness expansion, natural resource exploitation, and urban beautification and industrialization, that favored foreign corporations and the close associates and relatives of the president—typically at the expense of poor farmers, tribal minorities, and urban squatters—were criticized and opposed by progressive members of the clergy. Just as often, however, the armed forces were employed to silence criticism and to ensure the completion of government-sponsored economic projects with little regard for the wishes of those affected by the programs.

On numerous occasions the military used strong-arm tactics in support of the economic programs of the Marcos regime. For example, the military supported the efforts of Philippine Packing Corporation (PHILPACK), a subsidiary of the American Del Monte company, a multinational fruit-processing concern that has operated in the Philippines since 1926, to acquire an additional 14,000 hectares in Sumilao, Bukidnon, for its plantation operations. PHILPACK, backed by the PC, fenced disputed properties, drove cattle onto land to destroy crops, and employed armed guards to drive farmers off their plots. Approximately 80 percent of the population in the area affected by the expansion of the corporation were native Bukidnon.[2] The Office of the Presidential Assistant on National Minorities (PANAMIN), an agency charged with the task of protecting tribal minorities, sided with PHILPACK in the dispute despite provisions in Presidential Decree 410 guaranteeing tribal minorities the right to continue occupying ancestral lands in the public domain.[3] Previous attempts by farmers to secure titles to their land were thwarted by land speculators who had surreptitiously obtained the titles and who, as absentee landlords, had leased the property to PHILPACK without regard to the welfare of the tillers. Although the Philippine Constitutions of 1935 and 1973 limited the amount of land a foreign corporation could lease to 1,024 and 1,000 hectares, respectively,[4] a Crop Producer and Grower's agreement (essentially a disguised lease) allowed PHILPACK to obtain control over a larger land area, and empowered the corporation to initiate actions against third parties contesting the grower's right to lease to the producer, PHILPACK. The company was also assisted in its efforts to expand by local politicians and, critics charge, indirectly by Marcos' long, friendly association with the corporation.[5]

The Bukidnon Sugar Corporation (BUSCO) and the Tagum Agricultural Development Corporation (TADECO), a banana-exporting firm, also used coercion in acquiring additional land for plantation expansion in the provinces of Bukidnon (BUSCO) and Davao del Norte (TADECO). Both firms had close ties to Malacañang through Roberto Benedicto, the Philippine

[2]Vincent G. Cullen, "Sour Pineapples," *Signs of the Times*, 12 June 1976, pp. 17–24; *Philippine Times*, 1–15 February 1977, pp. 3, 6, 8, and 16–28; and Ben Langa-an and Nilo Langa-an, "Squatters in Their Own Land" (May 1980), pp. 40–41 (typewritten).

[3]*Presidential Decree 410*, 11 March 1984. A loophole in the decree provides "that the Government in the interest of its development program, may establish agri-industrial projects in these areas for the purpose of creating conditions for employment and thus further enhance the progress of the people."

[4]The Philippine Constitution of 1935, Article 13, Sec. 2; and the Philippine Constitution of 1973, Article 14, Sec. 11.

[5]Ronald K. Edgerton, "Social Disintegration on a Contemporary Philippine Frontier: The Case of Bukidnon, Mindanao," *Journal of Contemporary Asia* 13, no. 2 (1983): 163.

sugar czar, who was a major stockholder in BUSCO, and through Antonio Floirendo, the *Kilusang Bagong Lipunan* ([KBL] New Society Movement) party chairman in Eastern Mindanao, who owned TADECO. As a result, national and local government officials, the military, and PANAMIN readily facilitated the expansion programs of the companies by manipulating the law, by intimidation, by offering financial inducements, and, when necessary, by the use of violence.

In 1975, after having purchased disputed land in Barrio Paitan, Quezon, Bukidnon, BUSCO began destroying houses and evicting small farmers and indigenous Manobos. When the Manobos, who were occupying ancestral lands, continued to resist, BUSCO security guards and the PC returned in 1976 to demolish more homes and, on the orders of PANAMIN, to relocate forcibly the tribal residents onto a distant reservation. The Manobos were relocated without adequate monetary compensation from either BUSCO or the government. Moreover, once on the reservation the tribesmen were directed by PANAMIN, which held title to the reservation land, to plant sugarcane on 180 hectares.[6]

Methods identical to those used by PHILPACK and BUSCO were employed by TADECO in its expansion program. Opposition from small farmers and Ata tribesmen to selling or leasing land to TADECO was met with force, resulting in several violent incidents, including torture and murder. One example was the forcible ejection in late 1977 of nearly seven hundred families from barrio Tibungol, a settlement located adjacent to the TADECO plantation. Former residents maintained that Task Force *Pagkakaisa*, the Civilian Home Defense Force (CHDF), the 57th Strike Force, TADECO security guards, the army of PANAMIN, and prisoners on parole (presumably from the Davao Penal Colony [DAPECOL], part of which was farmed by TADECO), all participated in driving the occupants off the land. The media reported that the military was deployed to the area because of an infestation of rebels, and residents feared, according to one account, that "whoever refused to move out or surrender would be liquidated next."[7] The real reason for the ejection, however, was to make way for a TADECO tree farm of *ipil-ipil*, a quick-growing tree from which poles are made to prop up banana trees on the plantation. With the backing of the government

[6]ICL Research Team, *A Report on Tribal Minorities in Mindanao* (Manila: Regal Printing, 1979), pp. 22–23, 41–58; and Langa-an and Langa-an, "Squatters in Their Own Land," pp. 36–40.

[7]Philippine Inter-Agency Research Team on the Banana Workers, "Transnational Corporations and the Philippine Banana Export Industry: Its Effects on the Land and the People," Part 1 (Manila: LRC Series, 1978), p. 33 (mimeographed).

and military, TADECO's banana plantation increased from 171 hectares in 1969–70 to 4,504 hectares in 1976. By 1976, the corporation also was using an additional 3,480 hectares within DAPECOL.[8]

The Marcos regime repeatedly used the military and armed elements of PANAMIN elsewhere in the country to repress opposition to government development projects that threatened the livelihood of peasants and tribal minorities. Beginning in the mid-1970s, for instance, constabulary and PANAMIN forces were deployed in response to the protests of the Kalingas and Bontocs in the provinces of Mountain Province and Kalinga-Apayao over government plans to construct four dams on the Chico River and the protests of the Tingguians in the province of Abra over the activities of Cellophil Resources Corporation, a timber- and pulpwood-processing corporation owned by Herminio Disini. The Chico River Basin Development Project (CRBDP) threatened to dislocate 100,000 tribal Kalingas and Bontocs; the Cellophil project appropriated timber lands previously occupied and used by the Tingguians. Neither the Kalingas and Bontocs nor the Tingguians were consulted prior to the initiation of the projects, and given the record of broken promises to those affected by previous development programs, none of the regime's assurances of development-generated prosperity, adequate monetary compensation, and comparable relocation were believed by a majority of the minority tribesmen.[9]

Rather than reducing tensions, the introduction of PANAMIN and combat troops into the Chico River and Cellophil conflicts led to an escalating cycle of violence. Both PANAMIN and the military tended to view opposition to the projects as subversive and as a threat to national security. PANAMIN's inability to convince the minorities through bribery, deception, and intimidation to accept the hydroelectric dams prompted the regime to replace the agency in July 1978 with additional armed forces.[10] The military quickly assumed a larger voice in the administration of the

[8]Randolf S. David et al., "Transnational Corporations and the Philippine Banana Export Industry," in *Political Economy of Philippine Commodities*, ed. Third World Studies Program (Quezon City: University of the Philippines, Third World Studies Center, 1983), p. 32.

[9]Much of the discussion of the Chico River and Cellophil projects was drawn from Joanna Cariño, Jessica Cariño, and Geoffrey Nettleton, "The Chico River Basin Development Project: A Situation Report," *Aghamtao* 2 (December 1979): 37–91; Richard Dorral, "The Tinggians of Abra and Cellophil: A Situation Report," *Aghamtao* 2 (December 1979): 116–149; Anti-Slavery Society, *The Philippines: Authoritarian Government, Multinationals and Ancestral Lands*, Indigenous People and Development Series Report, no. 1 (London: Anti-Slavery Society, 1983), pp. 74–90, 102–119; "Tribal People and the Marcos Regime: Cultural Genocide in the Philippines," *Southeast Asia Chronicle*, no. 67 (October 1979); and Langa-an and Langa-an, "Squatters in Their Own Land," chaps. 4 and 5.

[10]Felix Casalmo (pseud.), *The Vision of a New Society* (Manila, 1980), pp. 44–46.

region. To break the resistance both to the CRBDP and the Cellophil project, the military harassed dissident villages, replaced recalcitrant elected officials, and, in some instances, jailed, tortured, and killed project opponents. The activities of the 60th PC Strike Force Battalion in Mountain Province and Kalinga-Apayao were so notorious that an open letter, containing documented cases of abuse, was sent to President Marcos in November 1978 asking that the unit be withdrawn from the region.[11] The battalion was eventually removed, but the militarization of the northern Cordillera nevertheless intensified in the face of steadfast opposition and the growing presence of the New People's Army (NPA), the military arm of the Communist Party of the Philippines (CPP), which moved into the region in 1976 in support of the minority tribesmen.[12] Although the government made a number of placating gestures, such as suspending or canceling much of the work on the Chico dam project and assuring the Tingguians that "development, economic growth, and technology" must be "subordinated to social and human needs,"[13] the conflict and violence surrounding the development programs continued. The regime's fundamental objectives for development in the Chico River basin remained unchanged; replacement military units rivaled the 60th PC Strike Force for repressiveness; and minority resistance, especially among the Kalingas and Bontocs, persisted unabated.

The political power of PHILPACK, BUSCO, TADECO, and Cellophil, as well as that of other agri-industrial and natural resource extraction firms, coupled with the support of the military, prevented small farmers and minority tribesmen, who were often poor and minimally educated, from successfully using the courts or local and national government agencies either to block the expansion of the companies or to obtain just compensation. As a last resort, many peasants and tribal Filipinos turned to the clergy for assistance through the Justice and Peace programs of the Catholic and Protestant churches. Attempts by priests, nuns, and pastors to assist peasants and tribal minorities dispossessed of their land or denied their rights met with opposition from the government and military. Arrests of church

[11]Open letter to "President Ferdinand E. Marcos, Malacañang Palace, Manila," from the Kalinga and Bontoc, Tabuk, Province of Kalinga-Apayao, 17 November 1978, reprinted in *Aghamtao* 2 (December 1979): 92–98.

[12]Sheilah Ocampo, "Breaching a Dam of Despair," *Far Eastern Economic Review*, 13 June 1980, pp. 23–24; and Richard Vokey, "Assault on the Peaks of Power," *Far Eastern Economic Review*, 13 June 1985, pp. 24, 26–27, 29.

[13]Comments attributed to Arturo V. Barbero, governor of Abra Province, in Albert Lee, "Tingguians Have Forged a Peace Pact to Wage a Non-Violent Rejection of an 'Intruder' in Their Land," *Panorama*, 25 March 1979, p. 33.

activists began immediately with the proclamation of martial law. In September 1972, a nun and eight priests, four of whom were Americans, including Fr. Vincent Cullen, who supported the Federation of Free Farmers (FFF) and the rights of Manobo tribesmen, were detained without charges.[14] In October 1972 two American priests, Bruno Hicks and John Peterson, were voluntarily deported for activities involving a church radio station on the island of Negros.[15] Hicks and Peterson were accused of advocating rebellion over the radio, but they denied the charges once back in the United States, saying the station was used as a forum for discussing and seeking solutions to peasant problems.[16]

A more widely publicized deportation case involving an American priest was that of Fr. Edward Gerlock. Angered by his criticism of martial law and by his support, as head of the Catholic church's social action center in Tagum, Davao del Norte, of small farmers' resisting the loss of their land to the expansion of TADECO, the PC arrested Gerlock in October 1973 on charges of subversion and inducing unrest among poor farmers and hill tribesmen.[17] Arguing that his missionary ministry required proclaiming the gospel "to all men at all times whatever the circumstances and consequences," Gerlock refused to leave the Philippines voluntarily.[18] Although cleared of subversion in January 1975, Gerlock was put on three years' probation, confined to the metropolitan Manila area, barred from participating in any political activities or any activities "inimical to the security of the Philippines," and required to report to the immigration office once a month.[19] He was eventually deported in November 1976—without a public hearing—for participating in several ecumenically organized rallies banned by the government.

Gerlock's confrontation with the regime was a harbinger of an increasingly troubled church-state relationship in the Mindanao-Sulu region that continued even with the termination of martial rule. In April 1981, Filipinos were shocked by the murder of Fr. Godofredo Alingal, a member of the Society of Jesus in the Diocese of Malaybalay in Bukidnon, and by a grenade explosion in Davao City's San Pedro Cathedral that killed 16

[14]Association of Major Religious Superiors in the Philippines (AMRSP), "Chronology of Church-State Conflicts in the Philippines," *Documentations*, 21 September 1975, p. 1 (mimeographed).

[15]*New York Times*, 5 October 1972, p. 8, and 20 October 1972, p. 8.

[16]*Los Angeles Times*, 11 November 1972, p. 25.

[17]*New York Times*, 28 November 1973, p. 5, and 10 January 1974, p. 40; and *Philippine Times*, 30 November 1973, pp. 1, 9, 12.

[18]*Philippine Times*, 15 December 1973, pp. 1, 7.

[19]*New York Times*, 14 January 1975, p. 2.

persons and injured more than 150.[20] Although the NPA was accused by the military for Alingal's death, and dissident groups including the NPA and the Moro National Liberation Front (MNLF) were initially blamed for the cathedral bombing, church officials and laymen were skeptical. Bishop Francisco Claver, for example, pointed out inconsistencies in the government's account of Alingal's murder, while at least two concerned citizens' groups of Davao protested the regime's conclusions about the bombing incident, questioning in particular the exoneration, prior to the conclusion of a full investigation, of a "lost command" operating in the area.[21] The government's credibility was weakened further by the knowledge that Alingal's Basic Christian Community (BCC) activities and social work in Kibawe, Bukidnon, had antagonized local officials and the military, and by the knowledge that the military had been linked to an increasing number of unsolved, violent incidents in Davao del Norte and Davao del Sur. Alingal's murder remained unsolved, and the MNLF, though officially blamed for the grenade attack, condemned the bombing as an "heinous act" perpetrated by persons "devoid of moral or religious scruples."[22]

Another manifestation of the tension between the churches and the regime in Mindanao was the expulsion of two missionaries of the Maryknoll Fathers in 1981. Fr. D. Edward Shellito was deported in June and Fr. Ralph Kroes was denied reentry in August 1981. Both were accused of "subversive activities" and branded as "undesirable aliens" because of their social justice work in the Diocese of Tagum, Davao del Norte. Shellito and Kroes irked the military and local authorities by publicizing military abuses against civilians, and by opposing the forcible expulsion of small farmers from their land to make way for the continued expansion of TADECO. The priests denied the charges against them, and were vigorously supported by the Maryknoll regional superior, Fr. James Ferry, who characterized Kroes's politics as "rather conservative" and pointed out that many cases of reported military misconduct handled by Kroes as head of the prelature's Justice and Peace Office were "brought to him by the people." Both deportations triggered protests by priests and laymen in the Davao region, and eventually the government reversed its decision and

[20]*Filipino Reporter*, 24–30 April 1981, pp. 1, 4, and 1–7 May 1981, pp. 1–2.

[21]A "lost command" is a military unit, usually made up of misfits, that operates outside of the normal chain of command, and is often associated with the murder of so-called "subversives" and persons considered antigovernment.

[22]*Ichthys*, 1 May 1981, pp. 1–11; 15 May 1981, pp. 5–7; and 24 July 1981, pp. 1–3; and *Impact*, December 1981, pp. 429–431.

allowed the missionaries to return.[23] The policy reversal on Shellito and Kroes, however, failed to bring about better relations between the regime and the churches in Mindanao and Sulu. On the contrary, tensions continued to mount: in April 1985, after military officials reportedly indicated that it might "be good to kill a Priest or a Sister"[24] in order to intimidate the clergy and the people, members of the CHDF murdered an Italian missionary, Fr. Tullio Favali, of the Diocese of Kidapawan, North Cotabato.[25]

Just as small farmers and minority tribesmen in Mindanao had done, the Kalingas, Bontocs, and Tingguians of Northern Luzon turned to the church for help in opposing the Chico River and Cellophil projects. At the beginning of 1975, following a year of bureaucratic intransigence and of unsuccessful attempts to obtain a meeting with President Marcos, representatives of the Kalingas and Bontocs asked Bishop Claver, himself a native Bontoc, for assistance. On 25 April 1975, the bishop wrote an open letter to the president expressing the concerns of those affected by the Chico River project and warning of an escalation of violence.[26] Earlier the bishop had indicated that the only way to avoid armed conflict was for the government to negotiate honestly with the Kalingas and Bontocs, giving ironclad guarantees of just compensation for the loss of their land and homes.[27] Within less than a month, on 10–12 May 1975, approximately 150 Kalinga and Bontoc leaders attended an ecumenical conference in Quezon City sponsored by the Share and Care Apostolate for Poor Settlers (SCAPS) of the Catholic church to discuss the opposition to the Chico River Basin Development Project (CRDBP). At the conclusion of the conference, the

[23]Sheilah Ocampo, "Briefing: Priests' Expulsion Causes Protest," *Far Eastern Economic Review*, 17 July 1981, p. 6; Sheliah Ocampo, "Briefing: Philippines Deports a Second Priest," *Far Eastern Economic Review*, 4 September 1981, p. 6; Sheilah Ocampo, "Philippines: Church and State," *Far Eastern Economic Review*, 2 October 1981, pp. 32–33; *Ichthys*, 28 August 1981, pp. 1–2; and *Philippine News*, 4–10 November 1981, pp. 1, 8.

[24]Orlando B. Quevedo, "Message of the Bishop of Kidapawan on the Killing of Fr. Tullio Favali, PIME," 12 April 1985, reprinted in *Simbayan* 4 (March 1985): 19.

[25]"The Death of Fr. Tullio Favali, PIME," and "Condemning the Assassination of Fr. Favali," *Simbayan* 4 (March 1985): 18–19, 35; Gingging Avellanosa, "A Priest's Ultimate Sacrifice," *MIPC Communications*, April 1985, pp. 41–43; *Political Detainees Update*, 30 April 1985, pp. 1, 9–10, 12; and Sheila S. Coronel, "Bloodshed in Tulunan—Part 1," *Panorama*, 16 June 1985, pp. 5, 56–58, and "Part 2," *Panorama*, 23 June 1985, pp. 3–4, 42–44.

[26]Francisco F. Claver to President Ferdinand E. Marcos, 25 April 1975, reprinted in Francisco F. Claver, *The Stones Will Cry Out: Grassroots Pastorals* (Maryknoll, N.Y.: Orbis Books, 1978), pp. 135–145.

[27]Francisco F. Claver to Pacifico Ortiz, secretary, Justice and Peace, Catholic Bishops' Conference of the Philippines, 15 February 1975, reprinted in Claver, *The Stones Will Cry Out*, pp. 124–128.

leaders of the Kalingas and Bontocs signed a *bodong* (peace pact) specifying the conditions under which the minority tribesmen would oppose the hydroelectric projects.[28]

Bishop Claver's concerns were echoed by other officials in the Catholic and Protestant churches. The clergy of the Vicariate of Mountain Province indicated in September 1975 that while they supported the development of the Chico River basin, they were opposed to the "almost total disregard for the people's rights" in the government's attempt to "push through" the Chico development project. In February 1976, as tension mounted, Bishop William Brasseur, along with priests and nuns of the vicariate, issued a statement calling for "mutual respect, justice and peace" in resolving the conflict.[29] Unfortunately, the pleas for a peaceful resolution of the dispute were ignored by the government, and violence ensued.

The regime's control of the press resulted in the distortion and the suppression of information concerning the Chico River controversy. Manila-based newspapers either ignored the dispute or printed articles favorable to the position of the government, while the *Baguio Midland Courier* was prevented from covering both sides of the story. Thus after 1975, church institutions were used with increasing frequency as channels through which the Kalingas and Bontocs communicated their opposition to the project and publicized the abuses of PANAMIN and the military. Since the military viewed the church's role in the conflict as subversive, it prevented the Vicariate of the Mountain Province from conducting a comprehensive study of the sociocultural effects of the project,[30] and with increasing frequency began to accuse priests, nuns, and pastors who supported the minority tribesmen of aiding and abetting the CPP/NPA. Church officials consistently denied the military's accusations: In August 1980, following the murder of the Kalinga tribal leader Macli-ing Dulag, allegedly by the military for his opposition to the Chico project, Bishop Brasseur stressed that "while it is the task of the church to preach the gospel, the church can not also close its eyes to the violation of the human rights of the people." The bishop went on to reiterate the church's call for a fifteen- to twenty-year moratorium on the development of the Chico River

[28]*Pagta Ti Bodong* (Sanctions of the Peace Pact), reprinted in Anti-Slavery Society, *The Philippines: Authoritarian Government, Multinationals and Ancestral Lands*, pp. 105–106.

[29]Montañosa Social Action Center, "The Chico River Basin Development Project: A Case Study on Development," pp. 23–24, 36 (typewritten).

[30]Casalmo, *The Vision of a New Society*, pp. 42–45.

basin and, should the project go forward, for just compensation and the protection of the rights of those affected by the dams.[31]

That the Tingguians also turned to the Roman Catholic church for assistance in opposing Cellophil quickly resulted in controversy with the military, which, after 1977, became identified with the corporation. A series of CMLC meetings beginning in 1977 failed to reduce tensions. Church officials who assisted the Tingguians were labeled as "subversives" and "antigovernment" agitators. Although the provincial commander, Colonel Constancio Lasaten, admitted at a CMLC meeting in May 1977 that "opposition to Cellophil" was not synonymous with disloyalty to the government and therefore did not constitute "subversion," nevertheless, in October 1978, he branded clergy opposed to the project as "snakes" and warned the Tingguians not to listen to them or other "outsiders" and "foreigners."[32] Lasaten's comments were made in the context of intensified military harassment of anti-Cellophil clergy and of Tingguians who had entered into *bodong* agreements against the project; the military viewed opposition to the project as a threat both to the government's development program and to national security.[33]

Increased military repression, however, stiffened the resolve of Tingguians opposed to the corporation and radicalized some members of the clergy. Between 1977 and 1979, for instance, the Tingguians moved from a *bodong* expressing conditional opposition to a *bodong* voicing complete opposition to the activities of Cellophil.[34] In 1979, four Catholic priests, including Fr. Conrado Balweg, having given up hope of effecting some kind of a peaceful compromise with Cellophil, went underground to join the NPA. The regime responded by increasing the presence of the military in Abra, resulting in additional repression that further exacerbated church-military relations as well as contributed to the growth of the NPA in the region.[35]

Just as had the clergy assisting small farmers and minority tribesmen, Catholic and Protestant church officials and laymen working among urban

[31]*Bulletin Today*, 16 August 1980, pp. 1, 10.

[32]Dorral, "The Tinggians of Abra and Cellophil," pp. 122, 130.

[33]Ibid., pp. 131–135.

[34]Ecumenical Movement for Justice and Peace, *Iron Hand, Velvet Glove* (Geneva: Commission of the Churches on International Affairs, World Council of Churches, 1980), pp. 24–32.

[35]Anti-Slavery Society, *The Philippines: Authoritarian Government, Multinationals and Ancestral Lands*, pp. 87–90; and *San Francisco Examiner*, 23 June 1985, pp. A1, A12–A14.

squatters and laborers ran afoul of the Marcos regime after the imposition of martial rule. Beginning in January 1973, Fr. Jose Nacu, who had served as chairman of the Friends of Zone One Tondo Organization (ZOTO), a militant squatter organization in Manila, was detained several times for alleged links to the NPA, and eventually spent two years in jail without being formally charged.[36] In November 1974, Cardinal Sin accompanied a delegation of squatters from the Tondo foreshore area to Malacañang for a meeting with the president over the eviction and demolition of their homes by the military.[37] Although Marcos temporarily suspended the eviction order and promised the squatters would be housed near their present places of work, church-state conflict over squatter problems continued and was heightened with the deportation in January 1976 of two Italian priests, Fr. Francis Alessi and Fr. Luigi Cocquio, on subversion charges.[38]

At issue in Tondo was the forceful eviction of squatters, coupled with the demolition of their shanties, to make way for the development of a large container facility and a large fish port in the foreshore area.[39] First Lady Imelda Marcos was also interested in cleaning up the squatter community eyesores in the name of urban beautification. The regime's promises to allow squatters to participate in the decision-making process as well as to relocate them in comfortable housing near their jobs were neither honored nor, in the case of the housing promise, realistic. Squatter leaders were jailed or forced underground for speaking out against the evictions, and the adjacent government housing project, Dagat Dagatan, was too expensive. With an estimated average of ₱37 a month available for rent ($1 equaled ₱7.50 at the time), squatters were unable to afford the ₱70 to ₱100 per month rent, much less drive a car into the space provided; even if they could, Dagat Dagatan was only large enough to accommodate a few of the estimated twenty-eight thousand squatter families living in Tondo. Squatters were also unhappy that the government would only rent newly developed housing in contradiction of a 1956 congressional bill (voided by Presidential Decree 814 in 1975) allowing qualified squatters to purchase lots.[40] Although most squatters were unable to purchase the land at ₱5 per

[36]*Pahayag*, March 1975, pp. 6–7; and *New York Times*, 15 January 1976, p. 8.

[37]*Philippine Times*, 16–31 December 1974, p. 28.

[38]Bernard Wideman, "Cracking Down on Dissent," *Far Eastern Economic Review*, 6 February 1976, pp. 11–12; and *Signs of the Times*, 6 February 1976, p. 10, 13 February 1976, pp. 19–20, and 20 February 1976, pp. 20–23.

[39]See Walden Bello, David Kinley, and Elaine Elinson, *Development Debacle: The World Bank in the Philippines* (San Francisco: Institute for Food and Development Policy, 1982), pp. 108–120.

[40]Coordinating Council of People's Organizations of Tondo Foreshore, Navotas, Mal-

square meter, the right to do so was viewed as a form of security against government harassment and eviction.

Catholic and Protestant church relations with the government and the military were also strained over the regime's policies toward wage-earners. As a result of a rash of riots and strikes in the late 1960s and early 1970s, Marcos banned strikes "in vital industries" after martial law in General Order 5 to allay the fears of foreign investors and to maintain exports in crucial foreign exchange–earning industries. In November 1975, prompted by a strike at the Manila La Tondeña Distillery, over wages and hiring practices, Marcos issued Presidential Decree 823 prohibiting "strikes, picketing and lock-outs" and outlawing the participation of aliens in all trade union activities.[41] The decree's banning of aliens was aimed at foreign priests who historically had played an active part in Philippine trade unionism and who supported the demand of seven hundred part-time laborers that they be hired permanently by La Tondeña rather than be laid off and rehired at regular intervals for lower pay than permanent employees for the same work. The regime's move against church labor organizers and its January 1976 deportation of Alessi and Cocquio for assisting squatters prompted sharp reactions from ranking members of the Catholic hierarchy. The ban on strikes was protested by three thousand priests and nuns, led by the archbishop of Manila, at a mass at the Santa Cruz church. After the deportation of the Italians, Julio Cardinal Rosales, then president of the CBCP, stated that the Catholic hierarchy would "do everything within its power" to see that foreign priests were not denied due process.[42] The Vatican radio termed the expulsions a "witchhunt" and charged Marcos with "repression,"[43] while government threats to impose stricter immigration regulations on foreign clergy were sharply criticized by Cardinal Sin.[44]

Pressure from the churches and the Civil Liberties Union of the Philippines (CLUP) prompted Marcos in December 1975 to restore the right to strike, under certain conditions, in industries not vital to the national security. Yet the amendment of Presidential Decree 823 failed to bring about labor peace: In fact, after 1975 labor unrest among wage earners rose, resulting in a significant increase both in the number of strikes and in

---

abon, "Philippine Squatters and Martial Law Remedies," prepared for the U.N. Human Settlements Conference, Vancouver, British Columbia, May–June 1976.

[41]Bernard Wideman, "Philippines: Tough Line on Strikes," *Far Eastern Economic Review*, 14 November 1975, pp. 47–48.

[42]*Philippine Times*, 16–31 March 1976, p. 20.

[43]Ibid., 1–15 April 1976, pp. 1, 6.

[44]Ibid., 16–30 June 1976, p. 8.

the number of strike notifications filed with the Ministry of Labor.[45] Moreover, the clergy's criticism of the regime's labor policies, especially the use of the military to repress disgruntled workers and labor organizers, increasingly irked government and military officials. Nowhere was this more dramatically underscored than on the island of Negros, where the clergy's support of poorly paid sugar workers was countered by considerable violence, much of it attributable to the military, including murder, false accusations against priests, and in 1985, the unsolved burning of the residence of Antonio Fortich, the Bishop of Bacolod.[46]

The repression of clergy and layworkers assisting poor farmers, minority tribesmen, and wage-earners was but a part of a broader pattern of military actions against church officials and institutions alleged to be engaged in antigovernment or subversive activities. Not only were individual members of the clergy harassed, detained, and deported, but the military also periodically staged major assaults against Catholic and Protestant church institutions and programs critical of the policies of the government and military, particularly as such programs were aimed at helping the poor.

Major Church-Military Clashes

There were at least twenty-two major military raids on church institutions between 1972 and 1984, averaging almost two a year, as Table 3 demonstrates. Many other military actions of lesser magnitude also occurred against persons and groups using church facilities for purposes the military considered subversive. Right from the start of martial law a minority of bishops, religious superiors, pastors, and other church officials protested military actions on church property and against religious persons. Such actions contributed to the formation of the Church-Military Liaison Committee (CMLC) in November 1973. But it was not until the raids against the National Council of Churches in the Philippines (NCCP) and the Sacred Heart Novitiate in June and August 1974, respectively, that powerful members of the Catholic hierarchy began to speak out sharply. The strong reaction was easily understandable: the raids invariably violated

[45]Edberto M. Villegas, "Notes on the Labor Code and the Conditions of the Industrial Working Class in the Philippines," The Philippines in the Third World Papers, Series no. 23 (Quezon City: University of the Philippines, Third World Studies, 1980), Table 1, p. 3.

[46]The Association of Major Religious Superiors in the Philippines (AMRSP), *The Sugar Workers of Negros* (Manila, 1975); Alfred W. McCoy, *Priests on Trial* (Ringwood, Victoria: Penguin Books Australia, 1984); and *Philippine Newsbriefs*, January–February 1985, pp. 9–10, and March–April 1985, pp. 6–7.

Table 3. Military raids on church establishments after 1972

Institution raided[a]	*Date*
Church padlocked in Antique	July 1973
Convent of the Good Shepherd Sisters, Davao City	September 1973
St. Joseph's College, Quezon City	October 1973
Our Lady of Holy Angels Seminary, Novaliches, Rizal	October 1973
Trinity College, Quezon City[b]	October 1973
National Council of Churches in the Philippines' Headquarters, Quezon City[b]	June 1974
Sacred Heart Novitiate, Novaliches, Rizal	August 1974
Radio Station DXBB, Malaybalay, Bukidnon	November 1976
Radio Station DXCD, Tagum, Davao del Norte	November 1976
Signs of the Times, Manila	December 1976
The Communicator, Manila	December 1976
Ang Bandilyo, Malaybalay, Bukidnon	January 1977
Loyola House of Studies, Quezon City	April 1978
San Jose Seminary, Novaliches, Rizal	April 1978
Live-in Christian Seminar at Convento/School, Villaverde, Nueva Vizcaya	August 1982
Social Action Center, Catbalongan, Samar	September 1982
Task Force Detainees Office, Jaro, Iloilo	September 1982
Parish House, Oringao, Negros Occidental	September 1982
Residence of Reverend Volker Martin Jurgen Schmidt, Davao City[b]	March 1983
Residence of Bishop Miguel Purugganan and Convent of the Franciscan Sisters, Ilagan, Isabela	August 1983
Urban Industrial Mission Leadership Training Seminar, Guevarra Beach, Iloilo City[b]	July 1984
Residence of Bishop Ireneo Amantillo and Diocesan Pastoral Center, Tandag, Surigao del Sur	October 1984

[a]As cities have an independent legal status in the Philippines, province designations are eliminated.
[b]Military actions involving Protestant institutions and personnel.

the CMLC agreement of December 1973; after 1974 they were often against institutions of articulate, activist religious orders; and they represented a threat to continued church autonomy.

Reasons for the Raids

All the military raids against church establishments after 1974 were aimed either at capturing "subversives," stopping "subversive" activities, or confiscating "subversive" documents.[47] The apprehension of wanted "subversives" and the confiscation of "subversive" materials were the major reasons for the June 1974 dual assault on the home of the Rev. Paul Wilson, an American missionary of the Christian Church (Disciples of Christ), and the NCCP headquarters in Quezon City. The raids resulted in the arrest of three foreign missionaries and several leaders of the NCCP. The foreigners detained included Wilson, his wife, Marilyn, and their ten-year-old son, James, as well as the Rev. Harry Daniel, an Anglican minister and resident of Singapore, who was the associate general secretary of the Christian Conference of Asia (CCA). Among the Filipino religious officials arrested were the Rev. La Verne Mercado, a Methodist and general secretary of the NCCP; the Rev. Roman Tiples, Jr., a priest in the *Iglesia Filipina Independiente* (Philippine Independent Church) and the executive director of the Division of Self-Development of the NCCP; and Ibarra Malonzo, an attorney and commissioner of the NCCP's Commission on Participation and Development, who formerly was also active in Christian youth programs. The constabulary also went to the home of the Rev. Henry Aguilan, executive director of the Commission on Development and Social Concerns of the NCCP, and to the residence of Carmencita Karagdag, youth secretary of the CCA and a former official of the NCCP. In the absence of Aguilan and Karagdag, the PC picked up Aguilan's secretary and driver and four members of the Karagdag family, including a sister, Josefina, who was later allegedly mistreated by the military. Aguilan subsequently turned himself in to the military, while Karagdag was abroad working for the CCA. The same evening as the arrests the offices of the NCCP were searched and church records were removed.

Two days later at a meeting of the CMLC, "the military refused to discuss the arrests or give any reason for them," but later claimed the apprehensions were due to the presence of Dante Simbulan, a graduate and former professor at the Philippine Military Academy and a critic of the Marcos regime, and other alleged leftists at the home of the Wilsons.[48] The military also claimed substantial quantities of "subversive" literature were discovered at the Wilson residence and at the NCCP headquarters. General Fidel Ramos stated that Simbulan, supposedly a leader of a "Maoist faction of the Communist Party," was "trying to drive division in the Armed Forces"

[47]While Cardinal Sin repeatedly bemoaned the lack of a clear definition of subversion by the government, Defense Minister Enrile, in a BBC documentary, "Collision Course," on martial law, defined subversion as "anyone who speaks or acts against the government." *Philippine Times*, 16–31 July 1977, p. 13.

[48]Frank Gould, "Cracking Down on the Pulpit," *Far Eastern Economic Review*, 8 July 1974, p. 10.

by convincing servicemen to defect and that Karagdag, Wilson, and Daniel were members of a Communist Party group "infiltrating" the NCCP.[49]

All of the Protestants denied the charges, and the regime declined to press its case in court. Instead, Wilson, along with his wife and son, and Daniel were subsequently expelled from the Philippines; all others arrested were eventually released from jail without trials. The Wilsons and some NCCP officials thought that among the reasons for the arrests was Marcos' irritation with the social justice and human rights activities of Protestant ministers and laymen. Protestant activists in Manila also suggested that the NCCP resolution to abolish martial law and restore civil liberties passed at the November 1973 annual conference, coupled with anti–martial law statements of Protestants at the May 1974 Agono Conference on development and social concerns, irked the government and military.[50]

A search for "subversives" also prompted the August 1974 raids on the Sacred Heart Novitiate, but in contrast to the NCCP/Wilson residence action, the 150-man ground and air assault at Novaliches failed to turn up Jose Maria Sison, chairman of the CPP, or Fr. Jose Nacu, a recent prison escapee, or other signs of subversion that would stand up in a court of law.[51] Eyewitnesses reported not only violations of the December 1973 CMLC agreement, but also the presence of plainclothes agents dashing "through the corridors, kicking open doors, pointing guns at people, [and] entering rooms without knocking" prior to presenting a search warrant to the novitiate superior.[52] Fr. Benigno Mayo, Jesuit provincial superior at the time, was mistakenly arrested on his way to the novitiate and interrogated briefly at Camp Crame without legal counsel. In the absence of Sison and Nacu, the military arrested Fr. Jose Blanco, reportedly secretary general of a "subversive" organization, *Kapulungan ng mga Sandigan ng Pilipinas* ([KASAPI = co-member] Assembly of Persons upon whom the Philippines Rely), and twenty members of the Student Catholic Action organization, who were attending a seminar. Reports in the controlled press also indicated that documents revealing a conspiracy by KASAPI were confiscated in the raid.[53]

[49]"Top Protestant Officials Arrested," Associated Press (Manila), 10 July 1974 (mimeographed).

[50]Interview with top official in the National Council of Churches in the Philippines, 23 July 1979.

[51]Association of Major Religious Superiors of the Philippines (AMRSP), Secretariat for Social Justice and Peace, "Operation Novaliches," 28 August 1974, pp. 1–2 (mimeographed).

[52]*Philippine Jesuit News*, special issue, September 1974, pp. 11–12.

[53]*Philippines Daily Express*, 27 August 1974, p. 1.

Beyond general charges of rebellion and inciting to sedition, the military's justifications for closing two Catholic radio stations, DXCD in Tagum, Davao del Norte, and DXBB in Malaybalay, Bukidnon, in November 1976 were slightly different but obscured by subsequent newspaper reports and military interrogations. DXCD was closed for allegedly transmitting "messages and information" to the "Communist Party of the Philippines as well as the New People's Army and United Front Organizations[s],"[54] whereas DXBB was seized as a suspected "haven, headquarters and/or hide-outs [*sic*] of lawless gangs, criminals and/or subversive elements."[55] Manila newspaper accounts of the closures, however, said that "both Catholic radio stations were being used by the CPP and the NPA in sending subversive messages" and that among those arrested were "top members" of the CPP.[56] Yet a review of the military case against DXCD includes mostly excerpts from non-Communist publications critical of martial law, the dissemination of which, church progressives argued, fell under the freedom of religion guarantees of the 1935 and 1973 constitutions.[57] Similarly, the sworn statements of Fr. Agustin Nazareno, then director of the Communications Media Center of the Prelature of Malaybalay, and two American priests, Frs. Calvin Poulin and the late Joseph Stoffel, following the DXBB raid revealed that the military was irritated over the airing of programs derogatory of the government and the armed forces. Of particular concern were statements against the 1975 and 1976 referenda.[58] The military later admitted privately "that the subversion-inciting-to-rebellion charges were baseless," but nevertheless maintained that the reopening of DXBB was up to President Marcos.[59]

While sixty-nine persons were rounded up in the Davao area around the time of the closing of DXCD as part of a broader crackdown (reportedly code-named "Operation Libra") on church progressives, no one was ar-

[54]Philippines (Republic), Headquarters Philippine Constabulary, Office of the Constabulary Judge Advocate, "Charge Sheet," sworn by Col. Hermilo N. Ahorro, Camp Crame, Quezon City, 20 January 1977, p. 12 (hereinafter cited as "Charge Sheet against DXCD").

[55]Philippines (Republic), Department of National Defense, Office of the Secretary, Camp General Emilio Aguinaldo, Quezon City, *Arrest, Search and Seizure Order, number 236*, 18 November 1976.

[56]*Times Journal*, 20 November 1976, p. 1.

[57]"Charge Sheet against DXCD," pp. 12–20.

[58]Sworn statements of Agustin Nazareno, Calvin Poulin, and Joseph Stoffel taken by Col. Alfredo Olano and Lt. Col. Cesar Navarro at station DXBB, Malaybalay, Bukidnon, 20 November 1976 (typewritten).

[59]Jose Sumastre, "Communications Media Center," in "Quinquennial Report Prelature of Malaybalay, 1981," by Francisco F. Claver (n.p., 1981), Appendix G, p. 76 (mimeographed).

rested in the DXCD and DXBB raids. This may have been due to Bishop Claver's reputation as a critic of the government as well as to the widespread publicity given the incidents and the subsequent protests by many Davao and Bukidnon residents. No evidence, according to Bishop Joseph Regan of Tagum, was given for the closure of DXCD. Priests in Malaybalay, moreover, averred that the DXBB raid represented a violation of the December 1973 CMLC agreement, because Bishop Claver was away and the local vicar-general was not notified until after the radio offices were entered. However, with the exception of the military mistakenly trying to confiscate two mimeograph machines not covered in the search warrant, the DXBB raid and interrogations were conducted in "a correct and courteous way."[60]

Shortly after the raids on DXCD and DXBB, the military closed the *Signs of the Times*, a mimeographed circular of the AMRSP; the *Communicator*, a Jesuit publication, in December 1976, and *Ang Bandilyo* (The Towncrier), a newsletter of the Prelature of Malaybalay, in January 1977. All three publications printed articles critical of the government and military not carried in the controlled media. A year prior to the raids, Hans Menzi, chairman of the Philippine council for Print Media (PCPM) and a close associate of President Marcos, ordered the AMRSP to "stop publishing" *Various Reports* and later its successor, *Signs of the Times*, neither of which were licensed by the council in accordance with Presidential Decree 576.[61] The AMRSP Executive Board defied Menzi's telegrams, claiming "a legitimate human and religious right" to circulate information for "theological reflection, conscientization and Christian response." The board indicated it would continue publishing even if a "specific decree outlawing *Signs of the Times*" were issued.[62] Thus the military closed *Signs of the Times* for violating the law and engaging in "activities inimical to national security."[63] The padlocking of the *Communicator* was more complicated, because it was duly registered and licensed according to Philippine law, had never been reprimanded by the government, and continued to be listed in the 1977 PCPM directory. Although Roberto Men-

[60]Francisco Claver, "Closure of Radio DXBB, Malaybalay, Chronicle of Events, November 19–22, 1976," 30 November 1976, pp. 1–3 (typewritten).

[61]*Presidential Decree 576*, 9 November 1974.

[62]A letter from M. Christine Tan, chairman, Executive Board AMRSWP, and Lope Castillo, acting chairman, Executive Board AMRSMP, "To all major superiors of religious men and women, to all our religious and to all our friends," 3 November 1975 (mimeographed); and *Philippine Priests' Forum* 8 (December 1976): 92–95.

[63]*Times Journal*, 6 December 1976, p. 1.

doza, executive director of the PCPM, notified General Ramos on 4 November 1976, that the *Communicator* "has printed articles violative of the PCPM guidelines as well as tending to agitate the people against the government,"[64] he later told the editor, Fr. James Reuter, that "your license has never been revoked. You have not been closed by the Philippine Council for Print Media. Your difficulty is only with the military."[65] Accordingly, the military charged that the *Communicator* (1) was often "openly distributed in anti-government mass actions/symposiums;" (2) "tended to highlight the outlawed Communist Party of the Philippines" and the "New People's Army . . . and the actions of known radical members of the religious sector;" (3) was "leftist propaganda" of "anti-government elements who do not only sow dissension among the readers but show irresponsibility in public reporting;" and (4) undermined "the faith of the people in the duly constituted authorities."[66] Fr. Reuter, in contrast, felt that the military's action was mainly in retaliation for an article about the death of a Quezon City shoemaker involving Major Rolando Abadilla, one of the Metrocom Intelligence and Security Group (MISG) commanders leading the raid against *Signs of the Times* and the *Communicator.*[67]

The official reason for closing *Ang Bandilyo* was "inciting to sedition, rebellion and subversion," but just as in the case of the *Communicator*, Fr. Nazareno pointed out that while the provincial commander of the PC, the Department of Public Information office, the provincial fiscal of Bukidnon, and the town mayors routinely received copies of *Ang Bandilyo* throughout 1976, none complained about the seditious nature of any articles. Yet because the newsletter regularly published stories critical of the government and military, many of which were read over DXBB, the military held that the reproduction of "sensational news items" tended to incite the people to civil disobedience, especially in the case of the 1975 and 1976 referenda, and to lead them to violence. The PC thus confiscated the newsletter's equipment and padlocked its offices, hoping in the process either to silence or to cow the church in Bukidnon.[68]

[64]Letter to Maj. Gen. Fidel V. Ramos, chief, Philippine Constabulary, Camp Crame, Quezon City, about *Signs of the Times* and *The Communicator* from Roberto M. Mendoza, executive director, Philippine Council for Print Media, 4 November 1976 (typewritten).

[65]James B. Reuter, "Counter Affidavit" against the PC-Metrocom, 20 October 1977, p. 1 (typewritten).

[66]Contained in the joint affidavit of Lt. Col. Rolando V. Abadilla, 1st Lt. Panfilo M. Lacson and 1st Lt. Dennis T. Nazaire against *The Communicator*, 9 March 1977 (typewritten).

[67]Reuter, "Counter Affidavit," pp. 3–4; and "The Shoemaker," *The Communicator*, 11 February 1976, pp. 1–4.

[68]Nazareno, "Sworn Statement," 29 April 1977, Cagayan de Oro City, pp. 2–6.

The Metrocom actions against *Signs of the Times* and the *Communicator* were generally carried out in an orderly fashion. The presence of Fr. Joaquin Bernas, the incoming Jesuit provincial superior and a noted Filipino constitutional lawyer, ensured that the military adhered strictly to the Arrest, Search, and Seizure Order (ASSO), which limited the raid only to the offices of the two publications, and that detailed lists of all confiscated materials were prepared.[69] The military complied with all Fr. Bernas' requests. In contrast, accounts of the *Ang Bandilyo* seizure suggest a Keystone Kops operation. From the outset disagreement arose over the right of the military to enter the publication's offices in the absence of Bishop Claver and over the omission in the ASSO of a specific address to be searched, which allowed the PC "flexibility" in hunting anywhere to stop the newsletter and similar publications. Church officials also accused the constabulary of surreptitiously taking a key to unlock the office (to avoid a break-in). Church officials later caught three military men escaping from a basement window where they were surprised by neighbors while trying to force a door with an iron bar. Nothing in the basement was connected with *Ang Bandilyo*. Thus, after the equipment was seized, Fr. Joseph Stoffel, the vicar-general, refused to certify either that "no unnecessary force was employed . . . nor was there anything lost or taken without prior receipt" or that the "search . . . was done in a very orderly manner," and wrote a letter of protest to Defense Minister Enrile.[70]

The assault on Loyola House of Studies and San Jose Seminary was carried out following protests over the outcome of the Interim *Batasang Pambansa* ([IBP] Interim National Assembly) elections in 1978. Leaders of the LABAN Party staged a march—illegal under martial law—two days after the vote protesting alleged election irregularities resulting in the complete victory of Marcos' KBL Party in metropolitan Manila. The regime responded by arresting six hundred of the protesters, including SocDem organizer and ideologist, Fr. Romeo Intengan, who had worked for the opposition and helped train poll watchers for LABAN. Once Intengan was behind bars, the military raided his office at Loyola House of Studies and another room in San Jose Seminary in search of "subversive materials . . . explosives, firearms and ammunition," and confiscated one or two thousand copies of *Malayang Philippines* (*Free Philippines*, an ephemeral newspaper published by the opposition just prior to the election) as well as a

[69]The Philippine Province of the Society of Jesus, "Arrest, Search, and Seizure Orders Executed against *Signs of the Times* and *The Communicator*: Background Events," pp. 25–47 (typewritten).

[70]Joseph I. Stoffel, "The 'Ang Bandilyo' Raid—Jan. 22, 1977—Malaybalay, Bukidnon," pp. 1–21 (typewritten).

large quantity of medicine used by Intengan, also a medical doctor, to treat the poor.[71]

The military's conduct of the raid on Loyola House of Studies and San Jose Seminary was especially regrettable because it resulted in tragedy. Not only was the assault in violation of the CMLC agreement, but two young men working in the office of Fr. Intengan were taken into custody before the military produced an arrest or a search warrant. One of those arrested, Teotimo Tantiado, a seventeen-year-old youth who had worked for the opposition in the April 1978 elections, died while in detention. Although an autopsy was inconclusive as to the cause of death, the Jesuits disputed a military press release, published in the Manila newspapers, that claimed foul play was ruled out by a Jesuit panel of investigators.[72]

Although church-military relations continued to be plagued by misunderstandings after 1978, it was not until late 1982 that the military again staged major assaults against church institutions suspected of being used for antigovernment activities. In August 1982, for example, two priests, Theodore Bandsma and Herman Sanderinck, of the Congregation of the Immaculate Heart of Mary (CICM), and three layworkers were arrested on charges of harboring Communists and possessing subversive materials during a raid on a live-in Christian seminar in Villaverde, Nueva Vizcaya.[73] The following month the military raided the Catholic social action center in Catbalogan, Samar, and the Task Force Detainees (TFD) office in Jaro, Iloilo, for alleged antigovernment activities. In addition the military breached the parish house of the Society of St. Columban in Oringao, Negros Occidental ostensibly in search of suspected "subversives."[74] During the raid in Catbalogan, Sr. Helena Gutierrez and two layworkers were detained, and in October 1982, Fr. Edgardo Kangleon, director of the social action center, was arrested.[75] The military action in Oringao led to the arrest of the so-called Negros Nine accused in the Pablo Sola assassination discussed in Chapter 4.

Evidently, the arrest of the CICM priests in Nueva Vizcaya and the raid

[71]James B. Reuter, "Death in Manila," April 1978 (typewritten); and "The PC-METROCOM RAID of Loyola House of Studies and San Jose Seminary, Monday, 10 April 1978. A Report," Appendix D, D.2, D.3, D.4 (typewritten).

[72]Reuter, "Death in Manila"; "PC-METROCOM RAID"; and Joaquin G. Bernas, provincial superior, Philippine Province of the Society of Jesus, "Arrest, Investigation and Death of Teotimo Tantiado, 17," 25 April 1978 (typewritten).

[73]*Political Detainees Update*, 15 September 1982, pp. 1, 6.

[74]*Political Detainees Update*, 15 September 1982, pp. 3, 6; 30 September 1982, p. 1; and 15 October 1982, p. 1; and *Columban Mission*, January 1983, passim.

[75]*Political Detainees Update*, 31 October 1982, p. 1.

on the TFD office in Iloilo were prompted by a fear that ideas and materials deemed subversive and sympathetic to the Communists were being disseminated. The reasons for the Catbalogan raid, however similar, were more complicated, and revolved around a $25 million development program in Samar funded by the Australian government. The Samar Concerned Citizens for Human Rights (CCHR), a Catholic social justice group, in cooperation with the National Secretariat for Social Action, Justice and Peace (NASSA) in the Philippines and the Catholic Commission for Justice and Peace in Australia (CCJP-Aust.), issued a report (under the auspices of the CCJP-Aust.) in March 1982 claiming that the project benefited the rich rather than the poor and facilitated, through road construction, increased military repression in Northern Samar.[76] The CCHR report was interpreted by Peter Hastings, an Australian journalist, in two articles in the *Sydney Morning Herald* in June and July as the work of radical priests and nuns bent on "violent revolution" in the Philippines.[77] Within days Defense Minister Enrile indicated that the military would investigate radical elements in the church in Samar, and he subsequently used the *Sydney Morning Herald* articles as justification for the action on the social action center in September. Enrile also averred in October 1982 that captured documents and admissions from layworkers indicated that the church in Samar was riddled with Communists.[78]

The jailing of Frs. Gore, O'Brien, and Dangan, along with the six lay leaders, in Kabankalan, Negros Occidental, as indicated in Chapter 4, resulted from the priests' support of the Federation of Free Farmers (FFF), criticism of the rich, and successful organization of Basic Christian Communities (*Kristianong Katilingban*), which represented a political power base outside of the control of the local and provincial political elites. Wealthy sugar planters and local politicians, including Mayor Sola, were alarmed by previously docile sugar workers and subsistence hill farmers, many of whom were members of BCCs, speaking out publicly against military abuses and governmental graft and corruption. The planters and politicians were further alarmed by a concomitant growth of the NPA, whose influence was spreading because of deteriorating economic conditions and increasing military misconduct. The growing militancy of the

[76]Concerned Citizens for Human Rights (Samar), *Samar Island and the Northern Samar Integrated Rural Development Project: Development for the Poor Samareños* (Sydney: Catholic Commission for Justice and Peace, 1982).

[77]*Sydney Morning Herald*, 29 June 1982, p. 1, and 7 July 1982, p. 7.

[78]*Asian Bureau Australia Newsletter*, November 1982, p. 1; and *Catholic Weekly* (Australia), 30 January 1983, pp. 10–11, 27.

poor resulted in the elite equating BCC formation with support for the Communists; as a consequence, they tried to use the assassination of Mayor Sola (who at the time of his death was under investigation for the murder of seven peasants found buried on his hacienda) as a pretext for getting rid of Gore and O'Brien and blunting the power of the BCCs.[79]

Military pressure against activist clergy and layworkers continued in 1983 and 1984. Among the most widely publicized incidents were the arrest in March 1983 of the Rev. Volker Martin Jurgen Schmidt, a German Lutheran missionary, in Davao City along with several layworkers, including Carlos "Karl" Gaspar, former executive secretary (1977–80) of the Catholic Mindanao-Sulu Pastoral Conference (MSPC); and the raids in August 1983 on the convent of the Franciscan Sisters of the Immaculate Conception of the Mother of God (CFIC) and on the residence of Bishop Miguel Purugganan in Ilagan, Isabela. The military suspected that the home of the Rev. Schmidt was the headquarters of the Southern Mindanao Regional Party Committee (SMRPC) of the CPP, and over a three-day period detained everyone visiting the residence. Although several of those picked up were released almost immediately, Schmidt and the three layworkers were arrested for subversion in connection with their work at the Ecumenical Center for Development, which the military considered a "communist front organization."[80] Similarly, Gaspar was jailed for his activities as executive secretary of the Resource Development Foundation, and was accused (prior to a trial) by government officials, including President Marcos, of being a Communist leader and a conduit for international funding of the CPP in Mindanao.[81] The military assault on the CFIC's convent and Bishop Purugganan's quarters in August 1983 were prompted by reports that the residences harbored not only Communists and "subversive" priests, including Fr. Conrado Balweg, a member of the NPA, but also contained "firearms . . . and voluminous subversive documents." However, the raids produced no arrests and unearthed only a few publica-

[79]McCoy, *Priests on Trial*; Niall O'Brien, *Seeds of Injustice: Reflections on the Murder Frame-up of the Negros Nine in the Philippines from the Prison Diary of Niall O'Brien* (Dublin: O'Brien Press, 1985); and Bruce Stannard, *Poor Man's Priest: The Fr. Brian Gore Story* (Sydney: Collins/Fontana, 1984).

[80]*Political Detainees Update*, 31 March 1983, p. 12, and 15 April 1983, pp. 1–2; *Asian Bureau Australian Newsletter*, April 1983, p. 7; and *Philippine News*, 20–26 April 1983, pp. 1–2.

[81]*Political Detainees Update*, 15 April 1983, pp. 3–5; and United States Foreign Broadcast Information Service (FBIS), *Daily Reports*, vol. 4, Asia & Pacific, 28 April 1983, p. P1. See also Helen Graham and Brenda Noonan, eds., *How Long? Prison Reflections of Karl Gaspar* (Quezon City: Claretian Publications, 1985).

tions on human rights, such as *Political Detainees Update* and *Katarungan* (Justice).[82] In addition, four of the six priests listed in the warrant given to Bishop Purugganan worked in the vicariate of the Mountain Province and previously had never been associated with Fr. Balweg's NPA activities.[83]

The 1983 raids were followed in July and October 1984, respectively, with a roundup of persons attending an Urban Industrial Mission (UIM) leadership training seminar at Guevarra Beach, a resort near Iloilo City, that was sponsored by the Convention of Philippine Baptist Churches (CPBC) and an assault on the residence of Bishop Ireneo Amantillo and the Diocesan Pastoral Center in Tandag, Surigao del Sur. The military gave little explanation for the raids beyond indicating to the Protestants that they were "looking for specific persons to be investigated"[84] and telling Bishop Amantillo that "they were chasing a fugitive" who went into his residence.[85] Yet in the Amantillo assault it became clear that the military also suspected that the bishop's house and the Diocesan Pastoral Center were being used to treat wounded rebels. In neither instance, however, was evidence produced to substantiate the military's actions, and in the case of the UIM roundup, a plainclothes soldier was reportedly caught trying to plant a hand grenade in a rice basin belonging to the seminar participants. No search warrants were produced, which represented a violation of PC/INP policy with regard to relations with the churches.[86] Yet when questioned on this point during the Amantillo raid, the officer in charge retorted: "There is no privacy over and above national security" and "This is an emergency. We are in a state of war."[87]

Church Reaction to the Raids

Within a month after the June 1974 raid on the home of the Rev. Wilson and the NCCP headquarters, a small group of Protestant pastors and church officials issued a "Statement of Concern and Appeal to the Authorities" about the raids and the fact that the Rev. Tiples, Attorney Malonzo, members of the Karagdag family, as well as others picked up by the

[82] *Political Detainees Update*, 15 September 1983, p. 1.

[83] *NASSA News*, special issue, September 1983, p. 6.

[84] Rudy Bernal, "Philippine Constabulary Elements Raid Baptist's Seminar in Iloilo," *NCCP Newsletter*, July–August 1984, p. 21.

[85] *MIPC Communications*, November 1984, p. 6.

[86] Fidel V. Ramos, "Policies on PC/INP Relations with Religious Organizations, Establishments and Personalities," 24 August 1984, reprinted in *NCCP Newsletter*, July–August 1984, p. 23.

[87] *MIPC Communications*, November 1984, p. 6.

military, were still in jail.[88] In criticizing the government, the statement noted that Muslim terrorists in the South received better treatment than the pastors and NCCP officials, whose presumption of innocence was guaranteed in both the 1935 and 1973 constitutions, and that the arrests violated the December 1973 CMLC agreement. The concerns of the Protestant ministers were echoed by others. Cardinal Rosales, a staunch supporter of the president, asked "that cases against Protestants, if any, be expedited and not allowed to drag out." In August 1974, the World Council of Churches in Geneva condemned the raids and jailings outright.[89]

The official responsc of the NCCP's Executive Committee appeared the following October. After noting the government's "recognitions and courtesies," the statement pointed out the raids violated the CMLC agreement of December 1973, defended the visit of the Rev. Daniel to the Philippines on religious grounds, and upheld the right of the church "to analyze and understand existing ideological doctrines and theories" for Christian educational purposes. The Executive Committee, moreover, denied flatly that the NCCP was "ideology-oriented or motivated."[90] The slowness of the official response, however, reflected divisions within the NCCP leadership; as a consequence of the trauma of the military raids and arrests, more conservatives were elected to the Executive Committee of the NCCP. Thereafter during martial law Protestant clergymen and NCCP officials demonstrated caution in criticizing the government, while other activist Protestants became convinced that the best way to bring about social justice was to establish grass-roots community organizations rather than continue to issue position papers on various aspects of the New Society.[91]

Reports in the controlled media that the Novaliches raid was conducted in a "peaceful and orderly manner" under the supervision of the novitiate superior, with the "full cooperation of the Catholic hierarchy," and that an auxiliary bishop of Manila, Hernando Antiporda, "witnessed the entire operation" drew a quick and sharp reaction from the Catholic church. Both Benigno Mayo, the Jesuit provincial superior, and Cardinal Sin, the archbishop of Manila, rebutted the media accounts, and at the same time, noted that Fr. Blanco and the detained students were being tried in the press for

[88] "Statement of Concern and Appeal to the Authorities," July 1974, pp. 1–5 (mimeographed).

[89] *Philippine Times*, 1–15 August 1974, p. 2, and 16–31 August 1974, pp. 2, 21; and Alex Pescador, "An Overview of Philippine Church-State Relations since Martial Law," *Pahayag*, March 1975, p. 8.

[90] "NCCP Statement on the June 74 Incident," *NCCP Newsletter*, November–December 1974, pp. 1–2.

[91] Interviews with top NCCP official, Quezon City, 23 July 1979, and religious activist, Quezon City, 13 July 1979.

"subversion" when no charges had been filed.[92] A week after the assault, the archbishop officiated at a vigil of prayer in Manila Cathedral, attended by an estimated five thousand persons. The government and military were generally conciliatory. The erroneous reports in the media were partially corrected in subsequent articles: Minister Enrile talked with a delegation from the church over the incident; and the president met with Blanco and the students at Malacañang. All those detained in the raid were eventually released. But as later events indicated, Mayo's hopes for a more open exchange of views with the military went unrealized.

The seizure of the Catholic radio stations and publications in late 1976 and early 1977 received a mixed response from the church. The stations and the *Communicator* remained closed; although the charges were finally dropped, the military continued to contend that "*nolle prosequi* [not choosing to prosecute] does not amount to exculpation."[93] Fr. Reuter was told by the military that "amnesty" (which he received via the Manila papers) ruled out the republishing of the *Communicator* because it did not preclude prosecution in the future. The Catholic hierarchy for the most part tended to remain aloof; in fact, the secretary-general of the CBCP, Bishop Cirilo Almario, considered a member of the conservative group of bishops, stressed that neither *Signs of the Times* nor the *Communicator* were officially connected with the CBCP.[94] But church officials directly affected by the closures responded vociferously and in the cases of *Signs of the Times* and *Ang Bandilyo*, defiantly.

The arrest of Catholic lay leaders and the closure of DXCD prompted a demonstration of two hundred priests and nuns in Davao, and pastoral letters on the military actions were read throughout the Mindanao-Sulu region. Bishop Regan met in Manila with church and government leaders; in a public forum with military officials, according to Ralph Kroes, he compared the arrests and raid with events "he experienced with the Communists in China," evidently offending and angering Minister Enrile.[95] In Malaybalay, Bishop Claver, as well as other Bukidnon priests, flatly denied

[92]*Philippines Daily Express*, 27 August 1974, p. 1; Mayo letter to Tatad, 31 August 1974; and the pastoral letter of Jaime L. Sin, archbishop of Manila, 29 August 1974, reprinted in *Philippine Jesuit News*, special issue, September 1974, pp. 15–16.

[93]Correspondence between Col. Cesar Navarro, PC commander, Malaybalay, Bukidnon and Gaudioso Sustento, director, Communications Media Center, Prelature of Malaybalay, and Francisco Claver, bishop of Malaybalay, 19 June, and 10, 11, 12, and 16 July 1978 (typewritten).

[94]*Bulletin Today*, 7 December 1976, p. 1.

[95]Ralph Kroes to James Ferry, 29 January 1980. Edward Gerlock also said Bishop Regan was a "roaring lion" in Manila following the closure of DXCD. Personal letter to me, 6 March 1980.

that DXBB had links with the NPA or that the church conducted a boycott movement against the 1975 and 1976 referenda. The bishop did admit to a policy of "speaking the truth out at all times" and of setting forth "moral and religious principles" to guide citizens in "forming their consciences" about participating in the referenda, but steadfastly maintained such activity did not represent "subversion."[96] Similarly, Fr. Reuter wrote a blistering counter-affidavit in October 1977, taking the military's case against the *Communicator* apart piece by piece; he assumed full responsibility himself for the publication. The AMRSP continued to assert its "human and religious right" to circulate information for internal consumption of the religious and for interested laymen, and began publishing again in November 1977 under the name *Ichthys*. Bishop Claver replaced *Ang Bandilyo* with a series of pastoral letters and then, when the charges were dropped, started the newsletter again.

Because of the death of Teotimo Tantiado, religious reaction to the military raid on Loyola House of Studies and San Jose Seminary was mainly one of sadness. The Catholic hierarchy largely remained silent on the raid, perhaps because many bishops were ambivalent about the activities of Fr. Intengan, the reason for the assault. The Jesuits, in contrast, denounced the raid and challenged the military's statement on the cause of Tantiado's death. When a new autopsy could neither prove nor disprove foul play, Fr. Bernas, the provincial superior, distributed the findings widely, stating he was "not satisfied" with the investigation. Other letters critical of the military were also circulated, and it was obvious from the presence of more than fifty priests and many other religious and seminarians at the funeral that doubt existed in the church about the military's version of the incident.[97]

The military arrests and raids after the termination of martial rule were part of what many felt was an intensified campaign of repression aimed at silencing critics of the regime within the Catholic and Protestant churches. Although emphasizing the need for reconciliation, especially after the assassination of former senator Benigno Aquino, Jr., in August 1983, most bishops and church officials directly affected by the military actions generally reacted with alarm, pointing out inconsistencies in the government's versions of events, and defending the church programs and personnel under attack. Bishop Alberto Van Overbeke of Bayombong, for instance, issued a strongly worded pastoral letter asserting that Frs. Bandsma and Sanderinck

[96]Francisco F. Claver, *The Stones Will Cry Out*, pp. 3–5.

[97]Bernas, "Arrest, Investigation and Death of Teotimo Tantiado, 17"; Reuter, "Death in Manila"; and Walter L. Ysaac, "Teotimo Tantiado," pp. 1–4 (typewritten).

were "neither criminals nor subversives."[98] Bishop Antonio Fortich of Bacolod consistently maintained the innocence of Frs. Gore, O'Brien, and Dangan, whose arrest and detention resulted in widespread protest by laymen and priests in Negros Occidental, including a twenty-four-hour hunger strike by five hundred *Kristianong Katilingban* members and a mass attended by an estimated six thousand. Cardinal Sin reportedly told Immigration Commissioner Edmundo Reyes, prior to the suspension of deportation proceedings in March 1983 against Gore, pending the outcome of the court case against him, O'Brien, Dangan, and the six lay leaders, that the charges against the Australian priest were "outlandish."[99] Nevertheless, the three priests were again detained in May 1983. Although released to house arrest almost immediately by President Marcos, the three returned to jail at their own request in January 1984 as a "matter of conscience and in solidarity" over the denial of bail for the six lay leaders.[100] Throughout the trial, priests and nuns familiar with the case remained steadfast in proclaiming the innocence of the three priests and six lay leaders, and a number of church leaders, particularly Bishop Fortich and Cardinal Sin, participated in behind-the-scenes negotiations with the regime which resulted in the charges being dropped in July 1984.

Priests in Samar also protested the Catbalogan raid and arrests. However, by December 1982 Kangleon admitted to being a member of the CPP, using the social action center as a cover for illegal purposes, and funneling funds from abroad into "underground activities"; he also identified others, including six priests, a nun, and seven layworkers, as being involved with the Communist movement.[101] The confession tended to substantiate the military's claims, and resulted in considerable publicity about Communist infiltration of the Catholic church in Samar and elsewhere in the Philippines. Kangleon's revelations were followed by his early release into the custody of the military vicar of the Philippines and his grant of "full amnesty" by President Marcos in October 1983.[102] Although Kangleon repudiated his alleged association with the CPP and denied he

[98]*National Catholic Reporter*, 1 October 1982, pp. 1, 15.

[99]*Columban Mission*, January 1983, passim; *Political Detainees Update*, 15 March 1983, pp. 1, 5, 8; and Sheilah Ocampo-Kalfors, "Philippines: A Tactical Withdrawal," *Far Eastern Economic Review*, 24 March 1983, p. 34.

[100]*Philippines News*, 11–17 May 1983, p. 4, and 25–31 January 1984, p. 6; and Sheilah Ocampo-Kalfors, "Briefing: Marcos Frees Six Detainees," *Far Eastern Economic Review*, 19 May 1983, p. 10.

[101]*Bulletin Today*, 13 December 1982, pp. 1, 20; and *Times Journal*, 31 December 1982, pp. 1, 6.

[102]*Filipino Reporter*, 6–12 January, pp. 1–2.

was "coerced, tortured, or drugged" into making the confession, some church officials remained skeptical about the admissions, suggesting that the military may have used force to obtain them.[103] Such skepticism was further heightened by circumstances surrounding Kangleon's death from an automobile accident in January 1984. Following the discovery of entries in the priest's diary damaging to the military, which again raised questions about his confession, church officials asked the government to reopen the case.[104]

The arrest and imprisonment of Schmidt and Gaspar, along with other church workers in Davao, drew criticism in the Philippines and from abroad, prompting Gaspar, in an April 1983 letter to Philippine bishops, not only to protest the circumstances of his arrest but also to deny any connections with the Communists:

> The truth is that I *am not* "a top ranking member of the CPP and head of the CPP Mindanao United Front Commission"; that the Resource Development Foundation where I work now is *not* "a front of the CPP"; that I have gone on trips abroad *not* "to contact communists in order to raise funds for the CPP." In most of these trips abroad I was with bishops, priests, nuns and lay churchworkers. They can testify to what I did abroad.
>
> I have told my military interrogators that the reason for my involvement in justice and development issues is because of my faith commitment. Most of them, in fact almost all of them, cannot comprehend why we would risk our lives because of our faith in Jesus Christ and our concern for our fellow men.[105]

Gaspar, Schmidt, and the layworkers subsequently joined other political detainees on Philippine Independence Day 1983 in a fast over prison conditions. Eventually a compromise with the military resulted in the termination of the forty-four-day fast in July 1983, but not before Gaspar and Schmidt were transferred to the Davao City jail as punishment for leading the hunger strike.[106] The following month the charges were dropped against the three layworkers, although they were not immediately

[103]*Bulletin Today*, 15 December 1982, pp. 1, 15; *Philippine News*, 29 December 1982–4 January 1983, pp. 1, 8; and speech of Louie G. Hechanova before the Rotary Club of Cebu, 6 January 1983 (mimeographed).

[104]*Philippine Newsbriefs*, September–October 1984, pp. 19–20; and "Church Requests to Reopen Case of Fr. Kangleon," *Impact*, January 1985, p. 10. See also Defense Minister Enrile's announcement of a reinvestigation in the *Bulletin Today*, 5 October 1984, pp. 1, 14.

[105]Letter of Karl Gaspar to Philippine bishops, 12 April 1983 (photocopied).

[106]*Political Detainees Update*, 30 June 1983, p. 1; 15 July 1983, pp. 1, 6–8; and 15 August 1983, pp. 1, 7.

freed. In September 1983 Schmidt was released in the "spirit of amity between nations" and allowed to leave the Philippines. Gaspar was returned from the Davao City jail to the Davao PC/INP Metrodiscom detention center in late September 1983, but, because the military considered his prosecution crucial, he remained in detention until acquitted of all charges in January 1985.[107]

Although the CFIC sisters and Bishop Purugganan admitted that, in general, the raids in Ilagan were conducted properly, they questioned the military's motives for the investigations. At the time of the assaults, however, Bishop Purugganan noted that the front-door latch to his residence was unnecessarily damaged and that the search warrant lacked a proper serial number and court seal. The 6 September 1983, "NASSA Statement of Protest" pointed out that the military's actions violated "the long-standing agreement between the church and the military that no raid of any church establishment shall be effected without prior coordination with the highest ranking religious leader in the area."[108] The military subsequently apologized, but the raids nevertheless drew swift and sharp rebukes from Catholic church officials, including Cardinal Sin. Bishop Purugganan refused to accept the explanation that the raids were simply a "mistake." Instead, he felt they were a "test" to see "how far the military can go with the Church" and "how much the Church can stand."[109]

The military actions against the Baptist-sponsored UIM seminar in Iloilo and against the residence of Bishop Amantillo in Tandag were likewise criticized by Protestant and Catholic leaders.[110] The UIM controversy was quickly resolved when General Isidoro de Guzman, commander of the Regional Unified Command (RUC) 6, apologized to the head of the Philippine Baptist church and pledged that in the future the military would follow PC/INP policies with regard to relations with church organizations and personnel.[111] Nonetheless, following the raids on the residence of Bishop Amantillo and the Diocesan Pastoral Center, the military refused to apolo-

[107]Maryknoll Justice and Peace Office, Maryknoll, New York, "Phone Message Received from Jack Walsh, M.M.—Davao City, Philippines, September 1, 1983" (photocopied), and letters from Karl Gaspar to friends, 25 September 1983 (mimeographed) and 16 February 1985 (photocopied).

[108]*NASSA News*, special issue, September 1983, p. 4.

[109]Ibid., pp. 1–6; and *San Francisco Sunday Examiner & Chronicle*, 11 September 1983, pp. A1, A17.

[110]*Bulletin Today*, 17 August 1984, pp. 1, 12; and *Philippine Newsbriefs*, September–October 1984, pp. 18–19.

[111]Johnny Gumgan, "Military Apologizes on Iloilo Church Raid; Church Leaders Consider Case Closed," *NCCP Newsletter*, July–August 1984, p. 23.

gize and continued to harass the church in Tandag, causing church leaders, including three bishops, priests, nuns, and layworkers, to stage a protest march and a rally where "the U.S.–Marcos dictatorship" was singled out "as the principal cause of the soldiers' high-handed policy."[112] Bishop Amantillo did little to conceal his anger at the incident, asking that if the military could disregard the rights of a bishop, "What can they not do to ordinary people?" The bishop indicated that he would file a case against the military as a "sign of protest." He also maintained that the military was "barking up the wrong tree" if they felt such an attack would "silence the priests," and warned that continued military repression against the church was likely to result in increased alienation of the people from the government.[113]

National Security, the Military, and the Churches

Military harassment of the clergy working among small farmers, tribal minorities, and wage laborers as well as the military raids on church establishments, especially the Catholic media closures, went to the heart of the church-military conflict: the churches' right of free expression and duty to expose injustices in preaching the gospel versus the military's responsibility to maintain law and order and to protect the national security. Why did these two not necessarily incompatible missions result in controversy in the Philippines? Part of the explanation lies in how government and military officials viewed the role of the churches in the New Society and New Republic. Basically Marcos and the generals sought to restrict the clergy to simply preaching the gospel. Although the government recognized the right of church officials to speak out on social issues, it nevertheless demonstrated an ambivalence toward church involvement in "politics": They encouraged the clergy to report military abuses and misconduct but cracked down when the criticism became too trenchant. Then, too, there was a significant erosion of professional standards within the military after 1972. Marcos, a native Ilocano, surrounded himself with a disproportionate number of generals and ranking defense officials from the Ilocos region of northern Luzon, and favored the promotion of officers personally loyal to him over those more professionally qualified. Such a politicization of the military resulted in a rise in graft and corruption in the armed forces, a

[112] *MIPC Communications*, November 1984, pp. 4–7.
[113] Ibid., pp. 6–7, especially the interview with Bishop Ireneo Amantillo.

demoralization within the ranks of the professional officers, and an increasing inability of the military to police itself, especially at the provincial and local levels.[114]

The position of the military with respect to the exposure of injustices by the clergy was made clear within a year of the declaration of martial law. At the second CMLC meeting in December 1973, for example, Generals Campos, Pecache, and Ramos took exception to a survey done by the Major Religious Superiors to assess the national situation in preparation for the AMRSP's annual meeting in January 1974.[115] The study, which examined a variety of issues such as land reform, labor conditions, peace and order, and the economy, was largely a negative assessment of martial law reforms. The generals complained that since the survey was not "a fair and a balanced picture" of the New Society, it reflected badly on the country internationally.[116] Similarly, military officials grumbled over the issuance of a critical statement about conditions under martial law issued by the Second Mindanao-Sulu Pastoral Conference (MSPC II) in April 1974.[117] General Ramos argued that the misuse of such statements by elements with "ulterior motives against the government" and their distortion in the foreign media tended to undermine peace and order and, ultimately, the reforms of the New Society. While agreeing with the right of the churches to preach the gospel, Ramos and the other generals stressed the need for "consultation" with the military (at the appropriate level) "before . . . preaching justice from the pulpits," because the message might unnecessarily anger the people.[118]

The need to maintain political order as prerequisite to the achievement of the development goals of the regime, including the continued attraction of foreign investment, was among the principal reasons for the military's restrictive view of the role of the churches in evangelizing for social justice. The military clearly identified with the position that any unnecessary delay in Cellophil's activities would "place the company in an uncompromising

[114]Carl H. Landé, "Philippine Prospects after Martial Law," *Foreign Affairs* 59 (Summer 1981): 1156. The extent to which Marcos promoted Ilocanos to the rank of general over other ethnolinguistic groups is questioned by Filipe B. Miranda, "The Military," in *The Philippines after Marcos*, ed. R. J. May and Francisco Nemenzo (London: Croom Helm, 1985), note 6, pp. 108–109.

[115]Association of Major Religious Superiors of the Philippines (AMRSP), "Summary of National Survey of Major Religious Superiors," 26 November 1973, pp. 1–30 (typewritten).

[116]Minutes of meeting no. 2 of the CMLC, 18 December 1973, pp. 1–4 (typewritten).

[117]Second Mindanao-Sulu Pastoral Conference (MSPC II), "To the People of God of Mindanao and Sulu," *MSPC Communications*, July 1974, pp. 1–2.

[118]Minutes of Meeting no. 7 of the CMLC, 24 May 1974, pp. 3–6 (typewritten).

[*sic*] situation with its foreign financiers," resulting in embarrassment of the regime as Cellophil's "principal guarantor."[119] Cellophil's dependence on international finance was typical of other development projects where military force was employed to obtain compliance. For example, the government, backed by the World Bank, contracted with Lehmeyer International of West Germany to conduct a feasibility study of the Chico River basin project.[120] The expansion of agribusiness corporations in Davao del Norte and Bukidnon was linked to multinational corporations in the United States and Japan.[121] Similarly, the development of the Tondo foreshore area involved Japanese interests and the construction of Dagat-Dagatan was a project of the World Bank.[122] Thus, church support for the rights of the Tingguians as well as for others who faced dislocation from development projects without consultation or just compensation was characteristically interpreted as a threat to Philippine national security requiring a military solution, namely, the increased use of force.

The close cooperation of the military with national and local political elites identified with the regime also facilitated the use of repression to achieve development policies. For example, the PC's Task Force Kanlaon on the Island of Negros was controlled by Roberto Benedicto, Philippine sugar czar and a close associate of President Marcos.[123] Other reports demonstrated close links between the military and Antonio Floirendo in Davao del Norte.[124] In 1977, as the controversy between Cellophil and the Tingguians intensified, Arturo Barbero, the thirty-three-year-old son of Carmelo Barbero, the deputy minister of defense, was appointed governor of the Province of Abra.[125] Significantly, many of the abuses of the military in these provinces (and elsewhere), including the harassment of clergy helping small farmers, tribal minorities, and wage-earners, not only went unpunished, but also were frequently justified in terms of national security and the need to eradicate subversion. Both Catholic and Protestant leaders increasingly criticized the use of force against critics of the regime, par-

[119]As quoted in Dorral, "The Tinggians of Abra and Cellophil," p. 131.

[120]Langa-an and Langa-an, "Squatters in Their Own Land," p. 73.

[121]See David et al., "Transnational Corporations and the Philippine Banana Export Industry," pp. 1–133; and Peter Krinks, "Corporations in the Philippine Banana Export Industry: A Preliminary Account," The Philippines in the Third World Papers, series no. 28 (Quezon City: University of the Philippines, Third World Studies Center, 1981).

[122]Bello, Kinley, and Elinson, *Development Debacle*, pp. 108–120.

[123]McCoy, *Priests on Trial*, p. 230.

[124]The Philippine Inter-Agency Research Team on the Banana Workers, "Transnational Corporations and the Philippine Banana Export Industry," pp. 31–36.

[125]*Focus Philippines*, 14 April 1979, 30–32.

ticularly after the termination of martial rule in 1981. During a 1981 visit to the Philippines, Pope John Paul II declared that national security considerations "never justify any violations of the fundamental dignity of the human person or the basic rights that safeguard this dignity."[126]

Even granting that the military may have had valid reasons for some of the actions against church institutions, subsequent events, particularly the interrogations following the DXBB and *Ang Bandilyo* raids, demonstrated that a central concern of the military was church criticism of misconduct by the armed forces. The sworn statement of Fr. Nazareno, for instance, cited examples of airing or publishing stories to the effect that (1) the PC did nothing when informed a Special Police group was extorting money from Bukidnon businessmen; (2) locally stationed soldiers were not arrested or separated from the service, as ordered by Minister Enrile, for indiscriminately discharging firearms; or (3) the PC allowed persons to languish in the provincial jail in violation of their constitutional rights and perhaps in contradiction to General Romeo Espino's orders to remove from the constabulary those who whitewashed military cases. The military argued in its "after operations" account that such reports on DXBB and in *Ang Bandilyo* tended to "incite the people to civil disobedience and possibly in some instances to violence"; ultimately, however, the Ministry of Defense chose not to press charges in court.[127]

That the military was less concerned about working closely with the church leaders (and others) to rectify reported abuses than in silencing critics indicated its inability to police itself. Given the record of human rights abuses by many Third World military (or authoritarian) regimes, it was unrealistic to expect that errant elements in the Philippine military would reform themselves. Thus Enrile's 1979 announcement that he had "constituted a three-man committee, composed of no less than my Deputy Minister for Civilian Relations, the Chief of Staff of the Armed Forces of the Philippines, and the Chief of the Philippine Constabulary, to look into any complaints about military abuse" was, if not simply a public relations ploy, more of a hope than a promise of future action.[128] Certainly the level of military abuses did not diminish after the termination of martial law in 1981. The regime's lack of will to reform the military was underscored

[126]Office for Human Development, Federation of Asian Bishops' Conference, *Papal Speeches on Social Issues in the Philippines* (Manila: Communication Foundation for Asia, 1981), p. 6.

[127]Nazareno, "Sworn Statement," 29 April 1977, Cagayan de Oro City, p. 6 and passim.

[128]Juan Ponce Enrile, "AFP's Role during the Transition Period," *NCCP Newsletter*, September–October 1979, p. 6.

additionally by the appointment of General Fabian Ver as chief of staff in 1981. Not only was General Ver credited with politicizing the military by favoring the appointment of generals personally loyal to Marcos, but also, as director general of the National Intelligence and Security Authority (NISA) as well as the head of various other military intelligence and security units during his career, including the Presidential Security Command (PSC), his name was long associated with the abuses of the Marcos regime.[129] Moreover, in January 1985 Ver and twenty-five others were indicted in connection with the August 1983 assassination of former Senator Benigno Aquino, Jr.;[130] although all of the defendants were acquitted in December 1985 following a Marcos stage-managed trial, many viewed the Aquino murder as but a single sensational incident in a continuing pattern of military abuse in the Philippines.

The Marcos regime often stressed the autonomy of the church and the right of the clergy to speak out on social issues. Right after the Novaliches raid the president reaffirmed the essence of the 1973 CMLC agreement regarding searches of church establishments. In a speech to the Protestant Wednesday Fellowship in September 1979, the defense minister stated that the defense leadership welcomed "complaints against military abuse."[131] Yet Enrile, who signed the ASSOs authorizing raids against church facilities, and other high military officials such as Generals Ver and Ramos were slow either to apologize publicly for the mistakes of the military or, more importantly, to prosecute officers for infractions of the law. Certainly, the periodic dismissal of officers and men from the service and the reluctance to try cases against the church were admissions of fallibility, but the lack of an open and ongoing debate with the church over social injustice was perhaps a better indicator of the military's self-perception. While admitting to mistakes, the military viewed itself as the bulwark of the New Society and the New Republic, and Marcos and Enrile repeatedly emphasized the armed forces' role in socioeconomic development and civic action. The hubris of the military generally resulted in crackdowns on its most vociferous church critics (frequently located in the most troubled regions of the country), rather than in concerted efforts to work with committed Christians towards rectifying social injustices, including military misconduct. As long as this situation existed, church activists continued to clash

[129]Fred Poole and Max Vanzi, *Revolution in the Philippines: The United States in a Hall of Cracked Mirrors* (New York: McGraw-Hill, 1984), pp. 124–129, 211–212.

[130]*New York Times*, 24 January 1985, pp. 1, 6. Of the twenty-six persons indicted, twenty-five were members of the armed forces.

[131]Enrile, "AFP's Role during the Transition Period," p. 5.

with the armed forces on issues of social justice. To do any less was a violation of their vows to preach the gospel to all men at all times regardless of the consequences.

Another result of increased militarization was the detention of a large number of political prisoners after 1972. The jailing of political dissenters in the name of national security and national development also exacerbated church-state relations. Suspects were often picked up and detained without charges, sometimes subjected to torture—if not "liquidated" by military security units—and routinely endured unsatisfactory prison conditions. Chapter 6 deals with the situation of political detainees in the Philippines.

6

Political Detainees in the Philippines

At the outset of martial rule, President Marcos ordered the arrest and detention of many persons, including political opponents, outspoken journalists and radio commentators, prominent businessmen, and church activists, who were considered a threat to the establishment of the New Society and the achievement of the regime's economic development goals. Within weeks the number of those jailed climbed to an estimated 30,000.[1] Two years later, in November 1975, the figure had risen to approximately 50,000, and in September 1977, the president admitted that some 70,000 persons had been incarcerated since the imposition of martial law.[2] Although comprehensive figures were never released by the government after 1977, at least another 5,000 persons were picked up and detained prior to the termination of martial rule in January 1981.[3] Because Marcos retained virtually all of his martial law powers, persons continued to be arrested and

[1]Testimony of Amelito R. Mutuc on behalf of the Philippine government before the U.S. Congress, House, Committee on International Relations, *Human Rights in South Korea and the Philippines: Implications for U.S. Policy, Hearings before the Subcommittee on International Organizations*, 94th Cong., 1st sess., 1975, p. 286.

[2]Amnesty International, *Report of an Amnesty International Mission to the Republic of the Philippines, 22 November–5 December 1975*, 2d ed. (London, 1977), p. 6 (hereafter cited as AI Mission, 1975); and United States Foreign Broadcast Information Service (FBIS), *Daily Reports*, vol. 4, Asia & Pacific, 7 September 1977, p. P1.

[3]The 5,000 figure was calculated from figures in FBIS, the *Bulletin Today*, and the *Sunday Express* from April 1978 to the end of martial rule in January 1981. I believe it understates the actual number of additional detainees since Marcos' September 1977 speech.

jailed on charges of "subversion," with an estimated 8,414 arrests having been made in the 1981–84 period.[4]

While most of those jailed after 1972 were released, confusion and disagreement abounded as to the number, status, and treatment of detainees in the Philippines. Just how many were political prisoners, for instance, was repeatedly disputed. Marcos remained steadfast in claiming that most of those arrested were "common criminals," such as thieves, kidnapers, and murderers. Although admitting the occurrence of isolated incidents of abuse by the military, he insisted that the regime adhered closely to international standards of human rights in its treatment of prisoners. In contrast, critics charged that many persons were picked up on flimsy (or manufactured) evidence, detained for so-called "subversion," jailed without charges, sometimes subjected to torture, and often forced to endure unsatisfactory prison conditions. After 1975, there were increasing reports of "salvagings" (a military euphemism for murder) and disappearances. To be sure, considerable controversy surrounded the detainee question in the Philippines, yet few attempts during and after martial law were made to analyze the problem.[5] In examining the political prisoner situation, I focus on the general context of detention, the treatment of detainees, the role of the Philippine churches, and the response of the Marcos government to criticism of its detainee program.

The Context of Detention

Presidential Proclamation 1081 concluded with sweeping provisions empowering the armed forces, through President Marcos as commander-in-chief, to enforce martial law. The military was charged with the prevention and suppression of violence and insurrection; with the enforcement of all presidential orders, decrees, and regulations; and with the incarceration of persons for a wide variety of crimes, including rebellion, national security violations, and public order offenses, under extant statues and presidential proclamations "as will be enumerated." Significantly, pris-

[4]Figure computed from the "Statement of Various Religious Leaders on the Situation in the Philippines," U.S. Congress, House, Committee on Foreign Affairs, *Hearings and Markup before the Subcommittee on Asian and Pacific Affairs, Foreign Assistance Legislation for Fiscal Years 1986–87* (Part 5), 99th Cong., 1st sess., 20, 27, 28 February, and 5, 6, 12, 20 March 1985, Table 2, p. 642.

[5]Notable exceptions are Justus M. van der Kroef, "The Philippine Political Prisoners and the United States," *World Affairs* 140 (Spring 1978): 315–326; and Felix Casalmo (pseud.), *The Vision of a New Society* (Manila, 1980), chap. 2, "Political Detainees."

oners were to "be kept under detention until otherwise ordered released" by the president or by a "duly designated representative."[6] Although the central thrust of Proclamation 1081 was aimed at eradicating the threat of Communism, few Communists of significance were picked up in the early days of martial law. Instead, initial roundups focused on the detention of persons considered "obstructions to the effective implementation" of New Society reforms.[7] Such jailings included major political opponents and prominent newspaper publishers, but most of those jailed, according to the government, were "subversives and student activists with suspected ties to Communist front organizations" and the NPA. Within two months of the declaration of martial law, the military admitted to the arrest of more than 6,000 Filipinos; later estimates were five times higher.[8]

The status of many detainees was a source of controversy. Marcos repeatedly maintained after January 1977 that no one had been arrested for his political beliefs. Yet earlier, in December 1974, he had stated during a nationwide radio-television address that there were "still 5,234 persons under detention all over the country as a direct consequence of the martial law proclamation. Of these, 4,069 [were] ordinary criminal offenders while 1,165 [were] political detainees."[9] Similarly, Estelito Mendoza, solicitor general of the Philippines, revealed in January 1976 that 4,000 detainees were being held on charges of "subversion." In July 1976 Deputy Minister of Defense Carmelo Barbero estimated the number of detainees at "4,000, 'a few hundred' of whom were political prisoners accused of subversion."[10] Thus, four years after the declaration of martial law government officials continued to equate "subversion" with the term "political prisoner," yet "subversion" remained ambiguously defined. Minister of National Defense Juan Ponce Enrile defined "subversion" in a 1977 BBC documentary as: "Anybody who goes against the Government or who tries to convince the people to go against the Government, that is subversion."[11]

In December 1974, Marcos employed "political detainee" to designate alleged violators of the Anti-Subversion Act of 1957 or persons charged with "rebellion, sedition, or insurrection and other crimes against the security of the state as defined in the Revised Penal Code." In January and

[6]*Proclamation 1081*, 21 September 1972.

[7]*Washington Post*, 28 September 1972, p. A26.

[8]*Washington Post*, 19 November 1972, p. A27; and Primitivo Mijares, *The Conjugal Dictatorship of Ferdinand and Imelda Marcos I* (San Francisco: Union Square Publications, 1976), chap. 3.

[9]*Bulletin Today*, 12 December 1974, p. 24.

[10]*New York Times*, 15 January 1976, p. 8; and FBIS, 3 August 1976, p. P3.

[11]Amnesty International, *Amnesty International Report 1977* (London, 1977), p. 210.

June 1977, he used "political detainee" to designate only those detained for political beliefs in the absence of any criminal charges.[12] Henceforth persons accused of "subversion," that is, political prisoners, were officially referred to as "national security detainees" or, more commonly, as "public order violators" (POVs).[13] As far as critics of the regime were concerned, especially given Enrile's definition of "subversion," arrest as a POV (particularly in the absence of specific, formal charges) generally was viewed as synonymous with being a political prisoner.[14] An examination of detention centers and prisons in the Manila metropolitan area and selected provincial areas between 1976 and 1980 revealed no less than five hundred political prisoners at the time of each report, and, according to those monitoring the detainee situation, the total number of political prisoners for each year surveyed was probably two or three times greater.[15]

Just as thousands were detained as suspected "subversives," security risks, and opponents of New Society reforms under martial law, thousands were discharged upon swearing allegiance to the government and pledging not to talk to the local or foreign media.[16] For instance, with the exception of former senators Diokno and Aquino, who spent two and seven-and-a-half years, respectively, in jail, most prominent politicians and other public figures were released quickly. By September 1977 Marcos claimed that 66,579 detainees had been freed since the inception of martial rule and that fewer than 5,000 persons remained incarcerated, only 598 of whom were "accused of subversion or rebellion."[17] The release of large numbers of detainees, however, did little to dissipate the atmosphere of fear or to instill confidence in military justice, as detentions and releases were fraught with confusion. Typical of the confusion were the government's announce-

[12]*Bulletin Today*, 12 December 1974, p. 24 and 4 June 1977, pp. 1, 5; and *Political Detainees Update*, 30 June 1978, p. 1. See also Free Legal Assistance Group (FLAG), *Legal Rights of Political Detainees under Martial Law* (Makati: Civil Liberties Union of the Philippines [1970s?]), p. 1.

[13]AMRSP, Task Force Detainees (TFD), *Pumipiglas: Political Detention and Military Atrocities in the Philippines* (Manila, 1981), p. 76 (hereafter cited as *Pumipiglas*).

[14]*Political Detainees Update*, 31 March 1979, pp. 11–15 and 15 May 1979, pp. 10–13.

[15]Association of Major Religious Superiors of the Philippines (AMRSP), Task Force Detainees (TFD), *Political Detainees in the Philippines* (Manila, 31 March 1976), p. 4 (hereafter cited as *Political Detainees, Book 1*); AMRSP, TFD, *Political Detainees in the Philippines, Book 2* (Manila, 31 March 1977), p. 1 (hereafter cited as *Political Detainees*, Book 2); AMRSP, TFD, *Political Detainees in the Philippines, Book 3* (Manila, 31 March 1978), p. 8 (hereafter cited as *Political Detainees*, Book 3); and *Pumipiglas, p. 3.*

[16]*See Philippine News*, 19–25 December 1974, p. 1, for an example of the government's release procedures.

[17]FBIS, 7 September 1977, p. P1.

ments of the release of 545 prisoners at Christmas 1975 and the release of 3,069 detainees between 27 June and 7 September 1977. An examination of the 1975 "list revealed that there were at least 14 duplications of names and 21 names of detainees who had been released more than three months before." Others listed were still under detention.[18] Analysis of the 1977 release data also reveals gross discrepancies. Of the detainees supposedly ordered freed by the president, 2,061 were unaccounted for in the lists published in the government-controlled press; of the remaining 1,000, fewer than 100 were verified as political detainees. And of these "*only 41 had actually been released since June 27th*." All other political prisoners had been let go before 27 June 1977: Some had been released years earlier and at least two had been dead for more than a year prior to June 1977.[19]

Part of the confusion over detentions and releases was due to the extensive powers enjoyed by local military commanders in arresting and jailing suspects. The martial law requirement that prisoners appear within three days before a military officer responsible for evaluating the evidence was regularly ignored as were provisions in the 1973 Constitution protecting the rights of arrested persons.[20] As a result, many arrests went unreported and many persons were held incommunicado in violation of established procedures. Even though an elaborate organizational structure for detainees was created at the commencement of martial rule, investigative officers were overburdened by the sheer volume of prisoners. The Regional Commands for the Administration of Detainees typically were unable (or unwilling) to distinguish between detainees charged with "subversion" or some other unspecified statutory violation. Thus, according to at least one informant with ties to the Philippine Constabulary (PC), the regime frequently found it convenient to "stash" prisoners while accumulating incriminating evidence. Clearly, many persons were arrested, held, released, and even re-arrested at the caprice of provincial and regional military commanders and of security agency officers.[21]

Arrests and detentions by local commanders and security agency personnel simply reflected the attitudes and policies of high government officials, including the president. In June 1975, Solicitor General Mendoza maintained in defense of martial law that "persons had to be detained as preventative measures either to remove them from possible complicity in

[18]*Political Detainees, Book 1*, p. 4.
[19]*Political Detainees, Book 3*, p. 2.
[20]The Philippine Constitution of 1973, Article IV, Secs. 1, 17, 20.
[21]Van der Kroef, "Philippine Political Prisoners," pp. 316–317.

the existing rebellion or protect them from those who may seek to destroy them and blame their death on the government."[22] In January 1977, Marcos upheld the regime's right to jail anyone without "evidence of a commission of an act but merely evidence of the fact that there is an intention to commit the act."[23] Similarly, in October 1977, Defense Minister Enrile issued an Arrest, Search, and Seizure Order (ASSO) for the apprehension of more than 100 suspects who "may have committed/are committing/about to commit acts tending to undermine national security and public order."[24] Translated into human terms, such attitudes and policies resulted in arbitrary jailings of many persons without charges, a fact documented time and time again. An analysis of several major sources of information on political prisoners revealed that 75 percent of the detainees were unclassifiable as to the kind of "subversion" for which they were arrested.[25]

Explanations abound for why detainees were arrested and held in the absence of formal charges. In many instances suspects simply irritated individual military commanders or persons with official connections.[26] But by far the largest number of political prisoners detained under martial law were perceived as opposing government reforms and programs. By definition such persons were "subversives," and were often picked up for "preventative detention," essentially a harassment-and-intimidation mechanism of the military. Frequent targets of arrest were members of the urban poor and peasant organizations, labor federations, church social action groups, student organizations, and tribal minorities who had voiced dissatisfaction with the regime.

The inauguration of the New Republic in July 1981 did not result in a significant reduction of the harassment, arrest, and repression of critics and opponents of the regime. The day before the lifting of martial rule, Marcos

[22]*Human Rights in South Korea and the Philippines*, p. 387.

[23]*U.S. Manila Post*, 15 January 1977, p. 4.

[24]As quoted in *Political Detainees Update*, 21 September 1978, p. 3.

[25]The sources consulted were: *Political Detainees, Book 1*; *Political Detainees, Book 2*; *Political Detainees, Book 3*; *Pumipiglas*; AI Mission, 1975; William J. Butler, John P. Humphrey, and G. E. Bisson, *The Decline of Democracy in the Philippines* (Geneva: International Commission of Jurists, 1977) (hereafter cited as ICJ Report, 1977); and Amnesty International USA, *"Disappearances": A Workbook* (New York, 1981). A content analysis of these sources produced a list of 783 political prisoners of whom 192 (25 percent) could be classified by type of subversion, ranging from alleged NPA membership to possession of "underground" literature.

[26]See, for example, *The Communicator*, 11 February 1976, pp. 1–4; and *Signs of the Times*, 26 March 1976, pp. 27–34.

substantially increased the penalties for rebellion, insurrection, and sedition with the issuance of Presidential Decree 1834.[27] Prior to and during martial law the maximum penalties for such crimes were long prison sentences, ranging from four years and two months in prison (before martial law) for involvement in a conspiracy to commit rebellion, insurrection, and sedition to seventeen years and four months in prison (during martial law) for leading a rebellion or insurrection. Presidential Decree 1834 increased the maximum penalties for all crimes involving rebellion, insurrection, and sedition to death (See Table 4). Furthermore, anyone convicted of organizing an illegal assembly or of engaging in "propaganda assaults against the Government . . . which tend to destabilize . . . or undermine or destroy the faith and loyalty of the citizenry thereto" was also subject to a sentence of death after January 1981. Such stiff penalties were designed, according to the International Commission of Jurists (ICJ), to continue the limitation of dissent and the suppression of opposition to the Marcos regime.[28]

Opposition to such harsh penalties was so widespread and intense that Marcos issued Presidential Decrees 1974 and 1975 on 2 May 1985, abolishing the maximum penalties of life imprisonment or death for rebellion, insurrection, and sedition and other crimes against the state. In tempering the penalties Marcos claimed that he was acting "in the spirit of national reconciliation," but others alleged that his gesture was prompted by a desire to avert an adverse ruling against the punishments in the Supreme Court.[29] Significantly, PD 1974 and PD 1975 reflected no substantive change on the part of the regime toward those considered enemies of the state, nor did the decrees result in the rebuilding of public confidence in the essential fairness of the government toward dissenters.[30]

Marcos' law enforcement philosophy of jailing anyone suspected of "an intention to commit" an illegal act continued after the termination of martial law, first, with the creation of a Presidential Commitment Order (PCO) in May 1981 and, second, by replacing the PCO with the promulga-

[27]*Presidential Decree 1834*, 16 January 1981.

[28]Virginia Leary, A. A. Ellis, and Kurt Madlener, *The Philippines: Human Rights after Martial Law* (Geneva: International Commission of Jurists, 1984), pp. 40–48 (hereafter cited as ICJ Report, 1984).

[29]Philippines (Republic), *Official Gazette* 81 (6 May 1985): 1793–1798; and *New York Times*, 6 May 1985, p. 10.

[30]See, for example, Lawyers Committee for International Human Rights, *"Salvaging" Democracy: Human Rights in the Philippines* (New York: Lawyers Committee for International Human Rights, 1985) (hereafter cited as Lawyers Committee Report, 1985).

Table 4. Penalties for rebellion, insurrection, and sedition, in years

Sentence	*Before martial law*	*Presidential Decree 942*, 1976	*Presidential Decree 1834*, 1981
Rebellion or insurrection (leaders)			
Minimum	6+	14+	life sentence
Maximum	12	17+	death
Rebellion or insurrection (participants)			
Minimum	6+	12+	life sentence
Maximum	8	14+	death
Conspiracy to commit rebellion or insurrection			
Minimum	4+	10+	life sentence
Maximum	6	12	death
Proposal to commit rebellion or insurrection			
Minimum	2+	8+	life sentence
Maximum	4+	10	death
Inciting to rebellion or insurrection			
Minimum	6+	12+	life sentence
Maximum	8	14+	death
Sedition (leaders)			
Minimum	6+	12+	life sentence
Maximum	8	14+	death
Sedition (participants)			
Minimum	4+	10	life sentence
Maximum	6	12	death
Conspiracy to commit sedition			
Minimum	2+	8+	life sentence
Maximum	4+	10	death
Inciting to sedition			
Minimum	4+	10+	life sentence
Maximum	6	12	death

Source: Virginia Leary, A. A. Ellis, and Kurt Madlener, *The Philippines: Human Rights after Martial Law* (Geneva: International Commission of Jurists, 1984), pp. 42, 44.

tion of a Preventative Detention Action (PDA) in July 1983.[31] The PCO initially appeared designed to circumscribe the government's authority to employ preventative detention against persons accused of national security violations. Yet, according to the Lawyers Committee for International

[31]*Letter of Instruction 1125*, 9 May 1981; *Letter of Instruction 1125-A*, 25 May 1981; and *Presidential Decree 1877*, 21 July 1983. The PCO and the PDA replaced the ASSO.

Human Rights, it "soon evolved into a license to order detention without any meaningful limits."[32] Arrests and detentions were routinely carried out in the absence of either the knowledge of the judicial authorities or the issuance of a PCO, as required by Letters of Instruction (LOI) 1125 and 1125-A. But when the constitutionality of the practice was challenged by twenty-two detainees in March 1982, Solicitor General Mendoza produced LOI 1211, issued a few days prior to the hearing before the Supreme Court,[33] negating a provision in LOI 1125-A that stated "where no commitment order is issued by the President, the accused under detention may be released on bail."[34] Furthermore, LOI 1211 provided that military commanders and law enforcement agency heads could, through the minister of national defense, request PCOs from the president to arrest and detain persons suspected of national security offenses, "(a) when resort to judicial process is not possible or expedient without endangering public order and safety; or (b) when the release on bail of the person or persons already under arrest by virtue of a judicial warrant would endanger said public order and safety." Significantly, those arrested with the PCO could be kept "under detention until ordered released by the President or his duly authorized representative."[35] The broad powers of LOI 1211 allowed President Marcos, through the military, to use the PCO in bypassing normal judicial procedures in arresting hundreds of persons deemed "subversive." Task Force Detainees (TFDs) revealed, for example, that at least 168 persons were arrested in 1982 and the first five months of 1983 with PCOs. Human rights investigators also reported that many of those arrested under PCOs were kept in preventative detention for periods longer than the maximum sentence of the crime for which they were accused. Others who were acquitted or who had completed their sentences continued to languish in jail pending the issuance of a release order by the president or one of his representatives.[36] Attempts to check the president's powers under LOI

[32]Lawyers Committee for International Human Rights, *The Philippines: A Country in Crisis* (New York: Lawyers Committee for International Human Rights, 1983), p. 51 (hereafter cited as Lawyers Committee Report, 1983).

[33]*Political Detainees Update*, 15 March 1982, p. 1.

[34]*Letter of Instruction 1125-A*, 25 May 1981.

[35]*Letter of Instruction 1211*, 9 March 1982.

[36]"Political Detainees: Living Evidences of Repression," Report prepared for an International Ecumenical Conference on the Philippines, Stony Point Conference Center, Stony Point, New York, 27 September–2 October 1983, p. 12; and Lawyers Committee Report, 1983, pp. 55–57.

1211 were set back in April 1983 by the Supreme Court's decision in the *Garcia-Padilla v. Enrile* case, wherein the court ruled that the

> judiciary can, with becoming modesty, ill afford to assume the authority to check or reverse or supplant the presidential actions. On these occasions, the President takes absolute command, for the very life of the Nation and its government, which, incidentally, includes the courts, is in grave peril. In so doing, the President is answerable only to his conscience, the people and to God. For their part, in giving him the supreme mandate as their President, the people can only trust and pray that, giving him their own loyalty with utmost patriotism, the President will not fail them.[37]

The justices stated further that the courts were unable to void a PCO "under the doctrine of 'political question,' " as its issuance was "the exclusive prerogative of the President under the Constitution."[38]

The unpopularity of the *Garcia-Padilla v. Enrile* decision reinforced a campaign by religious and civic leaders, including retired Supreme Court Justice Cecilia Muñoz-Palma and the Catholic bishops, to abolish the PCO. Muñoz-Palma stated flatly that the PCO was designed to stifle legitimate dissent, to cow opponents of the regime, and to perpetuate the "power and domination" of the Marcoses.[39] Other prominent Filipinos signed a petition warning that the continued use of the PCO "will eventually lead to the total loss of our people's human and democratic rights."[40] To forestall the reading on 7 August 1983, in all Catholic churches throughout the Philippines, of a pastoral letter of the Catholic Bishops' Conference of the Philippines (CBCP) condemning the PCO, President Marcos replaced the PCO with the equally effective PDA. The major difference between the PCO and the PDA was that under the latter a person initially could only be held for a year, not indefinitely, prior to a review of the case. The PDA still allowed the authorities, however, to bypass the judiciary in the arresting and detaining process and allowed the president, after considering the recommendations of the review committee (which he appointed) either to release, continue the detention of, or file information in court against the detained suspect. In addition, although Presidential Decree 1877 provided that a person who had been acquitted or had served his sentence "shall be

[37]*Garcia-Padilla v. Enrile*, 20 April 1983, as quoted in ICJ Report, 1984, p. 75.
[38]Ibid.
[39]"Political Detainees: Living Evidences of Repression," p. 15.
[40]*Political Detainees Update*, 31 May 1983, p. 3.

released from proper custody," it also stated that "if in the meantime there is evidence of the detained person continuing to engage in the acts for which he was detained he may be ordered further detained by the President."[41] Thus, just as in the case of the PCO, persons could be jailed indefinitely—and were—at the discretion of the president under the PDA.

Treatment of Detainees

Within two months of the declaration of martial law, a Command for the Administration of Detainees (COMCAD) was established by the Ministry of National Defense under General Order 16, and by March 1977, detainees were kept in about a hundred detention centers nationwide. In addition, many political prisoners were held in provincial jails (often with common criminals) and in concealed "safehouses."[42] Prison conditions varied considerably from one stockade to another, with the worst located in provincial areas and the best centered in the Manila metropolitan region. Although systematic information on the detainee prison system was never made available by the Marcos regime, numerous reports on individual prisons revealed what appeared to be a widespread pattern of neglect and abuse.[43]

Even the regime's "showcase" prison for political detainees, the Bicutan Rehabilitation Center (renamed Camp *Bagong Diwa* [New Thought] in mid-1978), opened in April 1976 with a capacity for housing two thousand detainees, was plagued with strife and problems from the beginning. On 14 June 1976, detainees commenced a fifteen-day hunger strike for (1) the release of two nursing mothers in accordance with existing Church-Military Liaison Committee (CMLC) guidelines; (2) continued social contact between male and female prisoners, some of whom were spouses; (3) access to cooking facilities for preparing meals; and (4) improvements in water service, recreational facilities, and visitation rights.[44] Similarly, in

[41]Presidential Decree 1877, 21 July 1983. See also Lawyers Committee Report, 1983, pp. 58–62; and Lawyers Committee Report, 1985, chap. 7.

[42]Juan A. Sison, "Human Rights under Philippine Martial Law," Paper delivered at an international seminar on "Problems of Law and Society," East-West Center, University of Hawaii, Honolulu, August 1977, p. 16; and *Political Detainees*, Book 2, p. v. A "safehouse" is an undisclosed residence where political prisoners are held (sometimes for months) while they undergo "tactical interrogations," a military euphemism for torture.

[43]See, for instance, *Political Detainees Update*, 6 March 1979, pp. 1–11; 30 May 1980, pp. 3–5; and 31 August 1980, p. 4; and *Ichthys*, 18 May 1979, pp. 12–13.

[44]*Pumipiglas*, p. 70; and *Signs of the Times*, 10 April 1976, p. 10; 19 June 1976, pp. 10–12; and 10 July 1976, p. 4.

October 1976 the detainees organized a protest fast over the continued detention of married women as well as the prolonged incarceration of others in the absence of formal charges.[45] In the fall of 1980 Bicutan prisoners went on a three-day fast and then on an eighteen-day fast protesting detainee release procedures, the ₱4.00 daily food allowance, insufficient water, poor garbage collection, a lack of bedding, and inadequate cleaning supplies.[46] The government eventually granted many of the prisoners' demands, yet the concessions resulted in military reprisals and harassment. Strike leaders were moved to other stockades without notification of relatives or lawyers, visitation rights were often arbitrarily restricted, and some detainees were placed in solitary confinement.[47]

The lifting of martial law did not result in any dramatic improvements in prison conditions for detainees. By March 1982, for instance, the detention center in Lahug, Cebu City, which was designed to house 250 prisoners, held 631 detainees, many of whom were common criminals. Overcrowding in cells as small as 5.5 by 5 feet, along with unsanitary conditions and inadequate food rations, contributed to the spread of respiratory diseases, such as pulmonary tuberculosis, and to considerable violence.[48] That the state of the Cebu City detention center was not unusual was underscored by reports from Philippine human rights groups about other stockades throughout the country[49] and by a report of a fact-finding mission to the Philippines in 1983 sponsored by the American Committee for Human Rights and five other scientific and medical organizations. In visiting six detention centers, the American team discovered

> overcrowding with common criminals and political detainees sharing the same cell; meager food rations (roughly 6 pesos or 42 U.S. cents a day); insufficient medicines for a variety of ailments including tuberculosis, anemia, gastroenteritis and colitis; and irregular visits by prison health personnel. These conditions were further aggravated by the fact that many detainees had been held for a year or more under such circumstances.[50]

[45]*Signs of the Times*, 9 October 1976, pp. 12–16.

[46]*Ichthys*, 26 September 1980, pp. 7–9; 31 October 1980, pp. 9–10; and 21 November 1980, pp. 16–18.

[47]*Signs of the Times*, 17 July 1976, pp. 1–8; 24 July 1976, pp. 3–5; 11 September 1979, pp. 10–12; 20 November 1976, p. 3; 8 September 1978, pp. 17–18; and 28 November 1980, pp. 3–4.

[48]"Political Detainees: Living Evidences of Repression," p. 28. Ironically, the Lahug facility was named the *Bagong Buhay* (New Life) Rehabilitation Center.

[49]Ibid., pp. 27–30; *Political Detainees Update*, January 1983, p. 3; and Bruce Stannard, *Poor Man's Priest: The Fr. Brian Gore Story* (Sidney: Collins/Fontana, 1984), chap. 6.

[50]*Report of a Fact-Finding Mission to the Philippines, 28 November–17 December 1983*

The team concluded that the conditions they observed failed to meet international norms for prison facilities established in the United Nations Standard Minimum Rules for the Treatment of Prisoners.[51]

The status of Bicutan was also affected by the termination of martial rule: On 18 January 1981, the rehabilitation center was closed down and the remaining thirty-two political detainees were sent to the national penitentiary in Muntinglupa.[52] Although protests over conditions in Muntinglupa resulted in a small part of Bicutan being reopened as a political prisoner detention center in April 1981, many of the previously granted privileges of the Bicutan inmates were not restored and new restrictions were applied.[53] Only after a twenty-one-day fast in November 1981 were the rights to mingle with other detainees within the detention area and visits from relatives (outside of the nuclear family) and friends again allowed.[54]

The government assiduously defended its political prisoner detention system. In December 1974, Marcos insisted that prisoners were well treated and that the International Committee of the Red Cross (ICRC) found Philippine prisons exemplary, while in July 1977, Defense Minister Enrile reiterated the claim, saying that in yearly visits to Philippine detention centers since 1973 the ICRC "invariably found conditions satisfactory."[55] In April 1979, Amante Bigornia, assistant press secretary, countered charges that some political prisoners endured "subhuman conditions" by highlighting the treatment of Marcos' archrival, former Senator Benigno Aquino, Jr., at Fort Bonifacio and the privileges enjoyed by detainees at Bicutan.[56] Contrary to the president's assertion, however, the ICRC frequently suggested improvements in Philippine prison conditions, especially with respect to better food and "overcrowding as well as sanitary, medical, leisure and visit facilities."[57] Although Aquino's Fort Bonifacio cell and the Bicutan Rehabilitation Center represented the best prison conditions in the country, Bigornia's statement was challenged. Aquino's wife, Corazon, now president of the Philippines, for example, denied that

(Washington, D.C.: Clearinghouse on Science and Human Rights, American Association for the Advancement of Science, April 1984), p. 10 (hereafter cited as Fact-Finding Mission Report, 1983).

[51]Ibid., p. 11.

[52]*Political Detainees Update*, 31 January 1981, pp. 4–6.

[53]*Political Detainees Update*, 15 July 1981, pp. 1–2; and "Political Detainees: Living Evidences of Repression," pp. 32–33.

[54]*Political Detainees Update*, 15 November 1981, pp. 4–5, and 30 November 1981, p. 7.

[55]*Bulletin Today*, 12 December 1974, pp. 1, 5; and Juan Ponce Enrile, "On Human Rights in the Philippines," *The Republic*, 1–15 July 1977, p. 6.

[56]*Ichthys*, 18 May 1979, p. 15; and *Bulletin Today*, 29 April 1979, p. 2.

[57]*Philippine Times*, 16–31 January 1975, pp. 16–17.

his cell was "carpeted" or that he had "access to the camp's officers clubhouse," emphasizing instead that the senator remained padlocked in solitary confinement under twenty-four-hour guard. Satur Ocampo, a well-known Bicutan detainee and a major figure in the CPP, pointed out factual errors in Bigornia's statement on the rehabilitation center and took issue with his characterization of the detainee situation in the country generally.[58]

Despite the conditions of some prisons, assignment to a military stockade may have been the least objectionable form of detention. Many political detainees were tortured in undisclosed "safehouses" and in security unit quarters prior to being turned over to COMCAD. Of 783 persons listed in major Philippine and international human rights publications between 1976 and 1981, 47 percent (367) were reportedly tortured by one or more of 234 named torturers, 36 of whom were mentioned in two or more torture cases.[59] Among a wide variety of torture methods, electric shock, beatings, strangulation, water treatment, scalding, mid-air suspension, ear-popping, sexual assault, cigarette burns, and psychological intimidation were frequently mentioned. The general pattern was for suspects to be picked up by military intelligence units, or more ominously, by "nonorganic" units or "lost commands" (defined as units outside the control of local military commanders and sometimes referred to as "loose commands") and taken to safehouses where they sometimes were held for months while being subjected to intense interrogation, often resulting in physical and psychological abuse, including torture.

Although Marcos stated flatly in December 1974 that "no one, but no one has been tortured" in the Philippines, numerous incidents of torture were recorded after 1972.[60] The reports of Amnesty International (AI) in 1977 and 1982, the International Commission of Jurists (ICJ) in 1977 and 1984, along with the reports of the Lawyers Committee for International Human Rights in 1983 and 1985 and the American Committee for Human Rights in 1983, all concluded that torture was widely used on political prisoners.[61] Among those most commonly tortured were opponents of the regime and critics of New Society and New Republic reforms. One of the

[58]*Bulletin Today*, 29 April 1979, p. 2; *Philippines Daily Express*, 1 May 1979, pp. 1–2; and *Ichthys*, 1 June 1979, pp. 11–15.

[59]See note 25.

[60]*Bulletin Today*, 12 December 1974, pp. 1, 5.

[61]AI Mission, 1975; Amnesty International, *Report of an Amnesty International Mission to the Republic of the Philippines 11–28 November 1981* (London, 1982) (hereafter cited as AI Mission, 1981); ICJ Reports, 1977 and 1984; Lawyers Committee Reports, 1983 and 1985; and Fact-Finding Mission Report, 1983.

more widely publicized torture cases during martial law was that of Trinidad Herrera, president of Zone One Tondo Organization (ZOTO) and an opponent of government development programs resulting in the forced relocation of Manila squatters. Because of her activities Herrera was denied an exit visa to attend the United Nations Conference on Human Settlements (Habitat) in Vancouver, B.C. in June 1976; she was ordered arrested and subsequently went into hiding until her capture in April 1977.[62] Once in custody Herrera was subjected to electric shock treatment (to her fingers and breasts) until she agreed to "cooperate" with the authorities, ostensibly by identifying other "subversives."[63] After the case came to the attention of the U.S. Embassy and the international press, Marcos ordered Herrera released and initiated court-martial proceedings against the military personnel involved. In the end, the accused officers were acquitted by a military court; Defense Minister Enrile advanced the theory that Herrera's injuries were "self-inflicted torture" aimed at discrediting the government.[64]

The use of torture against opponents of the regime was not noticeably reduced with the inauguration of the New Republic. In July 1982, Horacio Morales, Jr., former vice-president of the Development Academy of the Philippines (DAP) and allegedly a leading member of the National Democratic Front (NDF), charged that he was subjected to several forms of torture, including "the water cure and electric shock treatment," in order to force him, among other things, to sign a waiver of his rights to legal counsel.[65] Also at this time, a group of twenty-three political detainees filed a joint petition before the United Nations Commission on Human Rights' Sub-Commission on Prevention of Discrimination and Protection of Minorities; the petition accused the Philippine government of a variety of violations of human rights, including the use of torture.[66] TFD reported, as

[62]*Philippine Times*, 1–15 June 1976, pp. 1, 9. Herrera had been arrested four times previously in 1975 and 1976 for engaging in "illegal" activities such as attending rallies and demonstrations and passing out handbills. See *Various Reports*, 28 February 1975, pp. 20–23; and *Times Journal*, 8 July 1977, reprinted in mimeographed documents of the Herrera case distributed by the Catholic church.

[63]"Trining Herrera, Zoto Head, Tortured," 6 May 1977 news release from the National Office of Mass Media, Manila, Philippines, and letter of F. Soc Rodrigo to Jose Crisol, Undersecretary, Department of National Defense, 12 May 1977 (mimeographed).

[64]Letter of F. Soc. Rodrigo to Capt. Martin B. Razalan, Judge Advocate General Service, 3 August 1977 (mimeographed); Richard P. Claude, "The Decline of Human Rights in the Republic of the Philippines," *New York Law School Review* 24 (1978): 215–216; and Rodney Tasker, "Marcos Probes Torture Claim," *Far Eastern Economic Review*, 27 May 1977, pp. 11–13.

[65]*Political Detainees Update*, 15 August 1982, pp. 3, 6.

[66]See petition of Rogelio C. Aberca et al. v. Republic of the Philippines to the United

Table 5. Human rights violations in the Philippines, 1977–84

Year	*Arrests*	*Disappearances*	*Salvagings*	*Torture*
1977	1,351	17	51	—
1978	1,620	10	86	—
1979	1,961	48	196	—
1980	962	19	218	—
1981	1,377	53	321	—
1982	1,911	42	210	—
1983	2,088	145	368	644
1984[a]	3,038	137	445	449
1985 (Jan–Mar)	1,069	35	93	184

[a]Totals exclude data for November and December from Mindanao.

Sources: Statement of U.S. church leaders and the Church Coalition for Human Rights in the Philippines on the Human Rights Situation in the Philippines, submitted to the Subcommittee on Asian and Pacific Affairs of the Committee on Foreign Affairs, House of Representatives, 12 March 1985, reprinted in *Phildoc,* March 1985, Tables 2 and 3, p. 5A; and *Political Detainees Update,* 31 May 1985, p. 9.

Table 5 demonstrates, 1,093 cases of torture in the 1983–84 period, and maintained, via a July 1983 article in *Political Detainees Update*, that the infliction of torture against opponents of the regime was "state policy."[67] The pervasiveness of torture as an investigative instrument of military security units prompted the Free Legal Assistance Group (FLAG) and the Medical Action Group (MAG) to sponsor a conference in September 1984 on ways to stop the use of torture and on the need to establish a rehabilitation center for the victims of torture.[68]

Coupled with widespread allegations of torture were indications that "disappearances" and "salvagings" accelerated after 1975. Amnesty International estimated in 1981 that no less than 233 political detainees "disappeared" between 1975 and 1980 in the Philippines; out of the 783 cases mentioned previously, 23 percent (181) were classified as either "salvage" victims (20 percent) or murdered members of the New People's Army (3 percent).[69] Other sources place the number of "substantiated *salvagings*" in the 1975–80 period at 303.[70] Similarly, data from TFD revealed the

Nations Commission on Human Rights' Sub-Commission on Prevention of Discrimination and Protection of Minorities, received in the Human Rights Liaison Office, New York, New York, 29 July 1982, pp. 1–23 and Annexes A through Y (typewritten).

[67]*Political Detainees Update*, 31 July 1983, p. 2.

[68]*Political Detainees Update*, 15 October 1984, p. 5.

[69]"Disappearance," p. 63; and note 25.

[70]*Pumipiglas,* p. 3; and note 25. The discrepancy between the data from the sources in note 25, which includes *Pumipiglas*, and the figure cited on p. 3 of *Pumipiglas* is because all

occurrence of another 377 "disappearances" and 1,344 "salvagings" from the beginning of 1981 to the end of 1984 (see Table 5). An analysis of "disappearances" in the Philippines indicate three principal patterns:

> (1) those of people arrested without witnesses (or without positive identification of the arresting agents), who are never found again; (2) those of prisoners—usually arrested without an appropriate warrant—held in complete isolation for weeks or months, while their families cannot discover their whereabouts and the military authorities deny having them in custody, until they eventually reappear in one detention center or another; and (3) those of victims of "salvaging," who have "disappeared" until their bodies are discovered.[71]

The incidence of "disappearances" varied over time, indicating a generally rising trend after 1978, and shifted geographically, revealing a drop in the metropolitan Manila area after 1976 but an increase in Mindanao and regions outside of the capital after 1979. The reductions in the metropolitan Manila area were attributed to increased publicity, particularly by the international press, and to the greater accessibility of national political and military officials in the capital, whereas the increase in the provincial areas was "attributed to counterinsurgency operations directed by government armed forces against the New People's Army (NPA) and the Moro National Liberation Front." Documentation of "disappearances," especially in rural areas, was hampered by military intimidation, an absence of witnesses, and by self-imposed media censorship.[72]

The pattern of "disappearances" and "salvagings" was very much alike, but with an increase in the latter both over time and in the provincial areas of the country. Nevertheless, there was one important difference: Whereas government and military officials tried to deny knowledge of many "disappearances," the existence of corpses from "salvagings" required an official explanation. Thus suspects picked up by the military and later found dead were often reported either as NPA members killed in military engagements or as innocent victims of NPA "liquidations."[73] Numerous "salvagings" were also attributed to "lost commands" operating independently of local military units and frequently, according to some provincial commanders,

---

persons who " 'disappeared' between 1975 and 1980 were not listed in the various sources, a further indication that "disappearance" figures are probably understated.

[71]*"Disappearances,"* p. 64.

[72]Ibid., pp. 65–66.

[73]For a discussion of the government's explanation of "salvagings," see AI Mission, 1981, pp. 19–20; and Lawyers Committee Report, 1983, pp. 34–38.

secretly and without official authorization. But on both counts, such official reports were found wanting.

A typical example of "salvagings" blamed on the Communists was the October 1978 death of four Davao del Norte farmers killed by the military. Reports in the local Mindanao press and radio indicated that the farmers were members of the NPA, two of whom were allegedly NPA commanders. Yet several witnesses, including two *barangay* captains, who knew three of the victims well, signed sworn statements questioning the military's NPA membership claim, and more than fifteen hundred local citizens signed a petition attesting to the innocence of the farmers. A subsequent investigation revealed inconsistencies in the military's version of the incident. Furthermore, military witnesses, who signed affidavits identifying (from death photos) the victims as NPA members, were unknown locally and, significantly, were unavailable for cross-examination.[74] In early November, the Regional Judge Advocate General Office (JAGO) in Davao City found "no evidence to warrant the prosecution of respondents" and recommended that the "case be dismissed"; two days later, however, because of public pressure, the provincial commander ordered two of the soldiers involved in the incident disarmed and restricted to camp and recommended the same for three other soldiers from a companion Constabulary Security Unit (CSU).[75] Within a month one of the "restricted" soldiers was seen armed in the community, and in January 1979, the case was dropped by JAGO without explanation or public review. As compensation Deputy Minister of National Defense Carmelo Barbero, while on a visit to Davao del Norte in February 1979, promised the families of the victims ₱2,000 each—a standard sum for civilian casualties of military encounters[76]—but as of May 1982, none of the families had been paid by the government nor had the murderers been brought to trial, although one, according to a priest familiar with the case, was known to be "a hired murderer used by the P.C."[77]

[74]*Pumipiglas*, pp. 37–38; *Ichthys*, 8 December 1978, pp. 3–4; Police Captain Librado N. Chiong, "Investigation Report," Headquarters, Davao del Norte Constabulary/Integrated National Police Command, Tagum, Davao del Norte, 9 November 1978, pp. 1–7 (typewritten); and an interview with a church official of the Justice and Peace Office, Prelature of Tagum, 18 June 1979.

[75]Major Enrique J. Lacanilao, "Resolution/Preliminary Investigation Report," Headquarters, PC/INP Regional Command 11, Office of the Regional Judge Advocate, Catitipan, Davao City, 6 November 1978 (typewritten). The report was to the Judge Advocate General, AFP, in Camp Aguinaldo, Quezon City.

[76]*Ichthys*, 23 March 1979, pp. 23–24.

[77]Personal correspondence from a priest working in the Diocese of Tagum's Justice and Peace Office, 4 May 1982.

While admitting "minor cases of maltreatment" by undisciplined troops, the government consistently denied that "salvaging" was officially condoned.[78] But there were many reliable reports of "lost commands" operating as "liquidation squads" in Mindanao. Such units were reportedly composed of court-martialed soldiers, amnestied members of the MNLF, and other criminals whose records were expunged in return for killing "rebels" (NPA or MNLF members) or "subversives." In December 1975, a prisoner in Muntinglupa admitted to Fr. James Travis, an American priest, that the conditions of his release included the killing of three men in return for a "full pardon" from a death sentence and the restoration of his "civil rights." In February 1977, Fr. Travis intervened as a seven-member "lost command" shot up a logging camp in Davao Oriental "to collect 'protection fees' and . . . to 'liquidate' " one of the company's employees.[79] More recently, in early 1982, the heavily armed, 275-man "lost command" of Lt. Colonel Carlos "Charlie" Lademora gained notoriety for a variety of abuses, including extortion, rape, robbery, and murder, in the Province of Agusan del Sur in Eastern Mindanao.[80] Part of the command's reign of terror involved the intimidation of small farmers and minority tribesmen resisting relocation as a result of a joint venture plantation project of the Philippine government's National Development Corporation (NDC) and Malaysia's Guthrie Overseas Limited. At least twelve of Lademora's men were hired as security guards for the NDC-Guthrie project and, according to one report, "the rest dominate[d] security in the area."[81]

Although it was well known that "lost commands" in Mindanao were composed of criminal elements, the military seldom mounted campaigns against them, either denying the existence of such units or pleading a lack of jurisdiction. Lademora's group was no exception: He admitted that his men were misfits, "social outcasts," and "real bastards."[82] Yet the military

[78]*Bulletin Today*, 29 April 1979, p. 2; and Lawyers Committee Report, 1983, p. 39.

[79]Prepared statement of Fr. James M. Travis, U.S. Congress, House, Committee on International Relations, *U.S. Policy on Human Rights and Military Assistance in Indonesia, Nicaragua, Philippines, Thailand, and Iran, U.S. Voluntary Contributions to International Organizations and Programs, Hearings before the Subcommittee on International Organizations*, Foreign Assistance Legislation for Fiscal Year 1979 (Part 4), 95th Cong., 2d sess., 1978, pp. 161–164.

[80]Sheilah Ocampo, "Angels of Death," *Far Eastern Economic Review*, 19 March 1982, p. 21.

[81]Catholic Institute for International Relations (CIIR), *British Investment and the Use of Paramilitary Terrorism in Plantation Agriculture in Agusan Del Sur, Philippines* (London: CIIR, August 1982), pp. 8–11; and Guy Sacerdoti and Sheilah Ocampo, "Guthrie and the Angels," *Far Eastern Economic Review*, 19 November 1982, p. 12.

[82]Ocampo, "Angels of Death," p. 21.

not only did little to stop the abuses of Lademora's "lost command" in Agusan del Sur, but used the unit on so-called anti-insurgency missions. Doubts about denials by officials of the Marcos regime of any links between Lademora's command and the government were intensified by an Amnesty International report that the group was reorganized as a Special Unit of the Armed Forces of the Philippines (SUAFP) in the spring of 1980[83] and by other reports indicating that, despite orders from General Fabian Ver to dismantle the group, Lademora remained unaffected because of connections with top military officials, who valued the unit's combat skills.[84]

Evidence from elsewhere suggests that, just as in the case of Lademora's unit, few, if any, of the "lost commands" operating in the Philippines could have existed without the tolerance, if not the official sanction, of the military and government. Equally disturbing, too, were indications that special military units, such as Task Force Kanlaon in Negros Occidental, and paramilitary units "composed of fanatical religious groups and criminals"[85] were engaged in "salvaging" on a widespread basis. Again the victims of such "salvagings" in the rural areas were typically peasants and tribal minorities.[86]

The Role of the Churches

Although the declaration of martial law was greeted optimistically by most of the Roman Catholic hierarchy and by most leaders of the Protestant churches composing the National Council of Churches in the Philippines (NCCP), a small minority of Catholic and Protestant church officials were skeptical from the beginning. Within a week of the issuance of Proclamation 1081, sixteen bishops and nine religious superiors, expressing concern over the use of coercion to bring about the New Society, asked the president (among other things) to ensure "that those detained for whatever reasons be dealt with fairly and justly in civil courts of law" and that "the innocent

[83]AI Mission, 1981, pp. 46–47.

[84]Ocampo, "Angels of Death," p. 22; and Sacerdoti and Ocampo, "Guthrie and the Angels," p. 59.

[85]Lawyers Committee Report, 1983, p. 31; AI Mission, 1981, pp. 43–46. See also *Political Detainees Update*, 30 November 1984, p. 1; and "Church, Human Rights Groups Urge Disarming of Paramilitary Units," *Philippine News and Features*, 29 April 1985, pp. 11–13.

[86]Interview with Catholic church officials in Davao City, 15 June 1979, and in Tagum, 18 June 1979; and *"Disappearances,"* p. 67.

[be] released as soon as possible."[87] In October 1973 Bishop Francisco Claver of Malaybalay alerted President Marcos to the widespread arrest of church activists in Bukidnon, including the jailing of Fr. Vincent Cullen, an American missionary who was an organizer of the Federation of Free Farmers (FFF) and a defender of the rights of tribal Manobos.[88] In February 1973 Bishop Claver informed Archbishop Teopisto Alberto, president of the CBCP that in Bukidnon

> tenant farmers have been ejected forcibly from land in disregard of orders from the President's office; men have been killed in jail even before their guilt could be investigated and established; land-grabbing of one sort or another still goes on; and worst of all, the military wink at these crimes, in some cases are themselves implicated—but on the side of injustices.[89]

Similar concerns were expressed by Bishop Antonino Nepomuceno of Cotabato the following June in a request to Archbishop Alberto that the CBCP take a position on martial law at its July 1973 meetings.[90] While the hierarchy remained divided on martial rule, numerous reports of mysterious disappearances, arbitrary jailings, and the torture of political prisoners, along with the arrest of priests, nuns, pastors, and laymen engaged in Catholic and Protestant church social action programs, resulted in more church leaders questioning martial law and asking for an accounting by the government.

In November 1973, the Major Religious Superiors issued the results of a nationwide survey of conditions under martial law which stated:

> There are no accurate estimates on the number of political prisoners, but all regions report there are some. They are generally accused of subversion. There are frequent reports of physical torture from all regions of the country.

[87]Letter to President Marcos from sixteen bishops and nine religious superiors, 28 September 1972, reprinted in "The Philippines: The Church and Martial Law," *International Documentation Project on the Future of the Missionary Enterprise*, Dossier no. 5 (Rome: IDOC International, 1973), pp. 45–46 (hereafter cited as "The Philippines: The Church and Martial Law").

[88]Letter to President Marcos from Bishop Francisco F. Claver, 4 October 1972, reprinted in "The Philippines: The Church and Martial Law," pp. 46–47.

[89]Letter to Archbishop Teopisto V. Alberto from Bishop Francisco F. Claver, 7 February 1973, reprinted in *IDOC Bulletin*, no. 6, April 1973, pp. 11–13. The letter was simultaneously sent to President Marcos.

[90]Letter to Archbishop Teopisto V. Alberto from Bishop Antonino F. Nepomuceno, 29 June 1973, reprinted in "The Philippines: The Church and Martial Law," pp. 57–58.

> The families and relatives of prisoners are kept under surveillance. Extortion money is asked of prisoners for their release in a number of regions.[91]

The report concluded that there was a lack of "safeguards in matters of arrest, detention, and trial."[92] The same month the NCCP organized an Ecumenical Ministry to Political Detainees and Their Families, while the AMRSP, in cooperation with the CBCP's Justice and Peace Commission, established the Church-Military Liaison Committee (CMLC), which included among its activities a monitoring of "arrest, searches, detention, [and] subversive activities."[93] These steps were followed in January 1974 with the creation of Task Force Detainees (TFD) by the AMRSP at its annual convention. Headquartered in Manila, TFD quickly became a key organization for assisting political prisoners through a national network of priests, nuns, and laymen who monitored prison and detention center conditions. Its initial objectives included (1) providing material and financial aid to prisoners and their families; (2) obtaining the charges (if any) against suspects and assisting in court proceedings and release; (3) protesting instances of torture to the authorities; and (4) publicizing the political detainee situation at home and abroad.[94]

The rationale for organizing TFD was echoed in April 1974 by a statement from the Second Mindanao-Sulu Pastoral Conference (MSPC II) that criticized the practice of detaining suspects "without charges and the benefit of counsel" and the use of "torture in violation of the U.N. Declaration of Human Rights." The Mindanao-Sulu clergy recommended that a Citizens' Committee for Justice and Peace be established in every diocese to "stimulate sensitivity to unjust acts" by government and military personnel.[95] During an interview with foreign journalists in November 1974, Cardinal Sin expressed "deep concern" over the "indefinite detention of prisoners" in the absence of formal charges and any "prospect of an early trial." He declared: "We cannot jail a man indefinitely and still call ourselves Christian." He also asked the government for "a clear-cut defini-

[91]"The Philippines: The Role of the Church under Martial Law—National Survey by the Major Religious Superiors," *IDOC Bulletin*, nos. 15–16, January–February 1974, p. 9.

[92]Ibid., p. 13.

[93]*Political Detainees*, Book 1, pp. 31–32; and minutes from Church-Military Liaison Committee Meeting no. 1, 26 November 1973, p. 2 (typewritten).

[94]The "operational guidelines" of TFD are contained in a letter "To All Major Superiors of Men and Women," 25 April 1974 (typewritten).

[95]Statement of the Second Mindanao-Sulu Pastoral Conference (MSPC II), Cagayan de Oro City, 28 March–1 April 1974, reprinted in *MSPC Communication*, July 1974, pp. 1–2.

tion of what subversion is," and lamented the military's unsatisfactory response to church inquiries into the deaths of Marsman Alverez, the brother of a prominent Marcos opponent residing in the United States, and Santiago Arce, a Catholic lay leader and an organizer for the FFF in Abra.[96] In response, Defense Minister Enrile wrote the archbishop a long letter avowing that charges were filed against all political prisoners, denying that the military erred in the Alverez and Arce cases, and saying that the Red Cross found Philippine detention centers satisfactory.[97] President Marcos reiterated the substance of Enrile's letter in an address to the nation in early December 1974. TFD refuted point by point the assertions of both Enrile and the president.[98]

Undesirable prison conditions prompted several hunger strikes in 1974–75, beginning with those of Eugenio Lopez, Jr., and Sergio Osmeña III in November 1974 and those of Frs. Edicio de la Torre and Manuel Lahoz in December 1974. The charges of de la Torre and Lahoz that detainees were frequently tortured gained international attention and led Cardinal Sin to suggest that a joint church-military investigation be conducted.[99] Although General Ramos declined Sin's offer, the priests' accusations of torture were confirmed by a nun with medical training and by a subsequent military investigation, resulting in the dismissal of thirty-seven soldiers and the initiation of pretrial hearings against five officers.[100] Such revelations of the maltreatment and torture of detainees drew sharp protests from church officials and organizations throughout the country. In January 1975, for example, Protestants underscored the plight of political prisoners (including several priests and pastors) at an Ecumenical Worship on Human Rights at Manila's Cosmopolitan church, and the Mindanao-Sulu Secretariat of Social Action (MISSSA) issued a manifesto against torture that was highly critical of the military. Two days later the Major Superiors published an open letter condemning the military's infliction of "bodily harm and indignities" on political prisoners. In June 1975, three thousand persons joined an ecumenical worship for those suffering under martial law, including political prisoners, at Manila Cathedral. In July 1975, the Citizens Council for Justice and Peace (CCJP) in Davao City, in connection with numerous

[96]"An Interview with Archbishop Sin of Manila," *Impact*, January 1975, pp. 21–24.

[97]Juan Ponce Enrile to Jaime Cardinal Sin, Quezon City, 30 November 1974, reprinted in *Impact*, January 1975, pp. 33–34.

[98]*Philippine Times*, 16–31 January 1975, pp. 1, 9, 11, 16, 17, 19.

[99]For the letters of Frs. de la Torre and Lahoz and Archbishop Sin, consult *IDOC Bulletin*, no. 27, January 1975, pp. 2–4; and *Various Reports*, 27 December 1975, pp. 4a–4f.

[100]*Various Reports*, 31 January 1975, pp. 20b–20d; and *New York Times*, 19 January 1975, p. 7, and 5 February 1975, p. 10.

mysterious "disappearances," denounced the existence of "nonorganic" military units that engaged in "tactical interrogation" (i.e., torture) at undisclosed "safehouses."[101]

Protests by individual clergy and by church organizations over the treatment of political prisoners and the state of the detention centers intensified in 1976 and continued to February 1986, when President Marcos was ousted from power. An important weapon of the detainees for publicizing prison conditions, as previously mentioned, was the fast or hunger strike. TFD supported these strikes, and the AMRSP through its circular, *Signs of the Times*, published the detainees' demands as well as refuted inaccuracies in the Manila press about the hunger strikes.[102] The AMRSP also released its first annual report on political detainees in March 1976, followed by similar reports in 1977, 1978, and 1981; in 1977 the AMRSP began publishing *Political Detainees Update* and *Quarterly Reports on Political Detainees*.[103] In addition, the contents of reports from Amnesty International in 1975 and 1981, the International Commission of Jurists in 1977 and 1983, the Lawyers Committee for International Human Rights in 1983 and 1985, and the American Committee for Human Rights in 1983 underscored the fact that all of these organizations received help from church groups, especially TFD, in the Philippines.[104]

Concern for political prisoners and their families continued and deepened through the efforts of church-based organizations such as Operation *Paglingap* (Caring) and the *Kapisanan Para sa Pagpapalaya at Amnestiya ng mga Detenido sa Pilipinas* (Association for the Release and Amnesty of Detainees in the Philippines, also known as *Kapatid* [Brother]), which began publishing a monthly newsletter, *Pahatid Kapatid* (*Kapatid* News) in

[101] *Political Detainees,* Book 1, pp. 35–40; and AMRSP, "Excerpts from Statements/ Liturgical Celebrations of Various Christian Organizations/Authorities on Martial Law in the Philippines," *Documentations*, 21 September 1975, pp. 16–33 (mimeographed).

[102] *Signs of the Times*, 2 January 1976, pp. 8–10; 20 February 1976, pp. 4–6; 19 March 1976, pp. 3–11; 16 April 1976, pp. 3–6; and 31 July 1976, pp. 10–15. See also note 44 for additional citations on the Bicutan fast.

[103] Harry M. Scoble and Laurie S. Wiseberg, *Freedom of Association for Human Rights Organizations* (Washington, D.C.: Human Rights Internet, 1981), p. 90.

[104] While neither of the AI studies nor the studies of the 1977 ICJ mission and of the 1983 American Committee for Human Rights mission acknowledge direct assistance from Philippine church groups, they all contain material similar, and in some cases virtually identical, to reports produced by the AMRSP's TFD. The 1977 trip of the ICJ to the Philippines and the publication of its report, however, was funded by the National Council of the Churches of Christ in the United States. Both the 1983 report by the ICJ and the 1983 and 1985 reports of the Lawyers Committee for International Human Rights acknowledge receiving assistance from clergy and religious organizations in the Philippines.

1980.[105] Church groups began to focus more attention in the late 1970s on an increase in militarization and on a concomitant rise of "disappearances" and "salvagings." Indications of this shift of focus were the additions of comprehensive sections covering military abuses in the 1977 and 1981 annual reports of the AMRSP, and the creation in July 1979 of the *Kilusan Para sa Katarungan at Kapayapaan* ([KKK] Movement for Justice and Peace) to monitor "growing militarization." The KKK's first study of military atrocities in five areas in the Philippines was confiscated by the military, but eventually was published by the World Council of Churches in Geneva.[106] Other church officials and groups were also critical of the rise of "disappearances" and "salvagings." Sr. Mariani Dimaranan, head of TFD, spoke out sharply in 1979 while in Europe and the United States against military atrocities, and TFD supplied statistics and information for the Philippine section of AI's 1981 study on "disappearances."[107] A growing number of bishops, including the conservative Antonio Mabutas, Archbishop of Davao, likewise raised their voices in reaction to reports of increasing military abuses, and the CBCP issued a pastoral letter in October 1979 condemning the rising tide of violence in the Philippines.[108]

The termination of martial law brought almost no change in the number of human rights violations. Persons continued to be arrested and detained as Public Order Violators (i.e., "subversives"); conditions in some stockades continued to be rated substandard; and incidents of "disappearances," "salvagings," and torture attributed to the military continued to occur with undiminished frequency. Accordingly, church efforts on behalf of political detainees and in defense of human rights continued unabated. Church organizations were at the forefront of the First National Conference on Human Rights held in February 1982,[109] and they were a large segment of

[105]Information on *Paglingap* was obtained in a private conversation with Senator Jovito R. Salonga, 12 April 1981; information on *Kapatid* was contained in an undated letter and brochure received from Rosario M. Pinguel in 1982.

[106]*IDOC Bulletin*, nos. 8, 9, 10, August, September, October 1980, p. 17. For the KKK study see the Commission of the Churches on International Affairs, *Iron Hand, Velvet Glove: Studies on Militarization in Five Critical Areas in the Philippines*, Background Information, 1980/2 (Geneva: Commission of the Churches on International Affairs, World Council of Churches, 1980).

[107]*Philippine Times*, 21–27 April and 28 April–4 May 1979, pp. 1, 6–7. Sr. Mariani was a participant in a seminar that served as a basis for AI's 1981 book *"Disappearances."*

[108]Pastoral letter of Archbishop Antonio Ll. Mabutas, 16 August 1979, reprinted in *MSPC Communications*, October 1979, pp. 14–15; and "Exhortation against Violence," 7 October 1979, reprinted in *The Bishops Speak (1968–1983)*, ed. Richard P. Hardy (Quezon City: Maryhill School of Theology, 1984), pp. 207–212.

[109]*Political Detainees Update*, 28 February 1982, p. 3.

the Philippine Coalition for Human Rights (PCHR), which held a series of annual conferences after 1981 reviewing the human rights situation in the Philippines.[110] By 1984, TFD comprised a force of well over one hundred persons, the majority of whom were full-time workers, and counted "more than 40 units in the regional centers of Luzon, Visayas and Mindanao."[111] Individual members of the clergy also continued to publicize human rights violations and to participate in the establishment of new groups, such as the *Samahan ng mga Ex-detainee Laban sa Detensyon at Para sa Amnestiya* ([SELDA] Association of Ex-Detainees against Detention and for Amnesty), an organization of ex-detainees formed March 1985, to assist political detainees and their families.[112] The CBCP likewise issued two pastoral letters, one in 1983 and another in 1984, deploring the high incidences of violence, the lack of due process in arrests and jailings, and the maltreatment of detainees.[113] And in January 1986, drawing on data from a number of Philippine human rights organizations, the World Council of Churches published a report on a wide range of human rights violations, such as torture, disappearances, extrajudicial killings, and hamletization, still being committed by the Marcos government.[114]

The Response of the Regime

Government reaction to criticism about the treatment of political prisoners remained muted until late 1974. Yet behind the scenes several generals complained at CMLC meetings about the release of the Major Superiors' 1973 survey and the publication of MSPC II's 1974 statement on martial law. Although recognizing the church's right to preach the gospel, the generals argued that church officials should seek "consultation" with the military so that church statements on martial law would have "a little

[110]*Political Detainees Update*, 15 August 1982, pp. 1, 6; 31 August 1982, pp. 3–5; and 31 March 1983, pp. 6–7.

[111]*Political Detainees Update*, 15 January 1984, p. 5. Ross H. Munro, in "The New Khmer Rouge," *Commentary*, December 1985, p. 22, estimated that by late 1985 TFD operated on a large budget and maintained a staff of 280.

[112]*Political Detainees Update*, 15 March 1985, p. 8.

[113]"A Dialogue for Peace," 20 February 1983, reprinted in *The Bishops Speak (1968–1983)*, pp. 232–238; and "Let There Be Life," Tagaytay City, 11 July 1984 (mimeographed).

[114]Commission of the Churches on International Affairs, *Philippines: Testimonies on Human Rights Violations*, Background Information, 1986/1 (Geneva: Commission of the Churches on International Affairs, World Council of Churches, 1986).

more balance."[115] Following Cardinal Sin's interview with foreign correspondents in November 1974, however, the regime began defending more openly its treatment of political prisoners. As indicated previously, in a letter to Cardinal Sin, Enrile essentially exonerated the military of wrongdoing in the handling of prisoners and, like the generals, asked the archbishop to check with the Ministry of National Defense before speaking publicly on prisoner problems. Marcos, in an address to the nation in December 1974, ordered the release of 622 detainees, claiming that none were tortured.[116]

Within a month of the president's speech, after the hunger strikes of Frs. de la Torre and Lahoz established that torture was indeed inflicted on some detainees, reports of the punishment of abusive officers and soldiers began to appear more frequently. In January 1975, for example, the Ministry of National Defense announced the disciplining of 14 soldiers (out of 32) charged with abusing detainees. In June 1976 another 20 military men were ordered court-martialed for mistreating prisoners. Then in October 1976, Marcos announced that 2,700 members of the armed forces had been reprimanded for mistreating prisoners under martial law; a month later, he stated that 19 officers and 308 troopers were removed for misconduct, including abuse of prisoners, and that since September 1972 a total of 1,604 military personnel had been dismissed.[117] Similarly, in May 1977, Marcos ordered courts-martial for the alleged torturers of Trinidad Herrera, and the following year he revealed that by the end of June 1977, "2,083 members of the Philippine armed forces had been dismissed from the service and penalized for various abuses, including the torture and maltreatment of detainees. Of this number, 322 were also sentenced to disciplinary punishment."[118] In March 1979, Deputy Defense Minister Barbero, the person in charge of civilian relations in the ministry, disclosed that by December 1978 citizen complaints lodged against the military since the beginning of martial law totaled 4,512, resulting in the discharge of 2,917 officers and men. Another 704 were "reinstated on review and demoted," while the remaining 891 cases were pending.[119] In September 1982, during a state visit to the United States, Marcos admitted that 7,000 soldiers had

[115]Minutes from Church-Military Liaison Committee Meetings no. 2, 18 December 1973, pp. 1–4, and no. 7, 24 May 1974, pp. 1–27 (typewritten).

[116]*Bulletin Today*, 12 December 1974, p. 1; and *Impact*, January 1975, pp. 33–34.

[117]ICJ Report, 1977, p. 39; and AI Mission, 1975, p. 85.

[118]Ferdinand E. Marcos, *Five Years of the New Society* (n.p., Ferdinand E. Marcos, 1978), pp. 26–27.

[119]Richard Vokey, "Alarmed, Angry and Sick at Heart," *Far Eastern Economic Review*, 16 March 1979, p. 28.

been released from the armed forces since 1972 for misconduct.[120] Barbero later stated that of the 7,140 military personnel separated from the armed forces between September 1972 and May 1982,

> 1,145 were found guilty of *abuse of authority* (806 of these are for maltreatment/infliction of physical injuries); 1,930 for absence without official leave (AWOL); 532 for illegal discharge of firearms/indiscriminate firing (alarm and scandal without direct victims); 189 for drunkenness while on duty; 349 for immorality; 173 for illegal possession of firearms/explosives; 649 for murder/homicide (non-service-connected); and 2,173 for other offenses like estafa, non-payment of debts, non-support of dependents and the like.[121]

In addition to disciplining abusive military personnel and to ordering the release of large numbers of detainees, Marcos and Defense Ministry officials periodically announced other measures designed to ease the political prisoner problem. As early as the second CMLC meeting in December 1973, General Ramos assured church representatives that strict procedures guaranteeing all constitutional rights were followed in arresting and detaining suspects in accordance with General Order 2.[122] Three years later, while commenting on the AMRSP's 1976 report on political detainees, an aide to Barbero stated that commanders were now being made responsible for the misdeeds of subordinates. As an additional restraint on military misconduct, Enrile announced in October 1976 the termination of nighttime and weekend arrests (except, significantly, in cases of "subversion and other crimes against national security"). In February 1977 the Office of Detainees Affairs was created in the Defense Ministry to oversee the welfare of political prisoners.[123] In June 1977, expressing chagrin over the sluggishness of military justice, Marcos ordered a gradual phasing out of the military tribunals; in November 1977, he issued Letter of Instruction 621 to Minister Enrile outlining new procedures to protect the rights of persons arrested and jailed under martial law.[124] The president took another step toward "normalization" in December 1978 by restoring criminal

[120]*Asiaweek*, 1 October 1982, p. 31.

[121]Carmelo Z. Barbero, deputy minister of defense for civilian relations, to Thomas Hammerberg, secretary general, Amnesty International, 23 March 1983, p. 12, AI index: ASA 35/18/83.

[122]Minutes from Church-Military Liaison Committee Meeting no. 2, 18 December 1973, pp. 1–4, and attachment, "Arrest, Search, and Seizure," pp. 1–4 (typewritten).

[123]*Philippine Times*, 16–31 May 1976, p. 1; FBIS, 27 October 1976, p. P1; and *Political Detainees*, Book 2, p. 49.

[124]*Bulletin Today*, 4 June 1977, pp. 1, 5; FBIS, 3 June 1977, p. P1; and FBIS, 3 November 1977, p. P2.

jurisdiction to civil courts with LOI 772 and by establishing stricter guidelines for the issuance of Arrest, Search, and Seizure Orders (ASSOs).[125] In March 1979 both Enrile and Barbero reiterated a commitment to punish abusive military personnel and to deny promotion to lax commanders. And in December 1980, Marcos, in what the regime termed a humanitarian gesture, approved a two peso increase in the daily food allowance of political detainees.[126]

Marcos and other high government officials attacked domestic and international critics of the government's handling of detainees, and repeatedly underscored the regime's commitment to human rights and to the humanitarian treatment of prisoners. In response to the 1976 AI report, for instance, Enrile claimed that allegations of brutality were "highly exaggerated" and that most of those interviewed were "hardcore leaders and members of the Communist Party of the Philippines." In October 1976, Marcos asserted that instances of torture were infrequent and that such allegations were often nothing more than a defense strategy of suspects charged with murder and rebellion.[127] Similarly, in August 1977, Marcos defended the government's human rights record following the release of the ICJ report; in August 1978, he labeled the regime's foreign critics (especially American) as "moral imperialists." In December 1980, he even maintained that human rights violations in the Philippines were just "imagined" by some U.S. congressmen. At the same time, the president repeatedly stressed, especially after 1975, that all detainees were criminally charged (but he nevertheless periodically ordered the release of prisoners without charges), that there were no political prisoners in the Philippines (i.e., prisoners of conscience), and that martial law was established to protect civil liberties.[128]

That the reaction of the regime to criticism of human rights abuses remained essentially unchanged after the lifting of martial law was underscored by the publication of AI's 1982 report. When asked about the report during an official visit to the United States in September 1982, Marcos "conceded there had been 'some cases' of torture" and misconduct by the military, but at the same time, he maintained that AI's study was distorted

[125]FBIS, 8 December 1978, p. P1.

[126]Vokey, "Alarmed, Angry and Sick at Heart," p. 28; and *Pahatid Kapatid*, November–December 1981, p. 2.

[127]AI Mission, 1975, p. 59; and FBIS, 18 October 1976, p. P1.

[128]FBIS, 2 August 1977, p. P1; Rodney Tasker, "Marcos Courts His Critics," *Far Eastern Review*, 2 September 1977, pp. 20–21; FBIS, 29 August 1978, p. P1; and FBIS, 15 December 1980, p. P1.

and that those guilty of abuses were punished.[129] Other government officials reacted even more strongly to the report. Enrile accused AI of having "Marxist leanings,"[130] while Barbero, in the government's official response to AI, branded the report "a masterpiece of black propaganda and deception on a grand-scale" and suggested that the 11–28 November 1981 mission to the Philippines was influenced by the Communist Party of the Philippines (CPP).[131] Later, evidently in response to the 1983 publication of the report of the Lawyers Committee for International Human Rights, Enrile stated that much of the information was part of the propaganda effort of the Communists and that TFD itself was a front organization of the CPP.[132]

The regime's record on reducing abuses by the military and its rhetoric on human rights received careful scrutiny from a number of quarters. The ICJ mission's 1977 analysis of Defense Ministry records demonstrated a lack of "any reference to certain officers whose names repeatedly appear in interviews with detainees who claim to have been tortured," as well as a pattern of light sentences for military personnel found guilty of torture.[133] A review of data presented by Marcos in 1978 on cases against officers and soldiers accused of abuses, including torture and murder, revealed a similar pattern of leniency. From a total of seventy-nine cases, only one-third (twenty-seven) of the investigations were completed. All but three of the fifty guilty soldiers received mild punishment, with the stiffest sentences being six months at hard labor and dismissal from the service. Those punished were involved in only six (22 percent) of the twenty-seven completed investigations; the other twenty-one cases (78 percent) ended with no convictions. Although a number of officers were implicated in several of the seventy-nine cases, none above the rank of lieutenant were among those receiving punishment more severe than an administrative reprimand.[134] Similarly, Michael Posner, a member of the seventeen-day AI mission to the Philippines in 1981, claimed there was no evidence in Philippine military reports "that showed anyone dismissed because of human rights violations."[135] Additional reports showed that abusive soldiers frequently

[129]*New York Times*, 23 September 1982, p. 10.

[130]FBIS, October 1982, p. P1.

[131]Barbero to Hammerberg, 23 March 1983, pp. 1, 23.

[132]Lawyers Committee Report, 1983, p. 39; and *Political Detainees Update*, 30 April 1984, p. 9.

[133]ICJ Report, 1977, p. 39.

[134]Marcos, *Five Years of the New Society*, Appendix B, pp. 205–221; and Casalmo, *The Vision of a New Society*, pp. 23–28.

[135]*Matchbox*, November 1982, pp. 1–2, 13.

were merely transferred to assignments elsewhere; still others, though dismissed for maltreating detainees, apparently continued to serve the military in investigative capacities.[136] Thus Marcos' pronouncements on the humane treatment of detainees and the adherence to high standards of human rights were, in many cases, unable to withstand close examination. Contrary to government protestations, abuses of political prisoners appeared to be more of a pattern than isolated aberrations attributable to a few undisciplined troops.

The repeated arrest, detention, and mistreatment of political prisoners reflected a number of crosscurrents in Philippine society. One of the currents was an ambivalence—perhaps a cultural duality—on the part of the regime toward human rights. To be sure, the regime periodically released large numbers of detainees, announced the disciplining of abusive military personnel, improved conditions in some stockades (as a result of protests), and allowed international missions, such as the Red Cross, Amnesty International, the International Commission of Jurists, and the Lawyers Committee for International Human Rights, to investigate prison conditions. Yet at the same time, the implementation of human rights and political prisoner policies appeared half-hearted or otherwise flawed. At the August 1977 meeting of the World Law Conference in Manila, for instance, the president announced that he was "granting amnesty to all persons found guilty of subversion and who had committed crimes against public order"; concomitantly the conference's standing orders declared that "no pamphlet, printed or written materials of a political nature shall be circulated, issued or supplied to any person . . . without the prior approval of the Center Executive Committee."[137] Similarly, Deputy Defense Minister Barbero admitted that "a lot of unnecessary cruelty" had resulted from martial law, declaring that military abuses "make us sick at heart."[138] The record demonstrated, however, that the withdrawal of abusive military units from troubled areas was infrequent and done with obvious reluctance; and indeed replacement units were often just as abusive. At times Marcos and Enrile seemed to welcome criticism from the United States and from the Catholic and Protestant churches, only to lash out sharply on other occasions at State Department reports on human rights and to imprison (or otherwise harass)

[136]*Pumipiglas*, pp. 96–117.

[137]FBIS, 23 August 1977, p. P1; and Manila Conference on the Law of the World, Manila, Philippines, 21–26 August 1977, *Program*, p. 36.

[138]Vokey, "Alarmed, Angry and Sick at Heart," p. 28.

clergy critical of the regime.[139] In moving to terminate martial rule, as part of a normalization process, Marcos not only retained most of his emergency powers, but also expanded the coverage of the ASSO under fifty-two general categories to include crimes considered "pernicious and inimical to social and economic stability."[140] Marcos subsequently introduced the Presidential Commitment Order and Preventive Detention Action.

That these obvious contradictions apparently caused little consternation among government and military leaders was at least partially attributable to what Jaime Bulatao identifies as a "split-level" cultural phenomenon, which permits many Filipinos to evince contradictory conceptual and behavioral patterns without any (or very little) internal conflict. The phenomenon exists elsewhere in the world, yet Bulatao argues it is particularly prevalent in the Philippines as a legacy of simultaneous colonization and Christianization where foreign attitudes and behaviors, often learned in a foreign language, lack clear roots in the indigenous culture. Although it is important to pay homage publicly to the abstract, foreign principles, the inconsistency of violating them in practice "is either not perceived at all, or is pushed into the rear portions of consciousness."[141] Thus split-leveling allows for a Western conceptualization of human rights to exist side by side with an indigenous imperative to demonstrate group solidarity and obey authority, resulting in the coexistence of public assertions of humane treatment of political detainees and the absence of strong measures to punish violators, who may be members of closely knit military units under orders to catch "subversives."

Other crosscurrents contributing to repeated violations of human rights, including the harsh treatment of political prisoners, were differences among high government and military officials about how best to handle the problem of "subversion" and the tendency of local commanders to protect abusive officers and troops in order to retain the loyalty and esprit de corps of the unit. For some time, reports persisted about rivalries between moderates and hardliners in the defense establishment. Moderates included the Minister of Defense Juan Ponce Enrile and his former deputy, Carmelo

[139]Rodney Tasker, "Marcos Has His Day on Human Rights," *Far Eastern Economic Review*, 17 June 1977, pp. 11–12; Juan Ponce Enrile, "AFP's Role during the Transition Period," *NCCP Newsletter*, September–October 1979, pp. 5–6; and *Political Detainees*, Book 3, p. 2.

[140]FBIS, 18 November 1980, p. P1.

[141]Jaime Bulatao, "Split-Level Christianity," in Jaime Bulatao and Vitaliano R. Gorospe, *Split-Level Christianity and Christian Renewal of Filipino Values* (Quezon City: Ateneo de Manila University, 1966), pp. 1–18.

Barbero, along with General Fidel Ramos, acting chief of staff in 1984–85. The hardliners included General Fabian Ver, director general of the National Intelligence and Security Authority (NISA) and until his indictment in connection with the Aquino assassination, chief of staff (1981–84). The hardliners demonstrated sufficient power and influence to continue using harsh interrogation methods, including torture, on political prisoners and to thwart attempts by moderates from responding effectively to complaints about abuses of detainees, prison conditions, and human rights violations. Additionally, the hardliners were bolstered by the fact that the moderates, while professing high human rights standards, nevertheless expressed dissatisfaction with domestic criticism of the regime that was not first cleared through military channels.[142]

The punishment of abusive troops was further complicated at the provincial level by group solidarity within local military units, a fear of reprisals from discharged soldiers, and the prevalence of overlapping military jurisdictions in security cases. The head of the Justice and Peace Office of the Catholic church in Tagum, Davao del Norte, maintained in June 1979 that the armed forces were frequently unwilling to investigate charges of misconduct involving more than a single officer or soldier; he cited numerous cases, including the four farmers killed by the military on October 1978. The military, of course, disagreed. For instance, while contending that abusive troops in the 432nd PC Command in Tagum were appropriately disciplined, Colonel Teofilo Bulosan, the provincial commander, claimed at a CMLC meeting in February 1979 that he was considered too "pro-civilian" and was "already a subject for liquidation" by discharged soldiers, indicating the dangers associated with prosecuting abusive military personnel. Bulosan also lamented an inability to control the activities of other units operating in the Tagum area; as has been mentioned in the case of the four murdered farmers, the colonel only "recommended" disciplinary action against the three CSU soldiers involved in the killings, because they were part of another command.[143] Although church officials and human rights groups felt the lack of authority argument was disingenuous, the net effect was to condone (however unofficially and indirectly) the existence of abusive military units (such as the "lost command" of Col.

[142]U.S. Congress, House, Committee on International Relations, *Human Rights in the Philippines: Report by Amnesty International, Hearings before the Subcommittee on International Organizations*, 94th Cong., 2d sess., 15 September 1976, pp. 2–19.

[143]Interview with a church official for the Justice and Peace Office, Prelature of Tagum, 18 June 1979; and "Minutes of CMLC Meeting held at PC Headquarters, Tagum Davao on February 15, 1979 from 3:00–5:00 P.M.," pp. 1–8 (mimeographed).

Lademora and the CHDF group that in 1985 murdered Fr. Tullio Favali, an Italian missionary), and to reinforce the political power of the hardliners in the military.[144]

Conflict between the Marcos regime and the Catholic and Protestant churches over increased militarization and the jailing of large numbers of political dissenters was also accompanied by criticism among church leaders not only with the declaration of martial law itself, but also with many of the economic and political reforms associated with Marcos' "revolution from the center." Chapter 7 examines the varied reaction within the Catholic and Protestant churches to the imposition of martial rule and to the handling of the economy and the electoral process from 1972 to 1986.

[144]AI Mission, 1981, pp. 17–18; and "The Death of Tullio Favali, PIME," and "Condemning the Assassination of Fr. Favali," *Simbayan* 4 (March 1985): 18–19, 35.

7

The "Revolution from the Center" and the Philippine Churches

The initial reaction in 1972 of the hierarchies of the Catholic and Protestant churches to the declaration of martial law and the creation of the New Society was generally positive. Many church leaders accepted without question President Marcos' analysis of the various threats to the republic as well as evinced enthusiasm for proposed socioeconomic and political reforms of the "revolution from the center." The silence of the vast majority of church leaders over the loss of civil liberties and freedoms, along with the lack of concern over the growth of the military and the centralization of government control, underscored the basic conservatism of both Catholic and Protestant churches in the Philippines. Typical of the reaction of supportive Catholic and Protestant officials were statements by the Administrative Council of the Catholic Bishops' Conference of the Philippines (CBCP), headed by Teopisto V. Alberto, the conservative archbishop of Caceres, and Bishop Estanislao Q. Abainza, general secretary of the United Church of Christ in the Philippines (UCCP). The CBCP Administrative Council stated that "the Bishops of the Philippines recognize the right and duty of civil authorities to take appropriate steps to protect the sovereignty of the state and to insure the peace and prosperity of the nation," and called upon the faithful "to remain calm and law-abiding" and "to pray earnestly" for the "country's leaders and the Filipino people."[1] Bishop

[1]Reprinted in Felix Casalmo (pseud.), *The Vision of a New Society* (Manila, 1980), pp. 249–250. Although the statement was circulated under the auspices of the CBCP, it was approved only by the conference's Administrative Council, 27 September 1972, and not by the entire CBCP membership.

Abainza praised the "enforced discipline" of the New Society and enjoined Filipinos not to "minimize" the "positive effects" of martial law.[2]

Other conservative church leaders were equally enthusiastic. In November 1972, for instance, Rufino Cardinal Santos, the archbishop of Manila (1953–73), stated that the declaration of martial law and "the establishment of a New Society in our beloved country . . . should be hailed and welcomed by every peace-loving citizen" and that he was "fully in accord" with Marcos' "concern for . . . the restoration of peace and order and for the moral renewal and complete development of our people."[3] Similarly, in January 1975 during a speech delivered at Malacañang Palace at the investiture of Msgr. Domingo Nebres as a domestic prelate of the pope, Archbishop Alberto defended the Marcos regime as the "legitimate constitutional government to which every citizen is bound to render respectful allegiance"; he further maintained that there was "no doubt" that the "present political administration" was working for "the common good." Throughout the speech Alberto stressed the need for loyalty and obedience to the government and concluded by saying that "the habitual attitude of the loyal citizen is that of sympathetic faith not that of criticality and distrust."[4]

Catholic and Protestant church officials nonethless were not united in their attitudes toward martial law and the inauguration of the New Society. Even though the clergy agreed with the regime's stated goals of improving social justice and bettering the lot of the poor through economic development, significant minorities of clergy and layworkers in both denominations questioned the morality of martial law and the efficacy of the policies of the Marcos government. From the beginning of martial rule the president gave activist Catholics and Protestants cause for concern by harassing, jailing, and deporting priests, nuns, pastors, and layworkers engaged in social action programs sponsored by the churches and by allowing the military to raid church establishments suspected of being used for antigovernment activities or of harboring "subversives."[5]

Within a week of the proclamation of martial rule a group of progressive Catholic bishops and religious superiors issued a letter questioning the creation of a "new society" by "force" and "fiat," and asked that (1) basic civil liberties be restored; (2) political prisoners be tried "fairly and justly in

[2]As quoted in Barbara Howell, "Martial Law in the Philippines: Religious Reactions," *Christian Century*, 22 November 1972, pp. 1200–1202.

[3]Rufino J. Cardinal Santos, "The Church and the New Society," *Philippine Priests' Forum* 4 (December 1972): 11.

[4]Reprinted in *Philippine Priests' Forum* 7 (March 1975): 44–46.

[5]Howell, "Martial Law in the Philippines," pp. 1200–1202; and Rolando Yu and Mario Bolasco, *Church-State Relations* (Manila: St. Scholastica's College, 1981), p. 98.

civil courts of law"; and (3) martial law be limited to "a few months at the most."[6] A month and a half later, in November 1972, leaders of the AMRSP wrote Marcos expressing concern about "a general climate of uncertainty" resulting from "the sudden promulgation" and "uneven application" of regulations emanating from a "highly centralized" and "secret" decision-making process that permitted "no recourse."[7] A minority of Protestant church officials also expressed doubts about the efficacy of martial law,[8] while the Christians for National Liberation (CNL), which, as indicated in Chapter 4, was forced underground by the declaration of martial rule, advocated outright opposition to the Marcos regime through an intensification of the people's war.[9]

The apprehensions of the progressive Catholic bishops and religious superiors as well as the expressions of concern by Protestant officials were a harbinger of the regime's relationships with church progressives throughout the martial law period and after. Between 1973 and 1984, as discussed in Chapter 5, raids against church institutions averaged two a year, resulting in the closure of church radio stations and publications and the harassment and arrest of church personnel. Periodically after 1972 the so-called Christian-Left was attacked in the Marcos-controlled media, while clarifications and rebuttals from officials of both denominations were largely ignored.[10] Generally church activists responded defiantly toward government actions against church organizations and personnel, continually speaking out against military abuses of civilians, the jailing of persons for "subversion" in the absence of evidence, irregularities in the periodic referenda and elections, and the refusal of the government to restore basic freedoms. The same cannot be said of conservatives and moderates within the Catholic and Protestant churches, who, until the late 1970s, with few exceptions, were either supportive of the Marcos regime or only engaged in mild criticism of government policies that threatened vital church interests.

[6]Reprinted in Casalmo, *The Vision of a New Society*, pp. 251–253.

[7]AMRSP letter to President Marcos, 10 November 1972, as quoted in Yu and Bolasco, *Church-State Relations*, p. 99.

[8]Richard Deats, "Philippine Church-State Struggle Intensifies," *Christian Century*, 4 June 1975, pp. 574–576; and Cirilo A. Rigos, "The Posture of the Church in the Philippines under Martial Law," in *Southeast Asian Affairs, 1975*, ed. Institute of Southeast Asian Affairs (Singapore: FEP International, 1975), pp. 127–132.

[9]CNL, "Statement of Position," reprinted in "The Philippines: The Church and Martial Law," *International Documentation Project on the Future of the Missionary Enterprise*, Dossier no. 5 (Rome: IDOC International, 1973), pp. 47–49.

[10]Consult *Philippines Daily Express*, 9 September 1976, pp. 1, 6; 10 September 1976, pp. 1, 11; 11 September 1976, pp. 1, 9; 12 September 1976, pp. 1, 12; and 13 September 1976, pp. 1–2.

The desire to remain above "politics" and avoid conflict with the established authorities—historically a key policy of the Roman Catholic church—was reflected in support for martial law by the conservative mainstream of the Catholic and Protestant churches in the Philippines. That such a stance met with the approval of Rome is substantiated by evidence from the early years of martial law which indicated that elements within the Holy See often sided with conservatives in the CBCP against priests and nuns engaged in social justice activities considered "political" by the Marcos regime. In April 1975, for example, Arturo Cardinal Tabera, prefect of the Sacred Congregation for Religious and Secular Institutes, in a letter sent through Apostolic Nuncio Bruno Torpigliani (who was viewed by many as pro-Marcos), criticized the Executive Board of the AMRSP for "an almost exclusively socio-political emphasis" in its activities that tended "to obscure the spiritual ideal of apostolic religious life."[11] A year later, in October 1976, Sebastiano Cardinal Baggio, prefect of the Sacred Congregation for Bishops, in a letter addressed to Julio Cardinal Rosales, the conservative archbishop of Cebu, who, before his death in 1983, was considered close to Mrs. Marcos, admonished the association's leadership for its absorption in "activities of a socio-political character" that resulted in damaging good "relations between the Church and civil authorities."[12] Both letters also suggested that the association was uncooperative with the hierarchy and was thus responsible for engendering disunity within the Philippine Catholic church. The AMRSP justified its actions by citing numerous church documents exhorting the clergy to work for greater social justice, and underscored the fact that the bishops themselves were divided on what constituted undue political involvement in preaching the gospel. The AMRSP Executive Board, moreover, received the backing of a number of progressive bishops.[13]

Rome's support for the conservatives and in the CBCP desire to avoid antagonizing the Marcos regime was obvious. The papal nuncio never consulted the AMRSP Executive Board concerning disgruntlement about its leadership—reportedly because of the "delicate nature" of the information—before informing the Holy See, prompting Cardinal Tabera's letter.[14]

[11]Letter reprinted in Casalmo, *The Vision of a New Society*, pp. 297–298.

[12]Sebastiano Cardinal Baggio to Julio Cardinal Rosales, president of the CBCP, 25 October 1976 (typewritten).

[13]AMRSP Executive Boards, "To All Major Religious Superiors of Men and Women in the Philippines, June 24, 1975," (mimeographed); and Casalmo, *The Vision of a New Society*, pp. 293–296.

[14]AMRSP Executive Boards, "Minutes of the Meeting of the Members of the AMRSP Executive Boards with the Apostolic Nuncio," 10 May 1975, p. 3 (mimeographed).

Also, while on "unofficial" trips to the Philippines in 1977 and 1978, Cardinal Baggio met conspicuously with government officials. During the 1978 visit, for instance, he, along with Archbishop Torpigliani and Cardinal Rosales, joined President and Mrs. Marcos and other government dignitaries for the inauguration of "a minor basilica in Agoo, La Union, the home town of the Minister of Tourism." It was significant, as Casalmo points out, that the transformation of the Agoo church into the basilica cost millions of pesos at a time when the Philippines' annual per capita GNP was less than $500.[15]

Prior to the termination of martial law, conservative and moderate Catholic bishops, as well as Protestant leaders, failed to protest strongly the deportation of foreign missionaries engaged in social justice work among urban squatters and rural peasants. It is true that some of the missionaries were identified with leftist groups, allegedly with links to the Communist Party of the Philippines (CPP), and that other missionaries requested they be allowed to depart quietly. Such was certainly not the case, however, in the expulsion of Fr. Edward Gerlock, an American Maryknoll priest. Typical of the reaction of conservative and moderate bishops was a letter to Gerlock's mother from Cardinal Sin defending his (and the church's) inaction in behalf of her son. Although praising Gerlock's work among the poor, the cardinal stated that had he "chosen to engage the government in a direct confrontation, the consequences would have been dire. The Government could have ordered all Churches closed and all priests arrested, and all religious activities could have been suspended." Thus, he said, "for the sake of the Church in the Philippines . . . I chose to keep silence."[16] Sin's letter reiterated the low profile of conservatives and moderates in general on the expulsion issue; as such, it was in consonance with some conservatives' willingness to accept the assurance of President Marcos that "due process although summary" was followed in the deportation cases.

Progressive Catholic bishops and Protestant leaders consistently spoke out against the ejection of foreign missionaries but were largely unsuccessful in persuading their respective hierarchies to take a firm, united stand.[17] Following the termination of martial law in 1981, however, Cardinal Sin, along with other moderate bishops and religious leaders, began to protest more vocally against the regime's attempts to deport priests engaged in social justice work. This was clearly the case in the church's successful

[15]Casalmo, *The Vision of a New Society*, pp. 230–231.
[16]Jaime Cardinal Sin to Mrs. Angela C. Gerlock, 15 August 1977 (typewritten).
[17]Casalmo, *The Vision of a New Society*, pp. 254–257.

effort in getting the government to reverse its decisions in the deportation of Fr. D. Edward Shellito in June 1981 and the denial of reentry to Fr. Ralph Kroes in 1981.[18] Moreover, as we have seen, Sin was instrumental in preventing the deportation of Fr. Brian Gore in March 1983 and played a key behind-the-scenes role in the government's decision in July 1984 to drop the murder charges against Gore, O'Brien, Dangan, and six lay leaders accused in the March 1982 murder of Pablo Sola, the mayor of Kabankalan, Negros Occidental.[19]

Economic Reforms and the Church

From the outset of martial law, Marcos' resort to authoritarianism as a vehicle for imposing political order and for centralizing the regime's control as a means for bringing about greater social justice and economic development was questioned by activist clergy and layworkers.[20] Yet until the economic crisis of 1984, President Marcos seldom missed an opportunity to extol the economic accomplishments of the New Society. To be sure, as Table 6 demonstrates, Marcos was able to point to a number of significant economic achievements of the regime during eight years of martial rule, especially in the areas of GNP expansion, tax collection, infrastructure construction, export promotion, and rice and corn production. The expansion of the GNP, which increased from ₱55.5 billion in 1972 to ₱265.0 billion in 1980, was matched by an expansion in tax collection from ₱5.8 billion to ₱35.9 billion and an increase in the national budget from ₱7.0 billion to ₱55.0 billion. Concomitantly, exports earnings rose from $1.1 billion to $5.8 billion, while rice and corn production rose from 5.1 and 2.0 million metric tons, respectively, to 7.7 and 3.2 million metric tons. In the area of infrastructure construction, land brought under irrigation expanded by 548,000 hectares and additional roadways increased by 61,162 kilometers between 1972 and the termination of martial law.

Many of the accomplishments Marcos claimed for the New Society, however, were open to dispute on statistical grounds as well as in terms of the actual effects of the programs. Among the successes of the regime that Marcos recounted in *Proclamation 2045* at the termination of martial rule were holding the unemployment rate to 4.5 percent, increasing annual per

[18]See Chapter 4.

[19]See Alfred W. McCoy, *Priests on Trial* (Ringwood, Victoria: Penguin Books Australia, 1984), pp. 230–231.

[20]Yu and Bolasco, *Church-State Relations*, pp. 99–102.

Table 6. Selected indicators of economic progress under martial law, 1972 and 1980

Indicators[a]	*1972*	*1980*
GNP	₱55.5 billion	₱265.0 billion
Budget (national & local)	₱7.0 billion	₱55.0 billion
Tax collection	₱5.8 billion	₱35.9 billion
Exports	$1.1 billion	$5.8 billion
GNP per capita	₱1,428.0	₱5,484.0
Agricultural production (thousand metric tons)		
Palay	5,100	7,646
Corn	2,018	3,185
Agrarian reform		
Land transfer certificates issued	423	478,000
Tenant recipients	423	366,972
Hectares	682	571,784
Infrastructure Program		
Total irrigated land	780,000 ha.	1,328,000 ha
Total road kilometerage	90,756	151,918

[a]Figures in current prices.

Sources: Philippines (Republic), National Economic and Development Authority (NEDA), *1981 Philippine Development Report* (Manila: NEDA, 1982), pp. 2–6; and *The Philippines: Facts and Issues, January 1981* (Manila: Ministry of Information and the National Media Production Center, 1981), Appendix.

capita income from $214 to $755, advancing nutritional and health conditions, and improving housing opportunities.[21] Each of these claims was challenged, frequently with the regime's own statistics, not only by progressive clergy, whose analysis was bolstered by papal encyclicals and by CBCP pastoral letters calling for greater social justice, but by knowledgeable Filipino and American scholars as well.[22] Even accepting the government's figures on unemployment, although there is good evidence they were manipulated,[23] the president's statement only gave a partial picture of

[21]*Proclamation 2045*, 17 January 1981, in *Philippine News*, 21–27 January 1981, pp. 1, A.

[22]See, for example, Richard P. Hardy, ed., *The Philippine Bishops Speak (1968–1983)* (Quezon City: Maryhill School of Theology, 1984), pp. 52–77, 173–200; Jose V. Abueva, "Ideology and Practice in the 'New Society,'" in *Marcos and Martial Law in the Philippines*, ed. David A. Rosenberg (Ithaca: Cornell University Press, 1979), pp. 32–84; and Robert B. Stauffer, "The Political Economy of Refeudalization," in Rosenberg, pp. 180–218.

[23]In Appendix 2 (p. 88), Emmanuel S. De Dios et al., *An Analysis of the Philippine Economic Crisis: A Workshop Report* (Quezon City: University of the Philippines Press, 1984), point out that government statistics on unemployment were calculated on the assump-

the condition of Philippine labor in 1980: Additional statistics demonstrated that underemployment accounted for more than 20 percent of the labor force, or 3.4 million workers.[24] Also, the per capita income figure of ₱5,572 ($755 × ₱7.38) overlooked the fact that inflation during the martial law period considerably eroded the purchasing power of the peso.[25] The real wage index of average monthly earnings in selected nonagricultural industries in the Philippines dropped from 100 in 1972 to 93.2 for salaried employees and 86.7 for wage earners in 1980; the real wage rate index for skilled and unskilled laborers in Manila (the region of highest wages) declined from 100.0 in 1972 to 63.7 and 53.4, respectively, in 1980.[26] The drop in earnings and wages was further aggravated by the government's regularly intervening in collective bargaining to restrain wage increases in an attempt to make the country attractive for foreign investment. According to the Ministry of Labor and Employment, only about 10 percent of the nation's employers bothered to comply with minimum wage regulations.[27] Unfortunately, conditions of employment and real wages continued to deteriorate after the termination of martial rule. By the first quarter of 1983, unemployment and underemployment rose to 5.9 and 29 percent, respectively, of the workforce, while inflation averaged 50.3 per cent in 1984 and almost 25 per cent in 1985.[28]

The erosion of real wages was accompanied, as the figures in Table 7 indicate, by an increase in income inequality during the martial law years. Between 1971 and 1981 the percentage of total family income accounted for by the poorest 40 percent decreased from 11.9 percent to 9.3 percent, whereas families in the highest quintile accounted for a greater percentage of the national income in 1981 than in 1971. Moreover, concentration of income at the top continued, with the highest ten percent of families

---

tion that "anyone who worked *one hour* [emphasis added] in the preceding three months [was] considered employed."

[24]"Manila: A City of Contrasts," *NASSA News*, January 1981, p. 4.

[25]The value of the peso and the minimum wage rate fell further after 1981. By 1985 the purchasing power of the peso was equivalent to 15 centavos at 1972 prices and by mid-1984, controlling for inflation, the real minimum wage at ₱6.55 was below the effective wage rate of ₱8.00 per day in 1972. Figures reported in Ledivina Cariño, "Living in the Dark Times: How Ordinary Filipinos Cope with the Crisis in the Philippines," Paper presented at the annual meeting of the Association for Asian Studies, Philadelphia, 22–24 March 1985, pp. 13–14.

[26]De Dios et al., *An Analysis of the Philippine Economic Crisis*, Table 5, p. 21.

[27]*Ibon Facts & Figures*, 15 April 1980, pp. 3–4.

[28]*Asiaweek*, 15 February 1985, pp. 27–32; Jose Galang, "Confidence on the Wane," *Far Eastern Economic Review*, 31 October 1985, p. 110; and Jose Galang, "Slowed-down Slowdown," *Far Eastern Economic Review*, 23 January 1986, p. 56.

Table 7. Distribution of family income, 1971–81

	Percent of total income			
Percentiles	*1971*	*1975*	*1979*	*1981*
Lowest 40 percent	11.9	8.9	10.0	9.3
Lowest 60 percent	25.1	18.8	22.1	21.1
Highest 20 percent	53.9	64.3	58.0	58.6
Top 10 percent	36.9	49.5	42.0	42.0

Sources: Ma. Cristina G. Ginson, "Philippine Labor and the Economic Recovery Program," *Pulso* 1, no. 3 (1985): Table 1, p. 181; and Ellen H. Palanca, "Poverty and Inequality: Trends and Causes," in Ramon C. Reyes, ed., *Philippines after 1972: A Multidisciplinary Perspective, Budhi Papers* VI (Ateneo de Manila University, 1985), Table 5, p. 109.

receiving 42 percent of total family income in 1981, up 5 percent from 1971.[29] Along with heightened income inequality, the percentage of families below the poverty line rose from 44.9 percent in 1971 to 53.2 percent in 1975, and remained high into the mid-1980s.[30] As of February 1984, none of the legal minimum wages—the highest being ₱1,062.27 a month for nonagricultural workers in the Manila metropolitan area—reached "the lowest poverty-threshold estimate of ₱1,082.43 per month"[31] deemed necessary for the subsistence of a family of six, the average-size family. Clearly, the rich improved economically after 1972, but the poor increasingly found themselves worse off both in relative and absolute terms.

Marcos' assertions about advances in nutrition and health ignored reports from the Asian Development Bank (using 1971–75 data) that the Philippines ranked below India, Indonesia, and Bangladesh in average per capita caloric consumption and from the Ministry of Health that nearly four-fifths of all Filipino children suffered from some form of malnutrition.[32] Other data available at the time of the lifting of martial rule revealed that the Philippines not only lacked adequate sanitation facilities and plentiful

[29]Data for 1983 indicate a continuation of income inequality in the Philippines. See *Ibon Facts & Figures*, 31 May 1984, p. 3; and Ma. Cristina G. Ginson, "Philippine Labor and the Economic Recovery Program," *Pulso* 1, no. 3 (1985): 182. For a different view, consult Julieta L. Legaspi, "Commentary," *Pulso* 1, no. 3 (1985): 196–198.

[30]International Bank for Reconstruction and Development (World Bank), "Poverty, Basic Needs, and Employment: A Review and Assessment," confidential first draft (Washington, D.C., January 1980), Table 1.10, p. 36 (typewritten); Rehman Sobhan, "Inequitable Development: The Philippines Experience," *Asian Affairs* (Bangladesh) 5 (April–June 1983): 148–154; and *Ibon Facts & Figures*, 31 May 1984, p. 3.

[31]De Dios et al., *An Analysis of the Philippine Economic Crisis*, p. 24.

[32]Keith Dalton, "The Undernourished Philippines," *Far Eastern Economic Review*, 1 September 1978, pp. 35–36; and *Ibon Facts & Figures*, 15 December 1979, p. 3.

supplies of potable water—contributing to high incidences of common communicable diseases, such as gastroenteritis and colitis, whooping cough, diphtheria, tuberculosis, pneumonia, and bronchitis—but also had a shortage of medical resources and personnel, with a disproportionate number of doctors and hospitals being located in urban areas, especially metropolitan Manila.[33] Finally, the president's laudatory comments about the regime's human settlements program glossed over the fact that improvements in housing, particularly the *Bagong Lipunan* Sites and Services (BLISS) program, frequently resulted in the forcible relocation of squatters and typically failed to meet the needs of the very poor, who lacked sufficient income to purchase government constructed dwellings.[34]

The second, and perhaps more fundamental, area of disagreement with progressive church officials and layworkers focused on Marcos' "radicalization" and "restructuring" of Philippine society in the names of social justice and economic development. At the termination of martial law, the president emphasized how the regime's land reform program—the cornerstone of the New Society—had "liberated 523,153 farmers from the shackles of tenancy and transformed land ownership from a system of exploitation to a self-reliant and creative act."[35] At the outset of martial rule, Marcos had stated that land reform was the measure by which the success or failure of the New Society should be judged.[36] Others, including church activists, however, analyzed land reform statistics much differently. From the beginning, the land reform program excluded hectarage devoted to sugarcane, abaca, and other commercial crops, and thereby promised nothing in the way of economic relief to a significant number of tenants and agricultural laborers, many of whom were among the lowest-paid workers in the country.[37] Moreover, although the provisions of Presidential Decree

[33]*Ibon Facts & Figures*, 15 December 1980, pp. 1–5; and Cariño, "Living in Dark Times," p. 8.

[34]*Ibon Facts & Figures*, 15 October 1980, pp. 1–8, and 30 November 1983, pp. 1–8.

[35]*Proclamation 2045*, 17 January 1981, in the *Philippine News*, 21–27 January 1981, pp. 1, A.

[36]All of the Philippines was proclaimed a land reform area by *Presidential Decree 2*, 26 September 1972, and on 21 October 1972, Marcos issued *Presidential Decree 27*, the so-called Emancipation Decree, which provided for the transfer of land to the tiller.

[37]Benedict J. Kerkvliet, "Land Reform: Emancipation or Counterinsurgency?" in Rosenberg, pp. 129–132. For other critical analyses of the New Society land reform program, see David Wurfel, *Philippine Agrarian Policy Today: Implementation and Political Impact*, Institute of Southeast Asian Studies Occasional Paper no. 46, (Singapore, May 1977); and Linda K. Richter, *Land Reform and Tourism Development: Policy-Making in the Philippines* (Cambridge, Mass.: Schenkman, 1982).

27 potentially included 1,005,124 tenants on 1,462,570 hectares (1 hectare equals 2.47 acres) of tenanted rice and corn lands, the actual redistribution of land from the landlords to the farmers, according to the Ministry of Agrarian Reform, ultimately would affect only 396,082 tenants and 730,734 hectares of tenanted rice and corn lands upon the completion of Operation Land Transfer (OLT). The remaining tenants (609,042) and rice and corn lands (731,836 hectares) fell under the regime's Operation Leasehold (OLH).[38] By 1980, a mere 1,648 tenants involving 1,538.9 hectares, representing 0.4 and 0.2 percent, respectively, of all eligible tenants and hectarage under OLT, had received Tenant Emancipation Patents giving them full land ownership. During the same period of time, by comparison, thousands of hectares were acquired by corporations in compliance with General Order 47 and for agribusiness expansion to serve foreign export markets.[39]

The half a million "liberated" tenants Marcos referred to in Proclamation 2045, therefore, simply had received land-transfer certificates, not land titles. Under the terms of the certificates, they were required to comply with a series of regulations, such as purchasing the land within fifteen years at 6 percent interest, adopting expensive modern agricultural methods, and paying dues to a government-sponsored cooperative, that, in many instances, increased the cost of land ownership to the point where a large percentage of farmers defaulted on payments due to low net income and crop failures.[40] A reduction in funds for land purchases, a lack of adequate personnel in the Ministry of Agrarian Reform to monitor the program, and opposition from landowners likewise lowered the probability that the tenant emancipation process would have been accelerated in the future had Marcos remained in power.[41] The program did not result in a redistribution of wealth in Philippine society nor, as church activists and others pointed out, contribute to a significant reduction in the power of the landowning elites. Instead, it encouraged the growth of commercial farming, which, ironically, led to the displacement of many tenants and small farmers, as discussed in Chapter 5, and, in areas of agricultural mechanization, to a

[38]*Ibon Facts & Figures*, 30 September 1981, p. 3. Tenants who were ineligible to receive Certificates of Land Transfer (CLT) under OLT because they were sharecroppers of small landowners were protected from eviction under OLH.

[39]*Ibon Facts & Figures*, 30 November 1982, p. 7; and General Order 47, 27 May 1974.

[40]Kerkvliet, "Land Reform: Emancipation or Counterinsurgency?" p. 115; Casalmo, *The Vision of a New Society*, p. 65; and *Ibon Facts & Figures*, 30 September 1981, p. 2.

[41]*Ibon Facts & Figures*, 30 September 1981, p. 2; Richter, *Land Reform and Tourism Development*, chaps. 3–5; and Kerkvliet, "Land Reform: Emancipation or Counterinsurgency?" pp. 124–128.

loss of jobs for farm laborers.[42] Increased grain production, one of the main objectives of land reform, still did not meet demand; by 1984, the Philippines was again forced to import rice.

President Marcos typically blamed the country's economic difficulties on external factors. To be sure, oil price increases in 1973–74 and 1979–80 and the world recession in the early 1980s affected the Philippine economy negatively. But, according to De Dios et al., much of the nation's economic woe under Marcos resulted from the

> concentration of power in the hands of the government, and the use of governmental functions to dispense economic privileges to some small factions in the private sector. In turn, this sufficiently explains the more outward manifestations which have disturbed many observers of the recent economic scene, namely, (a) the generally expansionist fiscal and monetary policies over the past two decades; (b) the increasing role of the government in markets for products and financial assets; and (c) the trend towards a monopolistic structure in important sectors of the economy.[43]

In a departure from the conservative monetary and fiscal policies that characterized Philippine administrations from Roxas to Garcia, the Marcos regime, as indicated in Chapter 2, dramatically increased foreign borrowing and the government's role in the economy after 1972. The country's foreign debt jumped from $3,798.7 million in 1975 to $18,864.0 million in 1983, while the government's share of expenditures as a percentage of GNP advanced from 9.7 percent in 1966–70 to 17.7 percent in 1981–82.[44] Shifts in government capital expenditures away from infrastructure after 1975 to corporate equity investment and "other capital outlays," which together comprised 63.7 percent of all capital expenditures of the government in the 1981–83 period, underscored the problems of governmental economic mismanagement. The increase in equity investment was often used to bail out companies controlled by Marcos cronies. The rise of miscellaneous capital expenditures included many construction projects of questionable necessity, such as the Manila Bay reclamation project and building complex, the University of Life, several showcase medical facili-

[42]Philippine Ecumenical Writing Group, *Moving Heaven and Earth: An Account of Filipinos Struggling to Change Their Lives and Society* (Manila: Commission on the Churches' Participation in Development [CCPD], World Council of Churches [WCC], 1982), p. 10; Vincent G. Cullen, "Sour Pineapples," *Signs of the Times*, 12 June 1976, pp. 17–24; and Casalmo, *The Vision of a New Society*, pp. 68–70.

[43]De Dios et al., *An Analysis of the Philippine Economic Crisis*, pp. 10–11.

[44]Ibid., Table 19, p. 56, and Table 4, p. 11. The $18.8 billion figure for 1983 was subsequently revised upward by another $6.8 billion.

ties, and numerous official residences and government buildings, to provide amenities for high administration officials and to house an expanding bureaucracy.[45]

After 1972 Marcos used his decree-making powers and control over the government's financial institutions to intervene in the economy. Ostensibly this intervention was to accelerate economic growth but more often the result was the enhancement of the economic fortunes of favored individuals and companies. Between 1972 and 1980, according to De Dios et al., Marcos issued 688 presidential decrees and 283 letters of instruction that represented some form of intervention in the economy. Among the measures were twenty-four decrees and three letters of instruction that helped Roberto Benedicto and Eduardo Cojuanco establish monopolies in the sugar and coconut industries, which, as pointed out in Chapter 2, affected the livelihood of 40 percent of Filipinos.[46]

Marcos' reliance on traditional patronage politics to maintain political support significantly undermined the full implementation of the regime's economic development programs. Although Marcos continued to receive the support of the United States and the IMF and World Bank until after the Aquino assassination, the creation of monopolies controlled by his friends failed to stimulate growth. Instead, Marcos' clients mismanaged the monopolies for personal gain, while the technocrats, who also owed their positions to Marcos, remained silent or, in some cases, assisted in fabricating a more favorable view of the economy. Such policies alienated domestic businessmen outside of the president's patronage network, discouraged additional foreign capital, and ultimately eroded the regime's commitment to economic liberalization and export promotion. Nevertheless, Marcos continued to use the rhetoric of capitalist economic development and anti-Communism to justify his bureaucratic authoritarian rule, the maintenance of which required increasing amounts of repression.

The reaction of the Catholic and Protestant churches to the increasing income inequality and growing militarization, although at first uneven, became steadily more critical after 1972. In July 1973, ten months after the declaration of martial law, the CBCP issued a pastoral letter on "Evangelization and Development" that focused on the "scandal of poverty" in the country: the high unemployment and underemployment, gross income inequality, regressive tax structure, and extravagance of the rich. The bishops stressed the importance of equality, participation, and justice;

[45]Ibid., p. 34.
[46]Ibid., pp. 40, 83. See also Chapter 2, note 71.

while recognizing the potential of the regime's development programs for fostering "total human development," they warned of the "danger that basic human rights will be pushed aside and ignored, due process of law conveniently bypassed in the name of reform."[47]

A year later, in a July 1974 letter to Marcos, the Catholic bishops indicated that while they shared the President's vision for a new society—one characterized by "*social equality through the democratization of wealth* and *political equality through participatory democracy*"—and rejoiced in some of the initial successes of martial law, they were eager to see concrete results "toward the economic liberation of the many." The bishops also expressed concern about the spread of a climate of fear and stated that as a result of such fear,

> laborers and wage earners dare not organize themselves into free unions, or press for higher wages and better working conditions; ordinary citizens are beginning to slide back into despondency, and one of the initial benefits of martial law—confidence in the government and in government officials—is fast disappearing; even leading citizens in Church, business, and government circles, instinctively talk in whispers for fear of being accused of rumor mongering and taken to the nearest detention camp. Worst of all, the mass media licensed to operate can afford to be heard only when they speak of good news and speak in praise of the administration.

The bishops went on to call for an early lifting of martial rule, if only in selected areas of the country, and to join the Integrated Bar of the Philippines in expressing concern over human rights violations and the erosion of the independence of the judiciary.[48]

The CBCP also took issue with the regime's policies toward cultural minorities and the establishment of Basic Christian Communities (BCCs) in a pastoral letter released in January 1977. The bishops maintained that the programs of the Presidential Assistant on National Minorities (PANAMIN) "destroy rather than preserve the cultures" of tribal minorities; they criticized the harassment and intimidation, including arrests and detentions, of non-PANAMIN personnel working among tribal peoples and "the arrests of priests, religious and lay workers, and even the deportation of foreign missionaries" organizing BCCs.[49] The bishops again returned to questions of social justice in general as well as within various social subunits, such as

[47]Hardy, *The Philippine Bishops Speak*, pp. 52–77.
[48]CBCP to President Marcos, 24 July 1974 (mimeographed).
[49]Hardy, prepublication manuscript of *The Philippine Bishops Speak*, pp. 145–148.

the family, the school, the parish, the labor movement, and the political community, in a September 1978 pastoral letter, "Education for Justice."[50]

At the center of church-state disagreement on issues of social justice was a clash between the right of the clergy to defend dispossessed tribal minorities, poor farmers, and wage laborers in the normal process of evangelization and the regime's need to maintain national security, which frequently manifested itself in a disregard for the rights of anyone perceived as criticizing or opposing government development programs. The government and military tended to view the emphasis of the churches in establishing BCCs as subversive, first, because those engaged in organizing and running the communities, as pointed out in Chapter 4, frequently raised embarrassing questions about government policies and actions and, second, because a few of the communities had fallen under the influence of the CPP and its military arm, the New People's Army (NPA).

To be sure, the CBCP addressed a number of the country's fundamental economic problems during the first five years of martial law, yet the bishops as a group did little more than write letters and issue pronouncements that were themselves the result of compromises among the three major factions within the conference. In contrast, the AMRSP and several progressive bishops, who periodically issued statements and pastoral letters, were much more trenchant in their analysis and criticism of the regime's economic policies. In a report based on the results of a national survey conducted in October 1973, the Major Superiors criticized the regime's land reform program, labor policies, inability to control inflation, and ejection of squatters in the name of economic development.[51] Two years later, in January 1975, the AMRSP published a study of abuse and exploitation in the Philippine sugar industry.[52] The studies deplored the fact that the poor were forced to bear unequally the costs of the regime's economic development program; in a letter accompanying the release of the sugar industry analysis, the Major Superiors called on President Marcos to dismantle "*the plantation-type economy . . . which perpetuates an outdated feudal system of dependency*" in favor of more "*small-sized farms owned by the workers themselves*." They also praised the National Federation of Sugar Workers (NFSW), expressing "*support and confidence in its Christian orientation and leadership*," and suggested that the planters on the

[50]Hardy, *The Philippine Bishops Speak*, pp. 173–200.

[51]"The Role of the Church under Martial Law—National Survey by the Major Religious Superiors," *IDOC Bulletin*, nos. 15–16 (January–February 1974), pp. 3–15.

[52]AMRSP, *The Sugar Workers of Negros* (n.p., 1975?).

Sugar Industry Foundation, Inc. (SIFI) board of directors be replaced by workers.[53]

Both reports were controversial. The military expressed dissatisfaction at the 18 December 1973 Church-Military Liaison Committee meeting (CMLC) that the 1973 national survey portrayed martial law negatively and had been conducted without military approval.[54] In addition, the methodology of the study, which was based on a purposive sample, was criticized by social scientists affiliated with the Roman Catholic church.[55] The sugar planters of Negros were similarly irritated by the AMRSP's analysis of the conditions of labor in the sugar industry; Bishop Antonio Fortich, evidently under intense pressure from the planters, released a public statement, read by Armando Gustilo, president of the National Federation of Sugarcane Planters and an ally of the Marcos administration, at a sugar industry convention, attacking the study as full of "gross misrepresentations, generalizations, exaggerations, and patent inaccuracies."[56]

Criticism of the two studies, however, failed to deter the Major Superiors in their support for social justice. The 1973 national survey served as a basis for discussion at the January 1974 annual convention of the AMRSP; task forces were created within the association to respond to problems revealed in the survey. The initial task forces were an office for justice and peace, urban and rural task forces on conscientization of others, a task force on detainees, and a task force on data-gathering.[57] The sugar industry study prompted the Major Superiors to increase efforts in publicizing the conditions of the workers and in educating the poor to understand the structural conditions of their poverty and the need to work toward justice. Among the projects of the AMRSP were the publication of "a comic book in Ilongo with stories of workers being denied Medicare by greedy overseers or mountain farmers suffering from land grabbing,"[58] and a photo-essay

[53]AMRSP to President Marcos, 11 January 1975, in *The Sugar Workers of Negros*, pp. 156–165.

[54]Minutes of Meeting 2 of the CMLC, 18 December 1973, p. 3 (typewritten); and Yu and Bolasco, *Church-State Relations*, p. 108.

[55]Frank Lynch, "The AMRSP Survey: An Interpretive Note," 2 January 1974 (typewritten); Mary R. Hollnsteiner, "The AMRSP Survey: A Commentary Appended to Frank Lynch's Interpretive Note," 2 January 1974 (typewritten); and Asian Social Institute (ASI) Staff, "Comments on the Summary of the National Survey of Major Religious Superiors," ASI Communications Center [1970s?] (typewritten).

[56]Statement of Antonio Y. Fortich, 10 February 1975, in *The Sugar Workers of Negros*, pp. 184–185.

[57]"Main Activities of the AMRSMP, 1971 to 1975," pp. 3–4 (mimeographed).

[58]McCoy, *Priests on Trial*, p. 148.

pamphlet, *Pastures of the Rich*, that contained a series of photos depicting the arduous life of Negros sugar workers.[59] "Unlike traditional religious literature which blamed poverty on moral failings such as gambling or laziness," as McCoy points out, the comic book stories and the photo-essay portrayed "the workers as innocent victims of vicious exploitation."[60] Such efforts resulted in heightened state-sponsored harassment and repression of AMRSP's institutions and personnel working on behalf of the poor.

Among individual bishops who saw the Marcos regime's economic policies as exploitative, none was more outspoken than Bishop Francisco Claver of Malaybalay, Bukidnon. Not only did Claver agree that the AMRSP national survey, despite its shortcomings, presented the "best picture of the actual situation of the country under martial law," but he also took issue with the bright economic image presented in the controlled media and questioned the government's export-oriented development policy that favored foreign multinational corporations and their local allies.[61] He also protested government development schemes that threatened to dislocate poor farmers and minority tribesmen without prior consultation and without guarantees of just compensation.[62] While not so consistently critical as Claver, other bishops questioned the government's labor policies in specific instances:[63] In late 1974 Cardinal Sin and Bishop Julio Labayan, director of the National Secretariat for Social Action, Justice and Peace (NASSA), commissioned a study of industrial workers in the Manila metropolitan area that revealed the worsening conditions of labor under martial law.[64]

The growing concern among many church leaders for the bleak circumstances of the labor force was reflected in a message to Filipino workers issued at the June 1975 annual convention of NASSA which stated flatly that many of the regime's labor policies were against the interests of the workers. Among the policies singled out were an unjust wage structure, increased government control of labor unions, the banning of strikes, and the encouragement of foreign multinational corporations to take advantage

[59]AMRSP, *Pastures of the Rich* (n.p., 1975). The photo-essay was commissioned for the AMRSP convention in Bacolod City, January 1975.

[60]McCoy, *Priests on Trial*, p. 148.

[61]Francisco F. Claver, *The Stones Will Cry Out: Grassroots Pastorals* (Maryknoll, N.Y.: Orbis Books, 1978), pp. 117–119.

[62]Ibid., pp. 82–84, 124–128, 135–145.

[63]*Various Reports*, 21 February 1975, pp. 49–50.

[64]For a summary of the report, see "Labor in the Philippines," *Impact*, October 1975, pp. 339–344.

of cheap labor.[65] In November 1975 the Catholic and Protestant churches protested more forcefully the issuance of Presidential Decree 823, which banned all strikes and forbade individuals and organizations, "whether foreign or national," from providing assistance to labor.[66] More than two thousand bishops, priests, and religious cosigned a letter from Cardinal Sin protesting the decree, while other bishops, including Antonio Mabutas, the conservative Archbishop of Davao, who labeled certain aspects of PD 823 as "oppressive and inhuman," either wrote or cosigned statements critical of the decree.[67]

The widespread and vociferous reaction within the Philippine churches against PD 823 represented a watershed in church-state relations under martial law. Although the negative response to the labor decree did not herald immediate unity within the churches vis-à-vis the Marcos regime, increasingly members of the Catholic hierarchy and church leaders within the Protestant communities began to question the government's economic policies. In 1979, for example, the CBCP declared that the "existence of poverty and misery, of deprivation and injustices," coupled with "the denial and frequent violation of basic human rights, both personal and collective, in the name of defense and security of certain interest groups or the nation and state itself," were among the chief causes of the escalating violence within Philippine society.[68] The Catholic bishops again in February 1983 singled out the regime's economic policies for criticism, saying:

> The government has initiated a massive program of economic development aimed at correcting problems of poverty. But a number of its key developmental priorities,—e.g., heavy reliance on multinationals and its favoring of their needs over those of the people; its attention to tourist facilities and services, like lavish film festivals, over the services it can and should provide to rural areas, do not appear to lessen the number of our poor which is growing daily—their destitution more acute.[69]

The bishops pointed out further that economic corruption within the government and private industry was not only a major cause of poverty that

[65]*NASSA News*, August 1975, p. 1.

[66]*Presidential Decree 823*, 3 November 1975.

[67]See, for example, Jaime L. Sin to Ferdinand E. Marcos, 12 November 1975; and Antonio Ll. Mabutas to Ferdinand E. Marcos, 14 November 1975, in Committee of Christians for Justice and Human Rights, "Justice for the Filipino Workers: (Protests Against P.D. 823, Part I) (n.p., 1975?), pp. 3–5.

[68]Hardy, *The Philippine Bishops Speak*, p. 209.

[69]Ibid., p. 234.

deprived "the poor of benefits due them"; it also reinforced an "already much battered sense of justice" among those at the bottom of the economic system.[70] These statements and others indicate unequivocally that by the time of the Aquino assassination in August 1983 and the subsequent collapse of the economy, Philippine church leaders had lost faith in the ability of the Marcos regime's economic policies to create a more just and equitable society for the majority of Filipinos.

Political Reforms and the Church

In addition to praising the regime's economic achievements in *Proclamation 2045*, Marcos emphasized New Society political reforms, such as the establishment of *barangay* democracies, the promulgation of a new constitution, and government reorganization, and stressed the regime's "constant vigilance" against subversion and graft and corruption. He also maintained that "the election of representatives of the youth, labor, and agricultural sectors in the *Batasang Pambansa* and in the *Sanggunian*" represented a "widely accepted innovation in democratic government." He also maintained that "legitimate political dissent" had continued to receive "full protection" under martial rule.[71]

Progressive elements within the Catholic and Protestant churches, however, questioned the "innovativeness" of many New Society reforms. They argued that the reforms were geared primarily to perpetuating the president's power and were just as open to political manipulation by traditional elites as were political structures in the Old Society. They further parried Marcos' assertions about protecting civil liberties by documenting the harassment and jailing of many persons engaged in "legitimate political dissent."[72]

An interesting example of New Society political reforms was the manipulation of the *Kabataang Barangay*, the national youth council federation headed by Maria Imelda "Imee" Marcos, the president's eldest daughter, to bolster the power and influence of the Marcoses.[73] On numerous occasions during martial law, the *Kabataang Barangay* was employed to support decisions of the regime, including Imelda Marcos' appointment in

[70]Ibid.

[71]*Proclamation 2045*, 17 January 1981, in *Philippine News*, 21–27 January 1981, pp. 1, A.

[72]See, for example, Casalmo, *The Vision of a New Society*, chaps. 1–2.

[73]*Presidential Decree 684*, 15 April 1975.

1975 to the governorship of metropolitan Manila and the regime's threat in 1978 to close American military bases in the Philippines.[74] In praising the "innovativeness" of youth representation in the National Assembly and in the various *sangguniang bayan*, Marcos neglected to mention that many *Kabataang Barangay* chairmen had undergone secret training seminars that glorified the New Society and the president. Church progressives, who were among the first to reveal the existence of the secret indoctrination sessions, compared the content, structure, and goals of the seminars to the *Hitlerjugend* of the Nazis and the Red Brigades of China under Mao Zedong. They also deplored the antichurch orientation of the training.[75]

A more persistent bone of contention, however, was Marcos' use of the electoral process to maintain himself in power. Differences among the bishops were not initially apparent: In the 1973 constitutional plebiscite, believing that the "sanctity and secrecy of the ballot" was "inviolable," the CBCP stated that qualified Filipinos were "bound in conscience to . . . vote intelligently, conscientiously and courageously."[76] But the regime's manipulation of the constitutional plebiscite and the first two referenda prompted progressive Catholic bishops, along with other Catholic and Protestant church officials, to speak up more forcefully and more frequently.[77] Just prior to the 27 February 1975 referendum, the Mindanao-Sulu Secretariat of Social Action (MISSSA) issued a statement advocating a boycott of yet "*another mockery of Democracy*," maintaining that it was impossible to hold a valid referendum in the absence of "safeguards to basic human freedom and the sanctity of the ballot."[78] A number of bishops, including Claver, Nepomuceno, Varela, and Zafra, as well as the leadership of the AMRSP, supported the MISSSA manifesto, which was sent to President Marcos along with a covering letter from Bishop Claver. Claver, speaking for the original signatories of the manifesto, warned that unless the president provided a ninety-day period for "the freest discussion of issues" and established an independent body for the "counting and

[74]Casalmo, *The Vision of a New Society*, p. 117; and Sheilah Ocampo, "New Singer with an Old Song," *Far Eastern Economic Review*, 15 September 1978, pp. 13–14.

[75]See the letter of Joaquin G. Bernas, chairman of the Executive Board of the AMRSP, "'*Barangay Kawal*' Training: Prelude to Totalitarian Rule?," 22 May 1979, pp. 1–2 (mimeographed); *Signs of the Times*, 26 March 1976, pp. 9–12; and Casalmo, *The Vision of a New Society*, pp. 116–120.

[76]*Philippine Priests' Forum* 4 (December 1972): 91. For an indication of some of the disagreement among church officials over the constitutional plebiscite, see Yu and Bolasco, *Church-State Relations*, pp. 102–103.

[77]Rigos, "The Posture of the Church in the Philippines under Martial Law," p. 129.

[78]*Philippine Priests' Forum* 7 (March 1975): 57–58.

registering of ballots," there would be "no alternative but to openly declare our intention to abstain from participating in another referendum."[79] Concern for the conduct of the referendum was also echoed in a jointly signed statement by an ecumenical group of Catholics and Protestants requesting that certain conditions of freedom and honesty be met prior to and during the balloting.[80] Likewise, albeit in a milder tone, the CBCP issued a pastoral letter suggesting the implementation of safeguards, including freedom of the press and assembly, a suspension of penalties for not voting, and the organization of an independent body to supervise the election and canvass the results, to ensure meaningful participation.[81]

The call by progressive bishops and church officials for electoral guarantees and reforms in 1975 was but the opening salvo in what turned out to be a continuing battle over the regime's manipulation of referenda and elections. In advance of the fourth referendum on 16 October 1976, fourteen Catholic bishops, branding martial law as "a regime of coercion and fear, of institutionalized deception and manipulation," stated their unwillingness to participate in another "vicious farce . . . that further degrades and debases us and our people."[82] The bishops were again joined by the leadership of the Major Superiors, and a number of AMRSP-sponsored symposia were organized to express opposition to the referendum.[83] Other Filipino clergy and lay leaders, referring to themselves as the Concerned Citizens for Freedom and Justice, urged civil disobedience and postponement of the October 1976 referendum until civil liberties were restored. A year later another group of ecumenical activists, including members of the clergy, called for a boycott of the December 1977 referendum on Marcos retaining the dual powers of the president and prime minister after the interim *Batasang Pambansa* elections in April 1978.[84]

The call for a boycott of the October 1976 referendum-plebiscite by

[79]*Various Reports*, 24 January 1975. p. 2d.

[80]*Various Reports*, 7 February 1975, pp. 17–18; *Philippine Times*, 16–31 January 1975, pp. 1, 7, 18; and Bernard Wideman, "Marcos' Sometimes Referendum," *Far Eastern Economic Review*, 24 January 1975, p. 13.

[81]Reprinted in Casalmo, *The Vision of the New Society*, pp. 257–259.

[82]*Philippine Priests' Forum* 3 (September 1976): 93–94.

[83]*Philippine Priests' Forum* 3 (September 1976): 95; and *Signs of the Times*, 2 October 1976, pp. 3–5.

[84]A Representative Group of Filipino Citizens, *Manifesto on Martial Law and the Referendum of October 16, 1976*, Manila, 21 September 1976; *Katipunan ng Bayan Para Sa Kalayaan* (KABAKA), Alliance for Human Rights, and Philippine Organization for Human Rights, *The Citizens' Manifesto on the December 17, 1977, Referendum and the Five-Year Record of Martial Law*, Manila, 30 November 1977, in *Philippine Times*, 1–15 December 1977, passim; and *Christian Science Monitor*, 16 December 1977, p. 7.

progressive bishops, religious superiors, and other clergy coincided with increased attacks by the government on activist clergy and brought into sharper focus disagreements among progressive and conservative bishops within the CBCP. In early September, 1976, for example, the *Philippines Daily Express* published a series of articles on the so-called Christian-Left which were aimed at discrediting Catholic and Protestant clergy working among the poor.[85] In a letter to President Marcos on 20 September 1976, a number of Catholic bishops and religious superiors took issue with the substance of the articles, pointing out that it was the responsibility of the church "to stand up in defense of human rights and to support the just struggles of the poor and the oppressed."[86]

The stand of those in the Catholic church advocating boycott was countered on 28 September 1976 by a statement "in behalf of the Conference," issued under the auspices of the CBCP Administrative Council, headed by Cardinal Rosales and dominated by conservative bishops. The Administrative Council, indicating that it did "not want to prejudge the sincerity of the government when it solemnly gives assurances both of complete freedom in casting our vote, and of honesty in the actual counting of the votes," maintained it was "a moral duty: (a) to vote in obedience to a legitimately established law of the land; and (b) to vote in accordance with a well-informed conscience, after serious reflection on the issues involved."[87] The government interpreted the letter as support for the referendum-plebiscite, while the core of the CBCP's progressive bishops, along with a number of religious superiors and other clergy, wrote Cardinal Rosales challenging the Administrative Council's authority to disregard the voting guidelines agreed upon by the entire CBCP in 1975. The progressives pointed out that assurances of honesty and integrity in the conduct of previous referenda were ignored by the Marcos regime.[88] Following the referendum-plebiscite church officials again reported numerous election code violations and voting irregularities.

The wrangling over participation in the 1976 referendum-plebiscite was but a manifestation of the more fundamental disagreement among the prelates over the morality of martial law and the proper role of the Catholic church in Philippine society. The substance and the intensity of the dispute

[85]See note 10.

[86]Reprinted in *Signs of the Times*, 25 September 1976, pp. 4–5.

[87]Reprinted in Casalmo, *The Vision of a New Society*, pp. 260–261.

[88]Various letters to Cardinal Rosales from bishops, religious superiors, and clergy from 6 October to 16 October 1976 are reprinted in Casalmo, *The Vision of a New Society*, pp. 261–271. See also pp. 257–259 for the 1975 CBCP pastoral letter outlining the voting guidelines.

was reflected in the publication in November and December 1976 of two opposing statements—*Ut Omnes Unum Sint* (That All May Be One), signed by seventeen progressive bishops, and *Et Veritas Liberabit Vos* (And The Truth Shall Make You Free), released by two conservative archbishops—and in the October 1976 letter, mentioned previously, from Cardinal Baggio to Cardinal Rosales admonishing the AMRSP for engaging in political activities detrimental to felicitous church-state relations.[89] In *Ut Omnes Unum Sint*, the progressive bishops reviewed the disagreements within the CBCP over the martial law government of President Marcos, and suggested that cultural norms and "personal reasons . . . of friendship for and indebtedness to the First Family" inhibited most bishops from criticizing the government, which was "perforce, criticism of President Marcos."[90] They went on to outline a conception of the church that emphasized the importance of "the People of God, the Community of Believers," stating that

> if we are serious about the people . . . , we will have to pay more attention to their life situation, to their life problems, to events that help—or do not help—them to live a more human and Christian life. We do not deny the supremacy that the spiritual must have in the life of Christians. But accepting that supremacy does not mean either that we neglect the physical. The Church is people, not simply souls, disembodied, incorporeal. The Church is living men and women, flesh and blood, of the existential present. It is they who must live—and give witness to—the Gospel in the concrete realities of the Philippines today. Our preaching must take in those concrete realities.[91]

Such a notion of the church, according to the bishops, required that they (1) address the effect of martial law on the people; (2) concern themselves with the "moral dimensions to the art and practice of government"; and (3) in taking "seriously the social teachings of the Church," continue to work for social justice and to support human rights.[92]

Archbishops Francisco Cruces and Antonio Mabutas, speaking for the conservative bishops in *Et Veritas Liberabit Vos*, took umbrage at the content of *Ut Omnes Unum Sint*, accusing the seventeen bishops of maliciousness in their characterization of other bishops not willing to speak out against martial law, saying the progressives "simply cannot comprehend why there are people who are not strongly anti-martial law like them,

[89]Both statements are reprinted in Casalmo, *The Vision of a New Society*, pp. 271–287.
[90]"*Ut Omnes Unum Sint*," in Casalmo, *The Vision of a New Society*, p. 274.
[91]Ibid., p. 275.
[92]Ibid., pp. 275–277.

unless it is for vile, selfish and ignoble reasons."[93] The two archbishops then went on to praise the declaration of martial law for reestablishing law and order and stemming the spread of Communism. While recognizing the existence of "policies which are restrictive of some rights and freedoms," the archbishops nonetheless defended the government's record of rectifying abuses under martial law, pointing out that "hundreds among the military have been dismissed or severely disciplined for committing abuses."[94] They also emphasized the responsibility of the laity, guided by "the Gospel and the mind of the Church," to "act directly and definitively in the temporal sphere" without undue direction or involvement from the hierarchy, which smacked of "too much clericalism."[95]

Although unity within the churches toward martial law remained elusive throughout most of the 1970s, the regime's repeated manipulation of the referenda (and, after 1977, the rigging of other elections) resulted with increasing frequency in moderate Catholic and Protestant church leaders joining with the more activist, progressive clergy in questioning publicly the freedom and honesty of the electoral process in the New Society and the New Republic. Prior to the National Assembly election in April 1978, for example, Cardinal Sin encouraged the voters in the Archdiocese of Manila to be guided by the dictates of their conscience and to protect the sanctity of the ballot.[96] After the election, he requested all citizens who had witnessed fraud to come forward and file charges, and asked the Commission on Elections (COMELEC) to "conduct an unbiased and impartial investigation, and then, after due process, punish the guilty and absolve the innocent."[97] Significantly, the CBCP endorsed Sin's statement in a separate letter dated 10 July 1978.[98] A year later, in July 1979, in an interview with United Press International, Sin proposed that if Marcos were serious about normalization, he should declare his intention not to run for election again.[99] In April 1981, as a result of the controversy surrounding the constitutional plebiscite establishing a mixed presidential-parliamentary system of government, the Cardinal suggested that the scheduled 16 June

[93]Cruces and Mabutas, "*Et Veritas Liberabit Vos*," in Casalmo, *The Vision of a New Society*, p. 279.

[94]Ibid., pp. 279–280, 286.

[95]Ibid., p. 287.

[96]Sin's letter was reprinted in *Malayang Pilipinas*, 5 April 1978, pp. 1, 8.

[97]As quoted in the CBCP's open letter on the 7 April National Assembly election, in *Philippine Priests' Forum* 10 (September 1978): 71.

[98]Ibid., pp. 70–72. The Society of Jesus, among other church groups, also asked for an investigation into fraud during the election. See *We Forum*, 12 May 1978, pp. 1–2.

[99]*We Forum*, 14–20 July 1979, pp. 1, 5.

1981 presidential election be postponed until "the credibility of the government is restored." He maintained further that for Marcos to run unopposed "would be a farce reminiscent of one-candidate elections in totalitarian countries." Instead, he proposed that "the useless expenditure of uncounted millions of pesos" on the election be spent on underfinanced government projects to further the aims of the New Society and thereby restore the people's confidence in the government.[100]

While declining to join with church progressives in calling for a boycott of the referenda and elections held during the Marcos presidency, Cardinal Sin's criticism of Marcos' manipulation of the electoral process became increasingly trenchant after the termination of martial law in January 1981. Thus it was no surprise when he and the president locked horns over press reports on 10 June 1981 which quoted Marcos as saying that "according to an encyclical of Pope Pius XII, it was a mortal sin not to vote in an election" and another story on 15 June 1981, which maintained that the Catholic Women's League of the Philippines (CWL) was irritated by the "political agitation" of some Catholic leaders.[101] Sin clarified Pius XII's encyclical, stating that a refusal to vote as a matter of conscience must be respected by the state, and circulated a letter from the CWL repudiating the news reports in the controlled-press. Sin further accused the regime of a "deliberate, finely orchestrated campaign . . . to throttle the freedom of the church to speak on matters of Catholic morality." Such a campaign, Cardinal Sin argued, made a "mockery of the constitutional provision regarding freedom of religion."[102]

Following Marcos' reelection in June 1981, church-state relations deteriorated markedly as a result of the continuation of authoritarian rule and the government's contention that the churches—particularly the Roman Catholic church—were heavily infiltrated by Communists. Raids on church institutions and the arrest of priests, nuns, and laypersons suspected of leftist tendencies, as we have seen, increased dramatically in 1982. The government-controlled press, after July 1982, published numerous articles critical of alleged church radicals, but frequently declined to print rebuttals from church representatives. Within this context the CBCP voted during its

[100]United States Foreign Broadcast Information Service (FBIS), *Daily Reports,* vol. 4, Asia & Pacific, 24 April 1981, p. P5.

[101]As quoted in the opening remarks of Jaime Cardinal Sin to the CBCP, Baguio City, 27 June 1981 (typewritten). See also Anne S. Bagatsing et al., 18 June 1981, letter to Cardinal Sin from the CWL repudiating the press reports (typewritten).

[102]Jaime Cardinal Sin, "On the Church's Teaching Regarding Conscience and the Right and Duty to Vote," 11 June 1981 (typewritten); and FBIS, 30 June 1981, p. P3.

January 1983 meeting to withdraw from the CMLC, established in 1973 to resolve controversies between the Catholic and Protestant churches and the military. In February 1983, the bishops issued a blistering pastoral letter accusing the regime of repression, corruption and economic mismanagement. The bishops went on to warn that tensions were unlikely to ease in the absence of fundamental reforms which recognized "a certain pluralism of positions in the way . . . people strive for justice according to their faith."[103]

A recognition of the importance of pluralism in the political process, coupled with increased intolerance toward the regime's manipulation of elections, was reflected in the letters of the CBCP, the AMRSP, and statements of other church officials in advance of the 27 January 1984 plebescite and the 14 May 1984 *Batasang Pambansa* election. The CBCP's 8 January 1984 pastoral letter stressed the need to respect "the right of citizens not to participate in political exercises they consider contrary to the dictates of conscience"; underscored the importance of an honest and impartial electoral process, based upon a open exchange of ideas without fear "of threats of imprisonment or other forms of reprisal for exercising [the] right to free speech or peaceful assembly"; and pinpointed a number of steps the government should take to ensure a "proper climate of freedom and fair play."[104] The bishops, however, did not take a position either for participation or for boycott.

In contrast, the AMRSP, citing Marcos' refusal to relinquish his authoritarian powers, repeal a number of national security decrees and proclamations, and grant changes in the electoral code, issued a letter on 16 February 1984, advocating a boycott of the National Assembly election.[105] Other church leaders, such as Joaquin Bernas, president of Ateneo de Manila University and a former provincial of the Society of Jesus, and Cardinal Sin, advocated participation,[106] although neither Bernas nor Sin had any illusions about the essential fairness or morality of the Marcos government. Periodically during the campaign, Cardinal Sin irritated the government by calling on Marcos to grant the opposition's demands for electoral reform and by accusing the regime of repression against "dissenters and boycotters."[107] After the election, although Sin termed it "the freest, the

[103]Hardy, *The Philippine Bishops Speak*, pp. 232–238.

[104]Reprinted in *Philippine News*, 1–7 February 1984, p. 7.

[105]Reprinted in *Life Forum*, 16 (March 1984): 6–7.

[106]Joaquin G. Bernas, "Boycott or Participation: Confusion Twice Confounded," *Life Forum*, 16 (March 1984): 8–11.

[107]FBIS, 8 February 1984, p. P3; 24 February 1984, pp. P5–P6; 27 February 1984, pp. P4–P5; and 30 April 1984, pp. P4–P5.

cleanest and most honest one . . . since the imposition of martial law," he gave no credit to the regime, which he accused of being "bent on frustrating the voice of the people" through bribery, intimidation, and misappropriation of public funds. The cardinal attributed the outcome of the election, which resulted in the opposition's winning more than 70 of the 183 contested seats, to the vigilance of the people.[108]

Much of the success of the opposition was attributable to the activities of the National Citizens' Movement for Free Elections (NAMFREL), headed by Jose Concepcion, Jr., a businessman and prominent Catholic layman, long associated with the crusade for clean elections in the Philippines. With strong backing from business and civic organizations and from key elements within the Roman Catholic church, NAMFREL recruited an estimated 200,000 Filipinos nationwide to monitor registration and polling and to conduct a tabulation of the votes independent of COMELEC. By election day, NAMFREL had chapters in all but 15 of the 187 electoral districts. The role of the Catholic church in supporting NAMFREL was crucial. Several bishops, for example, served as NAMFREL regional and local chairmen, while priests and nuns throughout the country functioned as poll watchers on election day, often preventing intimidation and fraud. NAMFREL's national tabulation center was housed in De La Salle High School gymnasium in Greenhills, Metro-Manila. The support of the church also provided NAMFREL with a mantle of legitimacy that helped undermine attempts by the regime and boycotters to discredit the organization as a tool of the United States and contributed to the large turnout of voters on election day.[109]

The absence of open bickering within the CBCP and among various church leaders and institutions over whether to boycott or participate in the 1984 *Batasang Pambansa* election was followed in late 1985 and early 1986 by a demonstration of considerable unity among Catholic church leaders toward participation in the 7 February 1986, snap presidential poll, which had been announced by President Marcos in early November 1985 during an interview on "This Week" with David Brinkley. Not only did the hierarchy favor a free, fair, and honest election, but a substantial number of clergy, including bishops, individually supported the opposition ticket of Corazon "Cory" Aquino and Salvador "Doy" Laurel. Again Cardinal Sin, who assisted Aquino and Laurel in agreeing to form a united opposition

[108]FBIS, 1 June 1984, pp. P2–P3.

[109]Christian S. Monsod, "NAMFREL—Testing Democracy at the Grassroots," *Fookien Times Yearbook, 1984–85*, pp. 76, 78; *Christian Science Monitor*, 18 May 1984, pp. 1, 10; and *Asiaweek*, 1 June 1984, pp. 16–17.

ticket, was at the forefront of church leaders calling for participation and warning against fraud.[110] Prior to the election, for example, Sin issued two very strong pastoral letters, one on 28 December 1985 and another on 19 January 1986. In the first letter, which noted the "widespread violence and dishonesty" of referenda and elections held during the Marcos presidency, the cardinal emphasized that participation in the election was not just a political act, but was also an act of Christian faith, requiring high standards of honesty and integrity. Furthermore, he detailed what voters and polling officials needed to do to ensure a clean election; praised the work of the NAMFREL, pledging the church's cooperation to its efforts; stated that "to cheat or make others cheat" was "a seriously immoral and un-Christian act"; and then maintained that cheating and election violence together were "sins that cry to heaven for vengeance." Sin also advised against selling one's vote, but at the same time, said that the "acceptance of money to vote for a candidate" was not binding, as one was not "obliged to fulfil an evil contract."[111]

The second pastoral letter, while reiterating the need for honesty and integrity in the 7 February poll, was but a thinly veiled condemnation of the government's election tactics. The cardinal bluntly said:

> We already see many signs that show a very sinister plot by some people and groups (meaning the Marcos regime) to frustrate the honest and orderly expression of the people's genuine will. Already money has flowed freely into the hands of teachers, barangay officials and the common people to induce them to support particular candidates in a manner unworthy of free persons. Already we have seen, heard and read lies and black propaganda used by some quarters against opponents who are on the other hand deprived of adequate access to media, and are thus unjustly left defenseless. Already we hear of undue pressure exerted on hapless government employees to make them work (against the law!) for certain candidates.

Sin asked the voters to resist such election tactics and to vote for candidates "who embody the Gospel values of humility, truth, honesty, respect for human rights and life," warning again of divine retribution for perpetrators of violence and fraud.[112]

[110]FBIS, 12 November 1985, p. P9, and 16 December 1985, pp. P16–P17.

[111]Jaime Cardinal Sin and the Auxiliary Bishops of Manila, "Pastoral Letter," 28 December 1986, in FBIS, 10 January 1986, pp. P24–P26. Following the National Assembly election in 1984, Sin summed up his view on accepting "donations" from politicians when he said: "Take the bait but not the hook." See FBIS, 1 June 1984, p. P3.

[112]Jaime Cardinal Sin, "A Call to Conscience," 19 January 1986, in *Bulletin Today*, 19 January 1986, p. 10.

On 25 January 1986 the CBCP, headed by Ricardo Cardinal Vidal, who had been considered by many to be conservative, issued a statement on the snap presidential election that echoed much of what was contained in the two pastoral letters of the Archdiocese of Manila.[113] The bishops warned against any attempt to subvert the popular will of the people and asked the electorate to organize to prevent violence and fraud. Previously Cardinal Vidal had in a separate pastoral letter urged Cebuanos to vote according to their conscience, saying participation was "a sacred duty."[114] The response of the clergy and the electorate throughout the country overwhelmingly favored a clean and honest election, as indicated by voter turnout, citizen support of NAMFREL, and attempts to protect the sanctity of the ballots in the face of government intimidation and manipulation. Thus, immediately after the election, when it became clear that President Marcos intended to remain in office regardless of the outcome of the vote, the CBCP issued a statement labeling the polls as "unparalleled in . . . fraudulence," saying "intimidation, harassment, terrorism and murder . . . made naked fear the decisive factor" in the election. The Catholic hierarchy also accused the Marcos regime of "a criminal use of power to thwart the sovereign will of the people," and stated that "a government that assumes or retains power through fraudulent means has no moral basis." The bishops went on to recommend a "non-violent struggle for justice."[115] Following the revolt of Marcos' Minister of Defense Juan Ponce Enrile and Vice-Chief-of Staff Fidel Ramos, Cardinal Sin asked Filipinos to go to Camp Crame and Camp Aguinaldo in a demonstration of solidarity with the military dissidents. Tens of thousands—Protestants as well as Catholics—responded and within days President Marcos was forced into exile, ending a twenty-year rule that had become increasingly corrupt and abusive.[116]

The role of the Roman Catholic church in the 7 February 1986 presidential election, although unprecedented, was but a dramatic manifestation of a growing dissatisfaction among church leaders with the Marcos regime. It reflected a shift already taking place within the church toward more activism among conservative and moderate bishops, who composed the majority of the CBCP. Given the inability (or unwillingness) of Marcos to reform

[113]CBCP, "We Must Obey God Rather Than Men," 25 January 1986, in FBIS, 31 January 1986, pp. P31–P34.

[114]FBIS, 15 January 1986, p. P13.

[115]CBCP, "Post Election Statement," 13 February 1986 (n.p., Claretian Publications, February 1986). Evidently only 80 of 120 Catholic bishops were involved in drafting the CBCP statement. See FBIS, 13 February 1986, p. P21.

[116]Michael Richardson, "Inside Story of the Marcos Fall," *Pacific Defense Reporter*, April 1986, pp. 7, 29.

the system, the breach with the Catholic bishops, especially after the Aquino assassination in August 1983, was never repaired. In fact church-state relations became increasingly acrimonious, notwithstanding intermittent attempts at reconciliation, from 1982 until Marcos' departure from the Philippines. At the heart of the conflict was a fundamental disagreement over the best means of eradicating unjust structures and ameliorating conditions for the poor in a society that pitted the right of the churches to engage in social justice activities against the regime's economic programs, which were often justified in terms of national development and national security.

To be sure, the Philippines "developed" in terms of absolute increases in GNP, tax collection, exports, and infrastructure construction during the Marcos years. With respect to the promises of the "revolution from the center" for a more just, prosperous, and egalitarian society, however, the Marcos regime left the country more impoverished and with an external debt estimated at $26 billion at the beginning of 1986. The Marcos style of bureaucratic authoritarianism, with its heavy emphasis on the traditional patron-client relationships characteristic of Philippine politics[117] and reliance on the implementation of reforms from the top was more effective in widening the gap between rich and poor and in creating newly privileged groups—such as the "crony capitalist"—than on "radicalizing" and "restructuring" the system for the benefit of marginalized and dispossessed poor. New Society and New Republic programs like land reform, rural electrification and irrigation, and urban renewal were typically implemented in the absence of close consultation with affected local communities, resulting in unnecessary abuse and conflict and, by the end of the Marcos era, contributing to a dramatic growth in the CPP/NPA.

In contrast, progressives within the Catholic and Protestant churches consistently advocated people's participation in socioeconomic and political development as a means for liberating themselves from poverty and unjust structures. Although conservative and moderate church leaders often disagreed with the degree of involvement in what they considered secular affairs, they nevertheless recognized, if only formalistically, the legitimacy of the church's call for a preferential option for the poor. The articulation of support for the poor has returned the Philippine Roman Catholic church to the historical role of the early Spanish missionaries in protecting the population against the abuses of the regime. In supporting

[117]See Carl H. Landé, *Structure of Philippine Politics: Leaders, Factions, and Parties* (New Haven: Southeast Asia Studies, Yale University, 1965).

free and honest elections, especially in 1984 and 1986, the moderate and progressive leaders of the Philippine churches emerged, at least temporarily, as champions of the principles of democracy for which Filipinos have fought since the middle of the nineteenth century.

The conditions for the collision between the Philippine churches and the Marcos regime were rooted both in the changes in the Roman Catholic church brought about by Vatican II and subsequent papal encyclicals, which stressed that efforts to eradicate injustice and economic inequality were an integral part of preaching the gospel; and in Marcos' commitment, upon being elected president in 1965, to a neoclassical economic development model, which stressed economic liberalization and reliance on foreign investment and foreign borrowing. Even had Marcos and the technocrats implemented the development model flawlessly, church-state relations no doubt would have been tense from time to time; inherent within the model is a recognition that income inequality will rise in the short term before economic benefits begin to "trickle down" to the general population. Yet, as already discussed, the economic policies of the Marcos regime were so flawed and poorly implemented that only the Marcoses and a small segment of the elite profited enormously after 1972. The plundering of the economy by Marcos and his cronies and the deterioration of conditions for the poor and the middle-class contributed significantly to the exacerbation of church-state relations.

The economic development model pursued by Marcos and the technocrats offered other sources of tension in church-state relations. The need for political order, expansion of governmental capabilities, and depoliticization of the masses were all stressed in the political development literature of the late 1960s and early 1970s. Marcos justified the declaration of martial law in 1972 and the subsequent expansion of the military on this need for more political stability and discipline to stimulate economic development, especially to attract foreign investment and facilitate the acquisition of large loans from overseas banks and from the IMF and World Bank. The image of political stability created by martial law, however, was more apparent than real; although foreign investment and foreign borrowing increased initially, the abuses of the government, especially by the military, was eventually a major factor in the unraveling of the regime, including the alienation of influential elements within the Roman Catholic and Protestant churches.

Military and economic policies of the United States that facilitated Marcos' hold on power beyond a second term also fostered church-state enmity. The Nixon administration did nothing to discourage Marcos from declaring martial law in 1972. Officials in Washington and the U.S. embassy thought martial rule important for the achievement of political order and economic development, and, most important, for the maintenance of U.S. military facilities in the Philippines, especially Subic Bay Naval Base and Clark Air Force Base.[118] Washington's support for Marcos was demonstrated by substantial increases in military assistance, and although U.S.–Philippine relations deteriorated during the Carter Administration over human right abuses, the preservation of U.S. military bases remained paramount. Much of American military assistance to the Marcos regime helped the Armed Forces of the Philippines (AFP) conduct counterinsurgency campaigns that resulted in many civilian deaths, engendering increased criticism from Catholic and Protestant church leaders of Marcos and the AFP and of the U.S. government.

United States economic policy toward the Philippines also bolstered the Marcos regime. American advice and support during the 1960s helped shape the basic economic policy of the Marcos government; in the three years after the imposition of martial rule, U.S. economic assistance to the Philippines doubled. American backing likewise helped the Philippines secure large loans from international lending agencies after 1972. The ability to obtain large foreign loans allowed Marcos and the technocrats to deflect criticism of the economy by maintaining that the regime's economic policy had a "seal of approval" from the IMF and the World Bank.

American military and economic assistance, coupled with large foreign loans, provided a cushion for Marcos' economic excesses, while consistent American political support bolstered the political legitimacy of the regime. It is doubtful, for example, that Marcos could have diverted so much money from the economy or remained in power as long as he did in the absence of U.S. support. Nevertheless, Marcos himself was responsible for presiding over poorly conceptualized and inadequately implemented economic policies; for declaring martial law and establishing an authoritarian regime; expanding and politicizing the military, which resulted in a loss of professionalism and an increase in abuses; for plundering the country for the enrichment of his family and close political associates; and for manipulating the political system to perpetuate himself in power. Inevitably such decisions and policies, especially after 1972, resulted in conflict with the Philippine Roman Catholic and Protestant churches. The role of the Philippine churches in Marcos' fall from power underscored that in the absence of improvements in the quality of life of the poor, church-state relations in the Philippines will remain troubled into the indefinite future.

[118]Raymond Bonner, *Waltzing with a Dictator: The Marcoses and the Making of American Policy* (New York: Times Books, 1987), pp. 98–99.

Index

Library of Congress Cataloging-in-Publication Data

Youngblood, Robert L.
Marcos against the church : economic development and political repression in the Philippines / Robert L. Youngblood.
p. cm.
Includes bibliographical references and index.
ISBN 0-8014-2305-8 (alk. paper)
1. Philippines—Politics and government—1973–1986. 2. Religion and state—Philippines. 3. Philippines—Economic conditions—1946–1986. 4. Marcos, Ferdinand E. (Ferdinand Edralin), 1917– . I. Title.
DS686.5.Y68 1990
959.904′6—dc20 90–55135